The Underground Economy: Global Evidence of its Size and Impact

The Underground Economy: Global Evidence of its Size and Impact

edited by
Owen Lippert *and*
Michael Walker

The Fraser Institute
Vancouver, British Columbia, Canada

Canadian Cataloguing in Publication Data

Main entry under title:
The underground economy

Includes bibliographical references.
ISBN 0-88975-169-2

1. Informal sector (Economics)—Canada. 2. Tax evasion—Canada.
3. Informal sector (Economics) 4. Tax evasion. I. Lippert, Owen. II.
Walker, Michael, 1945,- III. Fraser Institute (Vancouver, B.C.)

HD2346.C2U62 1997   330.9   C97-910090-9

Table of Contents

Preface

A s a natural extension of its interest in the ways in which the private sector reacts to the activities of government, The Fraser Institute has long studied the underground economy. In pursuing this research, the Institute assembled a roster of experts in Vancouver in April 1994. They included government officials, accountants, economists, lawyers, federal police, politicians, and public policy analysts from Canada, the United States, Britain, Mexico, Chile, Peru, Russia, and Hong Kong.

The papers prepared for this meeting, as subsequently revised by the authors, constitute a unique collection of information about the underground economy and how it is manifested in a variety of countries. The purpose of this book is to collect these research findings to make them available to those who are interested in how this fascinating and increasingly prevalent segment of economic activity operates.

Section One collects papers that deal particularly with the underground economy in Canada. Rolf Mirus and Roger Smith were the first economists to measure the underground economy in Canada and their paper provides an up-to-date assessment of the size of this sector. While their calculation that the underground economy could be as much as 20 percent of the measured economy has received considerable attention, the estimates made by Mirus' and Smith's methods attract controversy and criticism by statisticians working for Statistics Canada and other statistical agencies. In his paper, Philip Smith provides Statistics Canada's views about the size of the underground economy. It is fair to say that these two papers represent the extremes of the measured range of the size of the underground economy. Philip Smith also provides the acronym UGE to describe the underground economy and henceforth in this preface we will use his abbreviation.

While Mirus and Smith estimate the UGE to be as large as 20 percent of the measured Gross Domestic Product, Statistics Canada offers an estimate in the range of 2.7 to 5 percent of the measured GDP.

In Section One's third paper, Peter Spiro provides a specific estimate of the impact that tax changes have on the size of the UGE. In particular, he analyzes the relatively significant impact of the Goods and Services Tax. According to Spiro, the introduction of the GST was the single most important factor contributing to a spurt in the growth of the UGE in 1991.

Bruce Flexman adopts a different approach to the UGE in his paper. He relies on surveys of opinion to infer how much people may be avoiding and evading taxation by reorganizing their activities. The survey also sought to determine people's attitudes towards the purchasing of smuggled goods and black market liquor and cigarettes. While the majority of citizens surveyed indicated that they would not engage in these kinds of underground activities, a very significant minority said that indeed they would. When asked whether they thought others would engage in such activities, the respondents were even more strongly of the view that other people participated in tax evasion. Perhaps the responses to these questions reflected in part the very strongly held view, revealed in the survey, that Canadians do not get value for the taxes they pay to governments.

The remaining two papers in Section One provide the views of Revenue Canada's Tim Gahagan, and British Columbia's Lois McNabb, who attempt to measure that provincial government's revenues in the face of changing behaviour by taxpayers. These two papers provide an interesting practical insight into the problems of tax evasion and tax avoidance.

Section Two of *The Underground Economy: Global Evidence of its Size and Impact* outlines a perspective of the UGE which is not often encountered, specifically, the view of law enforcement officials. The three papers in this section deal respectively with the size of the underground substance economy, the legal aspects of the UGE in the United States and an assessment of the economic activities of the Mafia.

In his paper, inspector Tim Killam of the RCMP points out that while the Statistics Canada estimate of the size of the entire underground economy is about $19 billion, police estimates suggest that trafficking in illegal drugs amounts to at least half of that figure. (Statistics Canada, like other agencies, does not include illicit activities in its UGE measurements, but includes only activities which, other than being clandestine, are legal.) Moreover, Killam is of the view that this is a very conservative, minimum estimate of the size of the illicit drug trade. One of the issues that Killam addresses in his paper is the very active smuggling which results from high excise taxation. This smuggling activity, Bruce Zagaris points out in his paper, has been facilitated by the increasing amount of international trade involving all of the major industrialized nations. The apparatus which has been established for legitimate trading activity also facilitates illicit trade.

Zagaris draws our attention to the fact that illegal trade in human beings in the form of illegal immigration is rapidly growing and may be the most profitable of the underground activities. Another outcropping of the UGE is more money laundering, which is, as Zagaris notes, an important component of the UGE. The increasing ability to communicate and the electronic transfer of funds makes money laundering an increasingly easy service for participants in the underground economy. Finally, Zagaris notes, there is an emerging problem called the "grey area phenomenon" or GAP. Essentially the GAP emerges when non-state actors and non-governmental organizations become the *de facto* "government" in a particular area. The activities of narcotics traffickers in Andean countries and the activities of private groups in U.S. innercities are examples of this sort of development.

John Burton, in his paper, points out that the Mafia is a natural private outgrowth of underground economic activity as well as an adjunct to ordinary economic activity. In effect, Burton maintains, the Mafia should be seen as a private protection industry. His analysis of the involvement of this industry is intriguing.

Section Three contains seven papers that analyze the underground economy in different countries and from different perspectives. Those who have an interest in the underground economy will be impressed by the diversity of experience in the countries discussed-from the United States and Britain to Mexico, Peru, and Chile, through to Russia and China. The findings of these papers are too numerous to summarize in this preface, but it is worth noting one of the conclusions in the paper by Edgar Feige, the father of UGE analysis.

Feige's paper is based on a study of the amount of U.S. currency held abroad. In the most careful analysis ever conducted of this issue, Feige concludes that the amount of U.S. currency held abroad indicates that there is an underground economy equal to the size of the U.S. economy hidden amongst the reported economic activities in the world's countries. Of course, much of that hidden economic activity is the subject of the country studies contained later in Section Three.

The fourth and final section of the book consists of two papers by two eminent Canadian economists—Jonathan R. Kesselman and Francois Vaillancourt. The papers have as their focus, once again, the Canadian economy and some policy implications of the UGE.

As was noted in the earlier discussion of the paper by Bruce Flexman, a majority of Canadians believe that they do not receive enough benefits for the taxation they are required to pay. In his paper, Francois Vaillancourt suggests that an obvious solution to the problem of tax evasion and the underground activity which accompanies it might be the adoption of user fees and user taxes. His analysis is that the wider use of these kinds of levies would open the way for reducing general tax rates that would in turn diminish incentives for tax evasion and therefore the size of the underground economy.

Jonathan Kesselman's paper poses some challenging questions for the avenues open to governments to reduce the size of the UGE. He provides an interesting analysis of the distribution of the costs and benefits of both tax evasion and the enforcement efforts which are pursued to stop it. Kesselman's analysis leads him to remind policy makers that, "even a relatively small underground sector could generate serious inefficiency and inequities." However, the effort to eliminate the UGE can also engender problems. One of the main public policy recommendations for tax authorities is that many of the problems of compliance with tax policy can be anticipated and to a large extent avoided in the design of the tax policies themselves.

Conclusions

The extensive discussions engendered by the papers in this book produced some interesting insights. For example, while the range of estimates of the underground economy was large, a more precise understanding of the definitional differences used to calculate the different estimates revealed that the range was much narrower than had first appeared. It was also pointed out by the Associate Deputy Minister of Finance for Canada, Don Drummond, that even if the smaller estimates—those in the five percent range—were more accurate, the implications are still important. In particular they are significant for the ability of governments to forecast current revenues and to accurately assess the possibilities for future revenue development.

The discussions also revealed that there are important implications for understanding the mechanisms of economic activity. Does the unemployment rate really mean what we think it means? In the Atlantic provinces, for example, where there has been evidence of considerably more underground economic activity than in the rest of the country, how do we account for the employment in the UGE? When we have a black economy, should we use the unemployment rate as an indication of economic cyclicality at all?

The search for the solution to the "problem" of the UGE led to two different lines of thinking. First, is this economic sector a problem or a solution? Some experts suggested that the tax wedge in the economy is killing economic activity which simply redevelops in the underground. In that sense, the underground is not a bad thing but a good one. Regulation often stifles business activity which then escapes partially or completely into the UGE. In other words, the UGE is, in fact, a measure of economic activity that is in some way a victim of tax and regulation policy and should not be regarded as a problem, but rather as a solution. Is society better or worse off as a consequence of a robustly growing underground economy?

The second line of thinking emerged from Canada's revenue Minister David Anderson, who pointed out that unsupported economic activity leads to unfairness in the distribution of the tax burden, a point which was further explored in the paper by John Kesselman written after the conference to reflect his reactions to the discussions. The fact is that the UGE represents a kind of uneven playing field when different taxpayers and different businesses comply with the tax system in different and unequal ways. This is certainly a problem.

But the attempt to deal with it, by making enforcement stricter or making the effective tax rate bite more decisively, may in fact produce further problems in the way of more evasion activity because, of course, the enforcement activity itself makes the effective tax rate higher. The studies of the underground economy in the various countries represented at this conference have led to an understanding of the enormous flexibility of the market economy to respond to unreasonable regulation or unsustainable tax rates.

We would be well advised to look more closely at the evidence from Peru and Chile. We now find that informality is as much as 50 percent of the economy in some developing countries. I think we have often tended, in North America at least, in looking at Latin America, to think that informality is a sign of some sort of cultural ineptitude. In fact, it is probably just the result of excessive regulation. The underground or informal economy, as they call it, is a natural consequence or expression of market adjustment rather than anything specifically cultural. And that is very important to understand as we begin to regulate the curvature of cucumbers and other things—that we can also produce a culture of evasion and a culture of avoidance and a culture of resort to the less efficient underground economy.

We also saw from the experience of Mexico that dramatic revenue increases can be a result of large tax rate reductions—that is, if those tax reductions are correlated with an appropriate public information program and an effective program of compliance or a change in effective compliance, so that, at the same time, you reduce the rewards of evasion and make a more effective effort to collect taxes. I suppose that the reverse situation is also true.

Finally, of course, and most importantly for researchers, there have been many suggestions for further research. There have been examples and there have been challenges thrown out by the people in government to get a better understanding of the ways in which the underground economy works. There has been a challenge to come to a more general agreement of how the UGE should be measured, and a plea for economists to collaborate to reach a consensus about the size and operation of the underground economy.

Among the most compelling pieces of evidence about the size of the UGE are the anecdotes that one encounters in everyday life. There has been a certain tendency for analysts to downplay this evidence. It is fair to say that the conclusion suggested by the evidence surveyed in this volume is that the everydayexperience evidence is fairly close to the mark. The UGE is a large and growing aspect of economic life in the world. The Fraser Institute has been pleased to support the research in this volume which has sought greater clarity about the issues of detection and measurement. However, the researchers have worked independently and the views they express may not reflect those of the members or trustees of The Fraser Institute.

—*Michael A. Walker*
Executive Director, The Fraser Institute

About the Authors

Michael Alexeev

Michael Alexeev is an Associate Professor at the Department of Economics of Indiana University. He received the M.A. equivalent in Economics and Mathematics from Moscow University in 1975 and the Ph.D. in Economics from Duke University in 1984. His current research interests lie mostly in the fields of comparative economics and economics of transition from socialism to a market economy with a particular focus on informal aspects of economic behavior. Since early 1992 Dr. Alexeev, who is a native of Russia, has been actively participating in the technical assistance programs to the former Soviet Union.

John Burton

John Burton is Professor of Business Administration and General Coordinator of the Strategic Management Research Group in the Department of Commerce, Birmingham Business School, University of Birmingham, UK.

He has previously held professorial posts at the Leeds Business School and the European Business School, and lecturing appointments with the Universities of Southampton and Birmingham, Kingston Polytechnic, and Boston University. From 1984-1987 he was a Research Director at the Institute of Economic Affairs, London; and in 1987 also a Special Adviser to the House of Commons Treasury and Civil Service Select Committee.

He is a co-founder of the magazine *Business Studies* (launched in 1988), and has contributed numerous articles in refereed journals. His books and monographs include: *Whither Sunday Trading?* (1994); *Retail Rents: Fair and Free Market?* (1992); (with D. Parker, Joint eds.) *Studies in Business and Management* (1991); *Would Workfare Work?* (1987); (ed.) *Keynes's General Theory: Fifty Years On* (1986); *Why No Cuts?* (1985); (ed.) *Hayek's 'Serfdom' Revisited* (1984); (With J.T. Addison) *Trade Unions and Society* (1984); *Picking Losers...?* (1983); *The Job-Supports Machine* (1979); (with J.M. Buchanan and R.E. Wagner) *The Consequences of Mr. Keynes* (1978); *Wage Inflation* (1972).

Edgar L. Feige

Edgar L. Feige is Professor of Economics at the University of Wisconsin-Madison. He has taught at Yale University, The University of Essex, Erasmus University and the University of Leyden where he held the Cleveringa Chair. He was appointed Fellow at the Netherlands Institute for advanced Study and Fulbright Scholar in Spain. He is the author of more than sixty publications in monetary and macroeconomics and is best known for his work on Underground Economies. He has served as a consultant to the United States Treasury Department, The Agency for International Development, the Supreme Soviet of the Russian Federation, the Board of Governors of the Federal Reserve System and on the Task Force on Economies in Transition of the National Research Council. He received his B.A. at Columbia University and his Ph.D at the University of Chicago.

Bruce P. Flexman

Bruce P. Flexman received a B. Sc. in Engineering and Mathematics from Queen's University and an M.B.A. with distinction from Cornell University. He is a chartered accountant specializing in GST and income taxes. Mr. Flexman is currently responsible for the Vancouver tax practice at KPMG and provides national technical leadership on GST matters. From 1991 to 193 he was on executive exchange with Revenue Canada acting as Deputy Director General for GST Policy and Legislation. He has also acted as technical advisor to the Senate Committee on Banking, Trade and Commerce in their deliberation concerning the introduction of the GST and was consulted by the Finance Committee on their review of alternatives to the GST.

Tim Gahagan

Mr. Gahagan is presently the manager, Underground Economy and Compliance Initiatives Section, Revenue Canada, in Ottawa. He holds a Bachelor of Mathematics degree from the University of Waterloo. Mr. Gahagan is also a Certified Management Accountant (CMA).

In his 20 years with Revenue Canada, Mr. Gahagan has held various positions in Hamilton, Edmonton, and Ottawa before assuming his present responsibilities in January 1994.

Enrique Ghersi

Enrique Ghersi was born in Lima, Peru, in 1961. He is a lawyer, journalist, and Professor at the University of Lima's Law School. Mr. Ghersi has been a member of Parliament since 1990, representing Lima. He is co-author of the bestseller *The Other Path* with Hernando de Soto. His weekly articles appear in over 40 newspapers from 20 countries.

Jonathan R. Kesselman

Jonathan R. Kesselman is Professor of Economics, University of British Columbia; Director, Centre for Research on Economic and Social Policy, UBC; Ph.D. in economics, MIT, 1972. Consultant to governments in Canada, Australia, India, New Zealand, and the United States; member, B.C. Premier's Forum on New Opportunities for Working and Living, 1994-95; member, Musqueam Indian Band Taxation Advisory Council (chair, 1992-96). He holds visiting appointments at the Institute for the Research on Poverty, University of Wisconsin-Madison; Delhi School of Economics, India; and the Australian National University as Professorial Fellow in Economic Policy of the Reserve Bank of Australia. Dr. Kesselman's areas of specialization include theoretical and policy assessment of taxation, income security, employment programs, and social insurance finance.

Timothy George Killam

Inspector Killam joined the Royal Canadian Mounted Police (RCMP) in 1976 and has since enjoyed a variety of policing and administrative experiences. He has five years experience in drug enforcement as an investigator and undercover operative. Inspector Killam spent nine years in a commercial crime unit investigating white-collar crime, including tax evasion and major frauds. In 1990, he was transferred to the RCMP Professional Standards Directorate, where he acted, on separate occasions, as advocate and solicitor in the roles of prosecution and defence. In 1993, he was appointed the Officer-in-Charge of the Anti-Drug Profiteering Program and a year later was transferred to his present position as the officer responsible for the RCMP Proceeds of Crime Program. He received an LL.B. (1990) and a Bachelor of Commerce (1985) from the University of Windsor and a Bachelor of Arts from St. Thomas University in 1976.

Owen Lippert

Owen Lippert worked as a policy and communications advisor in Ottawa for Kim Campbell when she was Justice Minister, and for Rob Nicholson when he was Science Minister. Prior to 1991, Dr. Lippert worked for the B.C. Premier's Office in Victoria. Owen Lippert earned a Ph.D. in History and Government from the University of Notre Dame, Indiana. He has taught at universities in the United States, Canada, Taiwan, and has independently advised the federal departments of Justice and Industry Canada as well as several private companies.

Lois McNabb

Lois McNabb is the director of the Economics and Trade Branch of the B.C. Ministry of Forests. From 1989 to 1996 she was director of the Fiscal and Economic Analysis Branch of the B.C. Ministry of Finance and Corporate Relations. From 1982 to 1989, she held various manager and director positions in the ministry. Prior to joining the B.C. government, Ms. McNabb was an economist in the revenue forecasting section of the federal Department of Finance. She graduated with a B.A. in Economics and Mathematics from McMaster University in 1974 and obtained an M.A. in Economics from the University of Western Ontario in 1977.

Rolf Mirus

Rolf Mirus is a Professor in the Faculty of Business and the Department of Economics at the University of Alberta. He served from 1984 to 1996 as Director of the Canada China Management Education Program link-ing the University of Alberta to Xi'an Jiaotong University. From 1989 to 1992 he was the Founding Director of the faculty's Centre for International Business Studies. Dr. Mirus obtained his Ph.D. in Economics from the University of Minnesota in 1973. He researches and teaches in macroeconomics, international finance, and international business; he has held visiting appointments at universities in Germany, Austria, China, Kenya, Pakistan, and the U.S.

Roger S. Smith

Roger S. Smith is a Professor in the Faculty of Business and the Department of Economics at the University of Alberta. He served as Dean of the Faculty of Business (1976-88) and as Acting Vice President (Academic) (1994-95). The years 1977-78 and 1995-96 were spent as a Visiting Scholar with Harvard's International Tax Program. He is currently Chair of the Board of Directors of the Banff School of Advanced Management. Dr. Smith received his Ph.D. in Economics from the University of California (Berkeley) in 1969. He worked for the IMF (1972-74), and has been a consultant to the IMF, World Bank, OECD, the Auditor General of Canada and other private and public organizations. His research and teaching is in the area of tax policy and macroeconomics.

Philip Smith

Philip Smith is an economist with a B.A. from McGill University and M.A. and Ph.D. degrees from Queen's University. He worked for several years at the federal Department of Finance as Director of Fiscal Policy and later, of International Finance and Development. For the past nine years he has worked at Statistics Canada, first as Director of National Accounts and Environment and currently as Director of Industrial Organization and Finance.

Peter S. Spiro

Peter S. Spiro is a Toronto—based economist specializing in macroeconomic policy issues, with wide experience working in both the public and private sectors. He has graduate degrees in economics from the University of Toronto and the University of Chicago, where he studied under Nobel laureates Milton Friedman and Gary Becker. He has published many research studies in professional journals, and is the author of a critically praised book, *Real Interest Rates and Investment and Borrowing*

Strategy. The opinions expressed in his contribution to this volume are personal and do not represent any organization with which he may be affiliated.

François Vaillancourt

François Vaillancourt holds a Ph.D. from Queen's University and is Professor, Department of Economics and Research Fellow, Centre de recherche et développement en économique (C.R.D.E.) at the Université de Montréal and Fellow, I.R.P.P. He teaches, conducts, research and has published extensively in the area of public finance and the economics of language. He has conducted research and acted as a consultant for organizations such as the Canadian Tax Foundation, the Conseil de la language française, the Department of Finance, the Economic Council of Canada, Statistics Canada and the World Bank.

Michael A. Walker

Michael Walker, Ph.D., is Executive Director of The Fraser Institute. Since 1974, he has directed the research activities of The Fraser Institute. He has written or edited 40 books on economic topics. His articles on technical economic subjects have appeared in professional journals in Canada, the United States, and Europe. He has been a regular columnist in the Vancouver *Province*, the Toronto *Sun*, the Ottawa *Citizen*, and the *Financial Post*. He taught at the University of Western Ontario and Carleton University, and was employed at the Bank of Canada and the Federal Department of Finance. He received his B.A. at St. Francis Xavier University and his Ph.D at the University of Western Ontario. He is a director of a number of firms and other enterprises.

Raymundo Winkler

Raymundo Winkler is the Director-General of the Center for Economic Studies of the Private Sector (CEESP), Mexico's leading private-sector economic think tank. He has a B.A. in Economics and post-graduate studies in Economic Development from the Instituto Politecnico Nacional in Mexico. Mr. Winkler has served in both the public sector, where he was in charge of the Department of International Economic Studies at the Ministry of Mines, Energy and State-owned Enterprises, and in the private sector, where he has been in charge of economic studies for several firms, including a mining company and DESC, one of the largest industrial conglomerates in Mexico. When Mr. Winkler joined CEESP, he was placed in charge of its research program, and while in this role published two books. He continues to write about short-term developments in the Mexican economy on a regular basis.

Yue-Chim Richard Wong

Yue Chim Richard Wong is Professor of Economics at the University of Hong Kong. He studied economics at the University of Chicago (A.B. 1974, A.M. 1974, and Ph.D. 1981), and was Visiting Scholar at the National Opinion Research Centre at the University of Chicago in 1985 and at the Hoover Institution of War, Revolution and Peace at Stanford University in 1989. His current research interest is in the economics of transition in China and the political economy of Hong Kong. He has authored numerous books and articles.

In addition to his scientific work, Dr. Wong is founding Director of the Hong Kong Centre for Economic Research; a free market policy research institution. The Centre is currently leading a 36-volume study entitled *Economic Policies for Hong Kong*: Beyond the Transition. He is a member of the Economic Advisory Committee, HK, Hong Kong Committee for Pacific Economic Co-operation Council, Industry and Technology Development Council, HK , University Grants Committee, HK, and Finance Committee of the Hong Kong Housing Authority.

Contact: School of Economics and Finance, The University of Hong Kong, Pokfulam Road, Hong Kong. Tel: +852-2547-8313, Facsimile: +852-2548-6319, Email: rycwong@econ.hku.hk.

Bruce Zagaris

Bruce Zagaris received his B.A., J.D., and LL.M. (tax) from George Washington University, his LL.M. (comparative) from Stockholm University, Sweden, and his LL.M. (international) from the Free University, Brussels. He did legal work in Europe and Africa for two years, including as a U.N. consultant in West Africa. He practiced customs law in San Francisco, and taught at the Law Faculty of the University of the West Indies before practicing law in Washington which he has done since 1978, currently as a partner with the law firm of Cameron & Hornbostel.

His practice includes counseling and defending white collar criminal cases with significant international elements. His work has a large focus on international tax law, including advising and negotiating agreements and serving as counsel in criminal tax litigation. He has also done a lot of work in the money laundering area.

He is an Adjunct Professor of International Criminal Business Law at Fordham Law School, New York City. He has written four books (three as editor) on international law and many articles. Bruce Zagaris is founder and editor-in-chief of the *International Enforcement Law Reporter*. He is chair, Committee on International Criminal Law, Criminal Justice Section, American Bar Association and chair, Committee on International Tax, Section of International Law & Practice, American Bar Association.

Section 1:
The Underground Economy
in Canada

Canada's Underground Economy: Measurement and Implications

Rolf Mirus and Roger S. Smith

Introduction

A recent headline in the *Globe and Mail* read, "US Tax Cheating Worth $150 Billion"; a regional newspaper featured the "Under-the-Table Economy" over a full two pages, and the Ontario Legislature's Standing Committee on Finance and Economic Affairs devoted more than a day to hearing expert evidence on tax evasion practices. These and other signs of heightened interest in the underground economic phenomenon raise some important questions.

How can our reported unemployment statistics be giving an accurate picture of labour market conditions when there is so much more economic activity than is being reported? Does the inflation rate truly reflect the prices Canadian households are paying? Are countries with large underground economies paying too little when their contributions to international organizations are based on official measures of GDP?

How will honest taxpayers react to mounting evidence that many others are not paying their share? Are we becoming a society in which it is widely acceptable to evade the GST? Should we be happy that the underground economy provides low prices for the poor (and the rich)? Could governments be basing policies on flawed statistics? Is a self-assessment system of taxation feasible in the long run when more and more people are seeing their neighbours participate in the underground economy?

The answers to these questions will in part depend on our assessment of the size of the underground economy. Moreover, actions to address this phenomenon will require comprehension of its underlying causes. Our aim here is to define what constitutes the underground economy, discuss some issues related to measuring its size and growth, and explore its causes and the implications for business and policy decision makers.

The underground economy: what is it?

As is well understood, the need to maintain a record of national production represents significant challenges for the government agencies charged with this task. One of the conventions among national income accounts statisticians is therefore to focus on market transactions for final goods and services, ignoring the considerable amount of output produced in the home.

The "observed economy," to use our term for officially measured output, can be computed by totalling all expenditures for newly produced goods and services that are not resold in any form. Typically, this includes consumer spending, investment spending by businesses, government expenditures at all levels for such goods and services (but not for transfer payments), and net exports. An alternative but economically equivalent approach is to focus on the cost of producing the output, inasmuch as costs are income for someone else, and arrive at total production, or GDP, by totalling all forms of income received.

The first hint of measuring difficulties comes when the income approach leads to a smaller GDP than the expenditure approach. This discrepancy suggests that, for example, some income is spent on consumer goods and thus captured in the expenditure measure of GDP, but not declared as taxable and hence not reflected in the income measure of GDP. However, this discrepancy loses its value as a proxy variable for unreported income when we realize that underreported retail sales—as a result of turning off the cash register, for example—can bias the expenditure measure in the downward direction. This possibility alerts us to the likelihood of unobserved economic activity that should be included in our GDP measure.

Testimony before the Ontario Legislature's Standing Committee pointed out that reported jewellery sales per capita were 33 percent higher in the US than in Canada and that Quebec sales were only 60 percent of Ontario's despite similar incomes and tastes. The absence of a sales tax on jewellery in the US explains the first difference and particular attitudes towards taxes in Quebec explain the second, suggested the expert witness, who had conducted a detailed investigation

Table 1: A Taxonomy of Types of Underground Economic Activities

	Monetary Transactions		Non-Monetary Transactions	
Illegal Activities	Trade in stolen goods, drugs; manufacture of drugs; prostitution, gambling, fraud		Barter, drugs, stolen goods, etc.	Produce or grow drugs for own use. Theft for own use.
	Tax Evasion	**Tax Avoidance**	**Tax Evasion**	**Tax Avoidance**
Legal Activities	Unreported income from self-employment, wages, salaries, and assets	Employee discounts, fringe benefits (cars, subsidized food, etc.)	Barter of legal services and goods.	Do-it-yourself work

Source: This table was provided by Professor H.G. Grubel.

for the industry association. These results indicated that as much as two thirds of the jewellery trade might be "underground."

Table 1 may be helpful for developing a better feel for what could be a reasonable consensus definition of the underground economy.

Illegal activities are not part of our GDP concept, although courts have ruled that resulting income is nevertheless taxable. And some illegal income is actually reflected in GDP because expenditures based on such income are included. Legal activities, whether money- or barter-based, should be included in GDP but may go unreported. The latter group involves the production of goods and services but may be structured as barter to leave no record and so succeed in evading taxes. A working definition of the underground economy would therefore be: economic activity which would generally be taxable were it reported to the tax authorities. Thus, the underground economy would include unreported rental incomes, skimming by owners of businesses, barter activities, off-the-books employment, and unreported income from home-produced goods.

How to measure the underground economy?

Obviously, anyone partaking in the underground economy is trying to escape detection: this makes measuring the phenomenon extremely difficult. If, however, we are to decide whether Canada's underground economy is worth worrying about or is growing so that it will be worth worrying about, or both, we must have an information base. Several approaches have been used to arrive at estimates, or "guesstimates," each with advantages and drawbacks. For example, it is plausible to expect estimates based on interviews and surveys, even when confidentiality is assured, to turn up a relatively small underground economy: respondents can be expected to err on the side of caution.

As already indicated, the discrepancy between the expenditure and income approaches to GDP compilation also yields a flawed estimate. Time use or availability studies, on the other hand, can provide some useful information. Statistics Canada researchers pondered how many additional hours could realistically be worked by occupations likely to have opportunities for unobserved economic activity and then added up the probable extra output. Since this approach does not cover the entire economy, its results, namely that there may be 2.9 to 3.5 percent more GDP than officially reported, can be viewed as a lower boundary for the then (1985) underground economy. In terms of 1992 GDP, this would have meant $20-24 billion.

Another frequently used approach for estimating the underground economy relies on an indirect route, attributing the increase in the ratio of currency to demand deposits over some base year to a need to hold cash for underground transactions. This approach results in a rather large underground economy for Canada, 21.6 percent for 1990 based on the 1937-1939 currency ratio. It is probably true that this type of estimate is biased in the upward direction due to the fact that the currency deposit ratio has increased, in part because financial innovations have substantially reduced the need to hold demand deposits. On the other hand, this approach does not capture cheque- and barter-based transactions.

The transactions method pioneered by Wisconsin economics professor Edgar Feige relies on the assumption that the ratio of total economic transactions to final transactions (GDP) is historically stable. This ratio permits us to estimate what GDP would have been had all final transactions been properly recorded. The underground economy, then, is the difference between the transactions-method estimate of GDP and the official GDP figure. On that basis, Canada's underground economy was in the order of 20 percent of GDP in 1984, the last year for which the necessary data on cheque clearing are available.

This method includes not only cash but also cheques as media of exchange in the underground economy—for example, a customer cheque endorsed by a contractor and used to settle a bill for building supplies. In other respects, however, this way of sizing the underground economy requires assumptions about the life of banknotes, the extent of purely financial transactions, and the structure of the economy that make it hard to accept its results as definitive.

Work on this topic by Vito Tanzi of the IMF uses a modified currency ratio method and relates it to the tax burden. This approach asks what the currency to deposit ratio would have been had historical taxation levels been maintained. For Canada in 1990, an extra $5 billion in currency were attributable to tax hikes since 1965. Multiplying this extra currency by the turnover speed of money (M1) produces an estimate of 12.8 percent of extra GDP that goes unmeasured and is tax-induced.

While the monetary approaches have been the domain of academics, some studies by the US Internal Revenue Service (IRS) have by and large resulted in the range of outcomes discussed so far. The latest of these was based on the Taxpayer Compliance Measurement Program that subjected 55,000 tax files to a detailed examination to identify amounts of income that should have been reported over and above what actually was reported. The IRS found unreported legal income of US$585 billion and illegal income of US$88 billion for 1992. These estimates also relied on audits and special surveys and assumed no change in non-compliance since 1982.

If Canadians behave similarly in an economy one tenth the size of the US, we get a $73 billion estimate for Canada (US$0.8/$) which translates as 10.6 percent of GDP. In the Canadian setting, Peter Spiro of the Ontario Ministry of Finance has found that since the introduction of the GST in 1991 cash holdings have inexplicably soared. This finding is entirely consistent with a boost in the size of the underground economy.

Further corroboration of this order of magnitude for the money-based (legal and illegal) part of the phenomenon under discussion in Canada has recently been produced by IMF researchers. Studying real per-capita currency holdings for eight countries with freely convertible currencies, they hypothesized that technology like credit cards and electronic transfer mechanisms should have reduced these holdings by 10 percent between 1970 and 1990. For Canada, this reasoning produced $4.7 billion in extra currency for 1990, and therefore, after multiplication by a turnover speed of 15 (M1), approximately $70 billion in additional GDP. This amounts to saying that whatever underground economy may have existed in 1970, it has grown by another 10.5 percent of GDP since.

All in all, then, a number of approaches suggest significant growth and an order of magnitude of 12 to 15 percent of GDP for Canada's underground economy when we include illegal activities but exclude barter-based transactions which our definition says should be counted.

Causes and implications

Granted that the above size and growth estimates are surrounded by large margins of error, it is nonetheless obvious that a federal deficit of $45 billion makes an additional unrecorded output of $70 to $100 billion the focus of some attention. Among the factors that may have caused the growth of the underground economy, personal taxes must figure prominently. As a share of personal income net of transfers, personal income tax rose from 15.2 percent in 1976 to 19.7 percent in 1990. There was a pronounced increase between 1980 and 1991 in Canada's total tax revenue as a share of GDP from less than 32 percent to almost 38 percent, and that was before the impact of the switch to the GST.

This same general period has also seen a decline in confidence in government and a higher unemployment rate that makes more people available for informal work. Additionally, the percentage of self-employed in the unincorporated and incorporated sectors grew from 11.1 in 1976 to 14.5 of total employment in 1990. While the small-business sector has thus proven itself to be the engine of growth, it may also be a breeding ground for much underground economic activity. In the US and the UK, only 60 to 65 percent of income in the self-employment sector is actually reported. This percentage is not likely to be much different for Canada.

Two other contributing causes of the underground economy are to be found in immigration and the globalization of portfolio investment. As regards immigration, annual newcomer numbers doubled between 1981 and 1992, while business immigrant numbers even quadrupled. Immigrants have to learn about our tax system, and again, US studies provide evidence that underground economic activity is more prevalent in recent immigrant communities because of their small-business nature and their tendency to foster informal business relationships. With respect to the increasing globalization of investment portfolios, the IMF recently observed that "reported portfolio investment income is the fastest growing, and now the largest, of all individual current account discrepancies." In plain English, worldwide interest and dividends reported as paid by corporations exceed those reported as income received by $33 billion, and that was in 1984!

Should we care? What can be done? A recent calculation by David Perry of the Canadian Tax Foundation shows that a 15 percent underground economy means $28.6 billion in forgone revenue: $15.8 billion at the federal level, $11.5 billion at the provincial level, and $1.3 billion for the Canada and Quebec Pension Plans. So much additional revenue potential in the face of massive deficits means that the Department of Finance cares. Clearly, we must care too when, as a result of widely observed underground economic practices, the tax system is perceived as unfair, attitudes deteriorate, and support for the public sector erodes. Yet quelling this growing underground economy is no easy task, especially as it has tended to establish itself slowly over time as a mindset with a powerful momentum.

Here, then, is a list of some things that can be done:

1. Broaden the tax base and lower tax rates to reduce the economic incentive to go underground. This may mean including food in the GST base and reducing RRSP deduction limits in return for lower rates of basic income tax.

2. Simplify the administration of the various taxes, including integration of the federal and provincial sales taxes.

3. Consider tougher enforcement. This is already happening as more auditors are being put to work by Revenue Canada. However, in response, we may expect some income-generating activity to be shifted to the non-taxable, do-it-yourself sector. In other words, don't expect miracles!

4. Increase international cooperation for the sharing of tax information. We already have this cooperation with the US, but big capital flows to and from Asia and Europe suggest that investment income reporting will become a more significant issue with those regions as well.

5. Build a better information base for the underground economy with the resources of Statistics Canada, the Department of Finance, and Revenue Canada.

There are, of course, some positive aspects to the underground economy, not least being the evidence that a more vital economy exists than we are led to believe by the official statistics. Its existence and growth, despite our lack of consensus on its extent, send a message to policy makers about the limits to which taxation can be pushed.

Assessing the Size of the Underground Economy: The Statistics Canada Perspective

Philip M. Smith

Introduction

A substantial body of opinion exists in Canada to the effect that a variously defined underground economy accounts for a large and growing share of total economic activity in the country. The news media have given the topic considerable attention in recent years.[1] Yet much uncertainty remains about how significant this phenomenon really is.

---

1   Among many recent examples which can be cited are the story "Underground economy runs deep, " in the June 24, 1993 issue of the *Vancouver Sun*; the August 9, 1993 cover story in *Maclean's* entitled "Cheaters: How Dodging Taxes Feeds a Growing Underground Economy, " and a feature item on the November 5, 1993 edition of the program "W5" on CTV.

A conclusion that the underground economy is large and growing has some serious implications: the recession and rising unemployment of the early 1990s may have been illusory, a sizeable portion of the population may be evading their fair share of the tax burden, and Canada's statistical system may be leading the country astray. A contrary conclusion also has important implications, especially if propensities for tax cheating are influenced by public pronouncements about its supposed prevalence. There is an urgent need to settle this matter one way or the other.

Unfortunately, this is no simple task. By its very nature, the underground economy defies measurement. Several methods have been tried to infer its approximate size, but none has attained wide acceptance. Some approaches—in particular, those relying on the assumed existence of a stable relationship between unreported economic activity and the stock of money—tend to indicate a large and growing underground economy, most often in the range of 10 to 25 percent of the observed economy. Other methods, based on more direct measurement techniques, point to a much smaller, albeit non-negligible underground economy, typically in the range of 1 to 5 percent of GDP.

We will consider four alternative definitions of the underground economy and examine the available evidence about its size. Statistics Canada believes that the underground economy is far smaller than the money demand studies have suggested.

Definitions

There are several definitions of the underground economy in common use,[2] serving various objectives. The public authorities are naturally most interested in sales or income not reported for tax or regulatory purposes, whereas statisticians are more concerned about economic activities belonging, but not captured, in the official GDP estimates. The

---

2   There are also many alternative adjectives —black, cash, covert, dual, grey, hidden, illegal, informal, invisible, irregular, marginal, moonlight, parallel, second, shadow, subterranean, twilight, under-the-table, unobserved, unofficial, unrecorded, unreported—which some people treat as synonymous and others use to draw distinctions. In this paper I use one term throughout: the underground economy.

differences in the various definitions of the underground economy turn on some questions of classification, which are schematized in Table 1.

Table 1: Classification of Production Activities with Examples

	Legal activities	**Illegal activities**
Market-based production activity	**A.** Production and sale of automobiles, housing, restaurant meals, roads	**B.** Production and sale of narcotic drugs, prostitution, some kinds of pornography
Non-market-based production activity	**C.** Household cooking and cleaning, imputed rent on owner-occupied dwellings	**D.** Growing marijuana for own use

There is an important distinction here between market-based and non-market-based activities. Most transactions included in the national accounts are market-based and monetary in nature. Household work, for example, is not included in GDP although it is quantified and valued separately by Statistics Canada. Non-market activities are included in a few exceptional cases totalling about 6 percent of GDP,[3] but the general rule admits only market-based economic activities. Since the tax base is confined to the market economy as well, most definitions of the underground economy will consider none but market-based activity.

GDP is explicitly a measure of economic output and so excludes transfers and capital gains and losses, which are not production. In this respect, the tax base differs somewhat. Although most of its components are domestic factor incomes or final sales, the tax base can also include other types of transactions—examples being capital gains, inheritances,

---

3   The exceptions are net rent on owner-occupied dwellings, food and lodging provided to employees in lieu of wages, food consumed directly on farms, income in kind to members of religious organizations, estimated services rendered by financial institutions without specific charge, and capital consumption allowances on residential property and government-owned capital goods.

and some transactions involving goods and services not produced domestically in the current period. Transactions of this kind are not part of domestic production and thus by definition are excluded from GDP.[4] Most researchers also exclude these transactions from their definitions of the underground economy, although Revenue Canada auditors would be unlikely to follow this practice.

A second important distinction is made between legal and illegal transactions. In the present context, the latter mean the production and sale of goods and services that are themselves illegal, such as certain narcotic drugs, some kinds of pornography, and solicitation for prostitution. Transactions that involve licit commodities being covertly traded to avoid tax or regulation are not deemed illegal for our purposes. In principle, GDP includes all production without regard for legality, though in practice there is usually no way of reliably measuring illegal output. Like the national accounts production boundary, the tax base makes no distinction between legal and illegal income.

At the most general level, the underground economy may be defined as the portion of the total economy that is unobserved due to the efforts of some businesses and households to keep their activities undetected. More specific definitions hinge on what is meant by "the total economy" and who the "observer" may be. Four different definitions of "underground economy" can be formulated on the basis of our classification of production activities (Table 2).

The first definition is based on what is, in practice, the production boundary for the Canadian national accounts. The second is identical to the first except that it also includes illegal activities (as defined above) that properly belong within the national accounts production boundary. The third definition is identical to the second except that the "observer" is the tax collector rather than the statistician. The reason for the distinction between definitions 2 and 3 is that the portion of market-based production missed in the national accounts is smaller than the portion

---

4   For example, cross-border shopping has no net effect on GDP, although it is part of the tax base. It enters personal expenditures for consumer goods and services and is netted out of GDP via imports. Trading margins on inported and used goods are treated as the production of services in GDP, but the base value of such goods, before margins, is netted out.

> ## Table 2: Alternative Definitions of the Underground Economy[a]
>
> 1. Market-based production of legal goods and services that escapes detection in the official estimates of GDP (part of A).
>
> 2. Market-based production of goods and services, whether legal or illegal, that escapes detection in the official estimates of GDP (part of A+B).
>
> 3. Market-based production of goods and services, whether legal or illegal, that escapes detection by the tax authorities (part of A+B).
>
> 4. Market- and non-market-based production of goods and services, whether legal or illegal, that escapes detection in or is intentionally excluded from the official estimates of GDP (part of A+B+C+D).
>
> [a]The symbols A through D are explained in Table 1.

that goes undeclared for tax purposes. Finally, a fourth definition broadens the production boundary to include non-market activities, household and volunteer work in particular.[5]

Available estimates for Canada

The international literature on the extent of the underground economy has been multiplying rapidly over the past fifteen years or so. In Canada, interest developed more slowly at first than in other countries, but the topic has come to be the focus of considerable attention.[6]

The earliest published Canadian study was by Rolf Mirus and Roger Smith (1981),[7] who reported widely varying estimates of the size of the underground economy based on hypotheses about the demand for

---

5 The term "underground economy" is less appropriate for this fourth definition, since household and volunteer work are by no means covert. One of the other terms alluded to in note 2 above, such as "invisible" economy, might be more suitable.

6 For selected readings on the size and implications of the underground economy in other countries, see Feige (1989) and United Nations (1992).

7 Some unpublished work on the topic has also been done at the Bank of Canada and the federal Department of Finance.

money similar to those used for the United States by Gutmann (1977), Feige (1979), and Tanzi (1980). Subsequently, Mirus (1984) provided additional estimates that were also based on assumptions about the relationship between the stock of money and the level of underground economic activity.

In these Canadian studies as well as in subsequent work by the same researchers, the applicable definition of "underground economy" is the second one, which includes all production activity missed in the official GDP estimates (including illegal activities) but excludes the portion captured in those statistics and missed by the tax authorities. In a volume published by the Royal Commission on the Economic Union and Development Prospects for Canada, Mireille Éthier (1985) reported another set of estimates based on the Tanzi approach.

In 1986, Seymour Berger of Statistics Canada published estimates of the size of the underground economy that were based on another methodology, similar in some ways to the one used by Carol Carson (1984) for the United States. In this procedure, the components of the income- and expenditure-based GNP estimates were considered separately and informed judgements were made in each case, based on expert knowledge about the quality of the surveys and other information sources used to derive the national accounts estimates, about how much unrecorded activity might exist. Berger concluded, as did Carson for the US, that the underground economy was considerably smaller than the money demand studies were indicating.

Three Université Laval economists—Fortin, Fréchette, and Noreau (1987)—tried a different approach: a direct survey of the 1986 underground economy. Their questionnaire, administered anonymously and completed by 2,134 respondents, contained questions on both the demand and the supply aspects of the underground economy. Some 31 percent of respondents acknowledged some kind of participation in the underground economy as purchasers or suppliers of goods and services. The average declared income of covert workers was about half that of the sample average, suggesting that underground activity is most often a part-time, low-income occupation. The Laval results pointed to total underground production equivalent to 1.4 percent of Quebec GDP.

Toward the end of the decade, Gilles Paquet (1989) reviewed the available evidence and offered his personal assessment that

Table 3: Estimates of the Underground Economy in Canada

Study	Date of study	Target year	Defini-tion	Method	Estimate (% of GDP)
Mirus and Smith	1981	1976	2	Money demand (Gutmann)	15.7
		1976	2	Money demand (Feige)	27.5
		1976	2	Money demand (Tanzi)	4.9 - 7.7
Mirus	1984	1980	2	Money demand	9.3
		1980	2	Money demand (Feige)	14.1
Éthier	1985	1981	2	Money demand (Tanzi)	5.7
Statistics Canada (Berger)	1986	1981	1	National accounts	2.8
		1981	1	National accounts	1.2 - 3.4
Fortin, Fréchette, and Noreau	1987	1986	3	Direct survey of households	1.4
Paquet	1989	1989	4	Subjective assessment	33 - 100
Mirus and Smith	1989	1982	2	Money demand (Feige)	10.5 - 12.8
Karoleff, Mirus, and Smith	1993	1984	2	Money demand (Feige)	19.3
		1990	2	Money demand (Gutmann)	21.6
		1990	2	Money demand (Tanzi)	14.6
Statistics Canada (Gervais)	1994	1992	1	National accounts	2.7
			2	National accounts	3.7
			3	National accounts	5.2
			4	National accounts	47.1

The estimates reported in this table are expressed as a percentage of measured GDP. Some authors record their results as a percentage of "total economic activity," defined as the sum of measured GDP and their estimate of the underground economy. In such cases the results have been converted using the formulas $x/(1-x)$, where x is the originally reported percentage. In addition, results originally reported as a percentage of GNP are shown here as a percentage of GDP (which is 2 to 3% larger than GNP). Note that although some researchers report time series estimates, this table shows only the value reported for the most recent year.

the underground economy broadly defined might represent, in the most conservative estimates, approximately one third of measured GDP and in the higher estimates as much as 100 per cent of measured GDP. It must be repeated that all such measurements are *extremely conservative* and that they do not begin to gauge the real size of the underground economy.[8]

It is hard to know what to make of this opinion, since Paquet provided no explanation of how his estimates were derived or why they were so much larger than all other published estimates.

More recently, Karoleff, Mirus, and Smith (1993) reported updated estimates based on the money demand approach placing the size of the underground economy in 1990 at 15 to 22 percent of GDP. Peter Spiro (1993) examined whether the introduction of the Goods and Services Tax in 1991 might have prompted a sharp increase in the underground economy and concluded, using an econometric equation for money demand, that the covert sector might have increased by 0.8 percent of GDP by 1992. Spiro did not, however, provide any estimate of the overall size of the underground economy.

The Statistics Canada perspective

In the light of all this, Statistics Canada took a fresh look at the size of the underground economy, focussing primarily on the first definition in Table 2. For the year 1992, the components of expenditure-based GDP were examined one by one for an assessment of how much spending might be missed at maximum, given the sources of information and statistical methods presently in use. Table 4 provides a summary of the analytical results that are summarized in the next few pages.

For some components—government expenditure, business plant and equipment investment outlays, inventory change, transfer costs on residential housing—there are strong *a priori* reasons for believing that the underground economy is not significantly skewing our official statistics. Governments do not make purchases underground. Business investment outlays are tax-deductible and financed openly in the capital markets: it is difficult to imagine why companies would deliberately

---

8   Emphasis on page 4 of original.

Table 4: Upper Limit on Underground Transactions Potentially Missing from Expenditure-Based GDP, 1992

	Official GDP estimates	Potential underground transactions	
	($ millions)		(%)
Personal expenditure on consumer goods and services	419,536	14,849	3.5
Government current expenditure on goods and services	148,377	—	—
Government investment expenditure	16,508	—	—
Business investment in fixed capital	113,440	3,578	3.2
Residential construction	43,992	3,578	8.1
New residential construction	20,934	1,883	9.0
Alterations and improvements	12,153	1,695	13.9
Transfer costs	10,905	—	—
Non-residential construction	30,189	—	—
Machinery and equipment	39,259	—	—
Business investment in inventories	-2,558	—	—
Exports	181,948	1,100	0.6
Merchandise	156,567	800	0.5
Non-merchandise	25,381	300	1.2
Less: Imports	185,751	1,038	0.6
Merchandise	147,588	1,038	0.7
Non-merchandise	38,163	—	—
Statistical discrepancy	-2,959	—	—
Gross domestic product at market prices	688,541	18,489	2.7

Source: Gervais [1994].

understate their investments.[9] Transfer costs—essentially, real-estate commissions—are measured in a way that precludes their being affected by underground transactions, even if some real-estate agents or companies are underreporting income to Revenue Canada.[10]

---

9   Machinery and equipment supply flows are also observed in the imports data and manufacturers' production survey responses. Non-residential construction activity is also monitored with information about construction materials shipments, building permits, the value of contracts awarded, and employment in the construction industry. Moreover, most non-residential construction is highly visible: hydroelectric projects, oil and gas drilling, office towers, shopping malls, roads, bridges, pipelines, and so on. There are many ways to cross-check the data for business investment spending.

10   An average commission rate is applied to the reported value of sales obtained from the Canadian Real Estate Association. The industry is self-regulating and monitored by provincial governments through the land registry system.

The export sector contains few goods or services concerning which underground activity is evident or suspected. Nevertheless, a review of the commodity detail for exports suggests that total exports might be understated by at most $1.1 billion, 0.6 percent, due to the underground economy. The case of imports is somewhat special, since this component is subtracted in the GDP calculation. Rather than implying an understatement of GDP, missed transactions would indicate that GDP is either overstated, if the imported goods and services still show up elsewhere in final demand, or unaffected.

One of the main sectors where underground activity is likely to be important is residential construction. New residential construction is essentially measured as the product of number of housing starts and average house value, appropriate allowances being made for construction lags. Starts are difficult if not impossible to hide, and the Canada Mortgage and Housing Corporation housing starts statistics are reliable. Average values, however, are taken from building permits and thus liable to some undervaluation. Assuming that, at a maximum, single dwellings and mobile homes might be undervalued by 10 percent and semi-detached row and apartment dwellings by 5 percent[11] implies an understatement that may conceivably be as great as $1.9 billion or 9 percent of the total measured amount.

For alterations and improvements to existing dwellings, there is reason to believe that the existing national accounts estimates are not subject to much, if any, undervaluation bias despite the fact that this activity is highly prone to tax evasion. The estimates derive from three basic data sources—an annual demand-side survey of 25,000 households, a survey of building materials sales by wholesale dealers, and building permits data—that can be cross-checked against one another. If, nevertheless, we insist on assuming a maximum 20 percent understatement of contract work for households—accounting for most spending on alterations and improvements, with landlords, tenants, and

---

11   Since municipalities issue the building permits and have a strong interest in ensuring they are not undervalued, the problem is not likely to be severe. Moreover, an adjustment for undercoverage is already built into the national accounts estimates.

cottage owners representing a small share—we come up with an under-estimation of up to $1.7 billion, or 13.9 percent of the measured total.

In the vast arena of consumer expenditure—60 percent of GDP—potential underestimation can be gauged from a detailed commodity breakdown (Table 5).[12] Three categories of commodities are identified: (1) those for which underground transactions are nonexistent or very unlikely to cause GDP measurement problems, (2) those for which underground transactions may cause us moderate measurement problems, mainly due to the "skimming" of business receipts, and (3) the ones that lend themselves comparatively easily to underground transactions and with which we could thus have serious measurement problems.

The first group, labelled in Table 5 as showing "no significant impact due to underground transactions," includes new motor vehicles, electricity, natural gas fuels, air transport, water charges, medical and hospital care, communications, cable television, urban transit, provincial lottery tickets, financial services, and the services provided by non-profit organizations. Overall, this group of commodities accounted for $187.1 billion in 1992 consumer spending, 45 percent of the total. Now these goods and services are virtually impossible to purchase "under the table." In most instances, the businesses selling them are large corporations or government business enterprises, companies unlikely to systematically understate their receipts. This first group also

---

12 The national accounts estimates for consumer expenditure are built up from many different data sources (see Statistics Canada, 1990, pp. 128-130). One important source is the *Survey of Family Expenditures* that involves detailed, face-to-face interviews with a random sample of about 10,000 households. In the most recent survey, for 1992, the response rate was 73 percent. Now it seems reasonable to assume that households heavily involved in the underground economy are likely to be non-respondents. Therefore, since the survey imputes income and expenditure values to non-respondents based on average reported values for respondents, the presence of underground activity would bias the results in a downward direction only if the average income and outlay of underground economy participants were significantly higher than those of respondents. The results of this demand-side survey are unaffected by the "skimming" problem alluded to in the paragraph.

Table 5: Potential Understatment Due to Underground Transactions in Personal Expenditure on consumer Goods and Services, 1992

	Official estimates				
	Excluding taxes	GST and PST	Including taxes	Potential under statement	Potential under statement (%)
			(Millions of dollars)		
No significant impact due to underground transactions					
New automobiles	8,817	1,279	10,096	—	—
New trucks and vans	4,481	618	5,099	—	—
Imputed food, farm, and non farm	936	0	936	—	—
Motor fuels and lubricants	11,413	784	12,197	—	—
Electricity	9,067	898	9,965	—	—
Natural gas	2,715	208	2,923	—	—
Other fuels	2,196	209	2,405	—	—
Gross imputed rent	59,258	0	59,258	—	—
Furniture and appliance rental	266	0	266	—	—
Janitorial services	722	0	722	—	—
Imputed lodging	553	0	553	—	—
Lodging in universities	251	0	251	—	—
Water charges relating to imputed rent	1,103	0	1,103	—	—
Water charges relating to paid rent	645	0	645	—	—
Travel payments	13,553	0	13,553	—	—
Less: travel receipts	8,059	0	8,059	—	—
Military pay and allowances abroad	310	0	310	—	—
Hospital care and the like	2,443	0	2,443	—	—
Special care facilities, operating expenses	3,588	0	3,588	—	—
Other health care	2,887	0	2,887	—	—
Bridge and highway tolls	101	0	101	—	—
Commissions of tour operators	494	20	514	—	—
Urban transit	1,276	0	1,276	—	—
Railway transport	124	8	132	—	—
Intercity and rural bus transport	512	24	536	—	—
Air transport	4,583	183	4,766	—	—
Telecommunications	5,539	772	6,311	—	—
Postal service	490	36	526	—	—
Lotteries	2,470	0	2,470	—	—
Pari mutuel betting	428	2	430	—	—
Cable television and pay television	2,072	266	2,338	—	—
Stock and bond commissions	967	0	967	—	—
Interest on consumer debt	5,872	0	5,872	—	—
Trust companies, imputed interest	988	0	988	—	—
Credit unions, imputed interest	556	0	556	—	—
Accident and sickness insurance	987	129	1,116	—	—
Automobile insurance, cost of service	1,876	82	1,958	—	—

Table 5: Potential Understatment Due to Underground Transactions inPersonal Expenditure on consumer Goods and Services, 1992

	Official estimates				
	Excluding taxes	GST and PST	Including taxes	Potential under statement	Potential under statement (%)
		(Millions of dollars)			
Life insurance, cost of service	4,082	52	4,134	—	—
Property insurance, cost of service	284	92	376	—	—
Bank service charges paid	2,369	23	2,392	—	—
Bank service charges imputed	3,602	0	3,602	—	—
Credit unions, cost of service	373	4	377	—	—
Pension funds, cost of service	581	0	581	—	—
Mortgage loan companies, cost of service	1,624	0	1,624	—	—
Mutual funds, cost of service	1,521	106	1,627	—	—
Universities, operating expenses	9,021	0	9,021	—	—
Private schools, operating expenses	2,350	0	2,350	—	—
Welfare organizations, operating expenses	4,162	0	4,162	—	—
Religious organizations, operating expenses	3,139	0	3,139	—	—
Trade unions, operating expenses	1,544	0	1,544	—	—
Political parties, operating expenses	207	0	207	—	—
Sub total	**181,339**	**5,795**	**187,134**	—	—
Impact primarily from "skimming" of business receipts					
Used motor vehicles	3,323	631	3,954	168.836	4.3
Motor vehicle parts and accessories	3,077	421	3,498	623	17.8
Motor vehicle maintenance and repair	3,612	405	4,017	862	21.5
Furniture	4,066	564	4,630	127	2.7
Floor coverings	439	60	499	67	13.4
Stoves, ranges and microwaves	805	110	915	15	1.6
Washers and dryers	597	81	678	16	2.4
Refrigerators and freezers	674	92	766	15	2.0
Other major appliances	793	107	900	38	4.2
Small electrical appliances	859	119	978	39	4.0
Garden tools and equipment	509	66	575	14	2.4
Household equipment repairs	263	30	293	43	14.7
Television sets, video equipment and accessories	2,376	319	2,695	79	2.9
Radios, sound systems and accessories	1,192	161	1353	41	3.0
Sporting and camping equipment	1,771	245	2,016	98	4.9
Musical instruments and supplies	1,642	216	1,858	86	4.6
Bicycles and motorcycles	1,198	161	1,359	45	3.3
Cameras and accessories	769	103	872	36	4.1
Office machines and equipment	1,228	169	1,397	23	1.6
Boats, motors, and accessories	632	88	720	36	5.0

Table 5: Potential Understatment Due to Underground Transactions inPersonal Expenditure on consumer Goods and Services, 1992

	Official estimates				
	Excluding taxes	GST and PST	Including taxes	Potential under statement	Potential under statement (%)
			(Millions of dollars)		
Trailers	526	68	594	19	3.2
Recreation equipment repairs and rentals	1,078	137	1,215	61	5.0
Watches and jewellery	1,784	241	2,025	121	6.0
Watch and jewellery repairs	95	12	107	13	12.1
Men's and boys' clothing	6,260	779	7,039	179	2.5
Women's, misses', and children's clothing	9,844	1,235	11,079	279	2.5
Footwear	2,743	321	3,064	102	3.3
Notions and smallware	342	43	385	15	3.9
Piece goods	622	78	700	17	2.4
Household textiles and furnishings	2,722	374	3,096	127	4.1
Luggage and leather goods	171	23	194	16	8.2
China, glassware, and crockery	1,506	202	1,708	93	5.4
Lamps, fixtures, and accessories	713	97	810	29	3.6
Silver and flatware	163	22	185	14	7.6
Hardware	2,233	306	2,539	164	6.5
Toys, games, and hobby supplies	1,789	241	2,030	105	5.2
Films and other photographic supplies	375	51	426	14	3.3
Stationery, books, newspapers, and magazines	4,067	368	4435	226	5.1
Pets and supplies	103	14	117	15	12.8
Pet food	805	106	911	57	6.3
Soaps and other cleaning supplies	1,831	239	2,070	65	3.1
Other household supplies	3,408	431	3,839	98	2.6
Flowers and plants	1,332	156	1,488	116	7.8
Cosmetics and toiletries	3,685	514	4,199	108	2.6
Drugs and pharmaceutical products	6,129	407	6,536	180	2.8
Food and non alcoholic beverages	42,039	440	42,479	1,522	3.6
Meals outside the home	17,461	2,036	19,497	2,335	12.0
Accommodation	2,463	292	2,755	301	10.9
Gross paid rent	20,832	0	20,832	220	1.1
Laundry and dry cleaning	1,002	76	1,078	173	16.0
Child care	3,512	0	3,512	137	3.9
Pet care	337	23	360	17.1224	4.8
Parking	761	36	797	9	1.1
Driving lessons and tests	234	16	250	13	5.2
Motor vehicle renting and leasing	1,173	152	1,325	60	4.5
Water transport	164	5	169	5	3.0
Taxis	307	20	327	35	10.7
Moving and storage	525	36	561	49	8.7

Table 5: Potential Understatment Due to Underground Transactions inPersonal Expenditure on consumer Goods and Services, 1992

	Official estimates				
	Excluding taxes	GST and PST	Including taxes	Potential under statement	Potential under statement
	(Millions of dollars)				(%)
Other recreational services	4,596	304	4,900	322	6.6
Movie theatres and drive ins	383	27	410	18	4.4
Photography	679	84	763	79	10.4
Other educational and cultural services	1,408	38	1,446	40	2.8
Legal, accounting, and other services	1,733	122	1,855	87	4.7
Hairstyling for men and women	2,168	143	2,311	410	17.7
Other personal care	530	38	568	103	18.1
Medical care, dental care, and the like	2,427	0	2,427	121	5.0
Funerals and burials	743	53	796	89	11.2
Sub total	**189,628**	**14,554**	**204,182**	**10,850**	**5.3**
Significant impact due to underground transactions					
Upholstery and furniture repairs	166	17	183	47	25.7
Dressmaking, repairs, and alterations	132	13	145	16	11.0
Shoe repairs	75	9	84	17	20.2
Alcoholic beverages	9,561	1,528	11,089	1,283	11.6
Service portion of alcoholic beverages	3,176	413	3,589	1,081	30.1
Tobacco products	5,779	4,069	9,848	1,090	11.1
Board paid	274	0	274	14	5.1
Lodging paid	701	4	705	35	5.0
Domestic services and household services	2,222	81	2,303	416	18.1
Sub total	**22,086**	**6,134**	**28,220**	**3,999**	**14.2**
All commodities					
Total	**393,053**	**26,483**	**419,536**	**14,849**	**3.5**

Source: Gervais [1994].

includes commodities for which the national accounts estimates are imputations.

The second group, labelled "impact primarily from 'skimming' of business receipts," includes items rarely purchased on the black market but often distributed by small businesses. Measured consumer spending on all commodities in this group amounted to $204.2 billion in 1992, or 49 percent of total personal expenditure. Small businesses selling these commodities may engage in "skimming"—the practice by which otherwise legitimate businesses fail to declare a fraction of their business receipts to Revenue Canada and presumably to Statistics Canada. For the portion of total sales to households[13] that is accounted for by small business—defined as all unincorporated businesses, without regard to sales, plus all incorporated businesses with annual sales below $1 million—some arbitrary assumptions, considered to be on the high side, are made: 15 percent skimming of gross business receipts in retail trade and taxicabs and 25 percent skimming of gross receipts for vending-machine operators, direct sellers, and selected businesses in services.

The above percentages are then applied to sales revenues for these types of businesses as reported to Revenue Canada. The results are distributed by commodity using information from the Statistics Canada *Retail Commodity Survey*. In the case of paid rent, an important commodity in this category, undercoverage cannot be very substantial in the national accounts because of the measurement technique used.[14] Overall, the assumptions about skimming imply a potential GDP understatement of $10.9 billion, or 5.7 percent of the before-tax value of consumer spending on this category of commodities.

The third and final group, labelled in Table 5 as receiving "significant impact due to underground transactions," includes a select list of nine categories in which unreported sales are likely to be fairly common. These commodities accounted for $28.2 billion in measured 1992 consumer spending. The most significant items in the group are alcoholic beverages, tobacco products, services associated with alcoholic beverages, and domestic and household services. For alcoholic beverages, the analysis considers illegal production of wine and the smuggling of spirits, using information provided by the Liquor Control Board of

---

13   Unrecorded sales to other businesses do not affect the measurement of GDP since they are intermediate rather than final output.

14   The method involves multiplying the total stock of dwellings, obtained from the census and updated with housing starts data, by a survey-determined average market rent. Because rent imputed on owner-occupied dwellings is included as well as paid rent, undeclared rents (such as on basement apartments) are captured nevertheless (although they may be misclassified as imputed rather than paid).

Ontario and the Association of Canadian Distillers, as well as markups on contraband spirits and wine by licensees. Tobacco smuggling is also analyzed, and since most contraband tobacco is produced legitimately in Canada, exported to the United States, and smuggled back into the country, the extent of smuggling can be tracked quite accurately from tobacco exports data. The potential undercoverage for the nine commodities taken together is calculated at $4.0 billion, or 18.1 percent of total pre-tax expenditure for the group.

For total personal expenditure on consumer goods and services, the results suggest that underground activity might be causing a maximum understatement of $14.8 billion, or 3.8 percent of spending before sales tax—3.5 percent of total consumer outlays. Half this sum is attributable to food and non-alcoholic beverages, alcoholic beverages and associated services, tobacco, and restaurant meals: most of the remainder is spread over a range of commodities distributed by small, unincorporated retailers or producers.

Assembling all the results, Gervais concluded that $18.4 billion, or 2.7 percent of GDP, was a reasonable upper limit on the possible size of the underground economy not captured in GDP as of 1992. However, she cautioned:

> It is only an estimate, not a measure, of the maximum value of the portion of underground production which may still be missing from GDP. Not all underground transactions constitute economic production, and therefore not all belong in GDP. Of the transactions that do belong, some are measured (even if undeclared or unreported), while others are missing. The 2.7 percent represents the upper limit of what could possibly be missing, not what is actually missing (which would be much less). If Statistics Canada was convinced that this amount was really missing, it would add it to GDP.

Reconciling the estimates

When considering the range of estimates of the extent of underground economic activity, it is important to recognize that definitions of this economy differ in the various studies and that these definitional differences may substantially account for the variances in estimated magnitudes.

The upper-bound estimates developed by Berger and Gervais[15] correspond to the first definition in Table 2 and constitute assessments of how much might be missing from Canadian GDP as it is presently measured. The indirect estimates from Karoleff, Mirus, and Smith, based on money demand functions, are market production-type estimates as well, but they also include illegal production. They are tied to official GDP estimates via their velocity of money assumptions and therefore correspond to the second definition of the underground economy.

How much of the difference between the double-digit estimates of Karoleff, Mirus, and Smith and the single-digit estimates of Berger and Gervais can be attributed to illegal activity? Unfortunately, there is little statistical information in Canada about the value of illegal production. Blades (1992), in his review of attempts to measure the underground economy in OECD countries, cites evidence that illegal production activity amounts to only about 0.1 percent of GDP in France and 1.5 percent of GDP in the United States. Noting that more things are illegal in the United States than in many other OECD countries and that heroin "is still essentially an American problem," he concludes (p. 13):

> For these reasons, it can be asserted with some confidence that for most OECD countries the inclusion of illegal production in GDP could not possibly add more than 1 percent and, on the evidence from France, probably much less than this.

Some detailed Statistics Canada calculations of a few years ago suggested that illicit domestic drug production and distribution margins in 1984 were between $1.3 and $2.7 billion, or 0.3 to 0.6 percent of GDP.[16] Including an arbitrary allowance for other illegal goods and

---

15 A large part of the Berger (1986) upper-bound estimate of 3.5 percent of GNP (3.4 percent of GDP) for 1981 was accounted for by suspected under-coverage of alterations and improvements to residential dwellings. Subsequently, the national accounts underwent an extraordinary historical revision to correct this problem. Adjusting Berger's estimate for this revision to the accounts yields an upper limit of 2.5 percent of GDP for 1981, slightly lower than the Gervais estimate for 1992.

16 The analysis, conducted by M.S. Gupta, examined the market for heroin, cocaine, marijuana, hashish, and chemical drugs, using partial information

services and adding a full 1 percent of GDP to the Gervais estimate for 1992 yields just 3.7 percent of GDP for the second definition, still much smaller than in estimates based on money demand.

The survey-based estimate reported by Fortin, Fréchette, and Noreau (1987) is associated with the third definition, which considers the underground economy from Revenue Canada's perspective. It differs in principle from Karoleff, Mirus, and Smith in including the portion of the Revenue Canada underground economy that is captured in the official GDP statistics. The national accounts estimates take full advantage of income, sales, and customs and excise tax data, but they also rely on other sources of information, notably household and establishment surveys.

How significant is this amount of undeclared (for tax purposes) but recorded (for national accounts purposes) activity? Table 6 shows a comparison of factor income statistics from the two sources. While adjustments have been made for conceptual differences between the national accounts and Revenue Canada income definitions, the comparison remains imperfect. The true amount of income from these sources that is captured in the national accounts but undeclared to Revenue Canada is probably somewhat smaller than indicated.[17] Assuming that the discrepancy is about 1.5 percent of GDP in 1992, then the size of the underground economy based on the third definition would be a maximum of 5.2 percent of GDP (3.7 percent for the second

---

from Health and Welfare Canada, the Addiction Research Foundation of Ontario, and the Royal Canadian Mounted Police. Reasonable assumptions were developed for numbers of users, average dosage per user per day, and average market price per dosage.

17 Total "other employment income" as reported on the personal income tax form, $1.9 billion in 1991, is omitted from this comparison. It includes several transfer-type items which do not belong in national accounts labour income, but it also includes tips, which are thought to be substantially underreported and do belong in labour income. Unfortunately, no tabulations are available for tips separately. However, the national accounts estimate for tips in 1991 is $2.1 billion. For farm income, there are a great many conceptual differences between the national accounts and personal income tax definitions relating to, among other things, cash versus accrual accounting and the measurement of depreciation.

Table 6: GDP Income Components National Accounts Versus Revenue Canada

	1983	1984	1985	1986	1987	1988	1989	1990	1991
Employment income									
National accounts	200.4	215.7	232.3	248	269.4	295.6	319.5	334.3	339.4
Revenue Canada	196.9	212	228.3	243.6	264.7	290.5	314.4	329.4	334.4
Difference	3.5	3.7	4	4.4	4.7	5.1	5.1	4.9	5.0
Difference as a percentage of GDP	0.9	0.8	0.8	0.9	0.9	0.8	0.8	0.7	0.7
Farm income									
National accounts	2.6	3.4	2.8	3.9	2.9	4.3	3.0	3.5	3.2
Revenue Canada	1.7	2.0	1.8	1.7	2.1	2.1	2.0	1.5	1.4
Difference	0.8	1.4	1.0	2.2	0.8	2.1	1.0	2.1	1.8
Difference as a percentage of GDP	0.2	0.3	0.2	0.4	0.1	0.4	0.2	0.3	0.3
Paid rental income									
National accounts	0.8	1.2	1.2	1.4	1.3	1.4	1.4	1.4	1.4
Revenue Canada	0.6	0.7	0.9	1.0	1.0	0.8	0.4	0.4	0.3
Difference	0.2	0.5	0.4	0.4	0.3	0.6	1.0	1.8	1.7
Difference as a percentage of GDP	0.1	0.1	0.1	0.1	0.1	0.1	0.2	0.3	0.2
Other unincorporated business income									
National accounts	13.1	14.4	15.8	17.2	19.2	20.8	22.4	22.9	24.0
Revenue Canada	10.7	12.1	13.2	14.3	15.9	17.8	19.1	20.1	20.1
Difference	2.3	2.3	2.6	3.0	3.3	3.0	3.3	2.8	4.0
Difference as a percentage of GDP	0.6	0.5	0.5	0.6	0.6	0.5	0.5	0.4	0.6
Total									
National accounts	216.8	234.6	252.1	270.6	292.8	322.1	346.3	362.1	369.9
Revenue Canada	210.0	226.8	244.2	260.5	283.7	311.3	336.0	350.6	355.4
Difference	6.9	7.8	8.0	10.1	9.1	10.8	10.4	11.5	12.5
Difference as a percentage of GDP	1.7	1.8	1.7	2.0	1.7	1.8	1.6	1.7	1.9

Source: Gervais, 1994.

definition plus 1.5 percent). This upper bound is substantially higher[18] than the conceptually comparable direct-survey estimate from Fortin, Fréchette, and Noreau of just 1.4 percent of GDP, which is appropriately viewed as a lower bound.

Finally, Paquet makes it clear in his commentary that his 100 percent of GDP estimate, if not his 33 percent estimate, applies to the fourth and

18 It would probably be higher still if account were taken of the difference between corporation profits and miscellaneous investment income as measured in the national accounts and the corresponding income aggregates as indicated by tax compilations. However, it is extremely difficult to properly compare these aggregates.

broadest definition of the underground economy. How does this compare with other estimates?

Recent work by Chandler (1994) on the imputed value of household work provides three alternative estimates of the extent of this kind of activity. The first, 41.4 percent of GDP, uses a replacement cost approach: time spent working in the home is valued in terms of the potential cost of similar services in the marketplace. The second estimate, 46.3 percent of GDP, is based on an opportunity cost: the time spent is valued in terms of the forgone gross earnings of the person doing the work. The third estimate, 30.6 percent of GDP, is similar to the second but relies on forgone earnings net of income tax as the basis of valuation. For our present purposes, the first approach using a replacement cost estimate is the most appropriate.

To this must be added an estimate of the value of volunteer work, broadly defined to include unpaid work both for volunteer agencies and directly for other households. Statistics Canada's time use survey for 1992[19] showed the amount of time spent on volunteer work as 1,175 million hours, equivalent to 4.7 percent of total hours spent on household work. No estimates are available for the value of this volunteer work, but if the same average value applied as in the case of household work, it would be equivalent to 2.0 percent of GDP. Using the fourth definition, then, the underground economy would be equivalent to 47.1 percent of GDP (3.7+41.4+2.0)—a significant number, but well short of Paquet's 100 percent "ballpark" figure.

Comments on the monetary approach

The attempt made here to compare various estimates of the size of the underground economy is less than fully successful because the huge gap between the indirect, money demand-based figures and the more direct statistical estimates remains largely unexplained. The two approaches are so different—one depending on monetary theories and the other on

---

19   See Statistics Canada, *Initial Data Release from the 1992 General Social Survey on Time Use*, uncatalogued, April 1993.

the statisticians' ability to assess the reliability of their product—that it will probably never be possible to properly reconcile them.

The money demand method is strictly a macro approach that tells us nothing about the differential impact of underground activity by sector, by industry, by commodity, or by region. Its validity cannot be tested by focussing on particular parts of the economy where underground activity is thought to be especially prevalent: the approach yields only an estimate of overall size. The procedure rests on strong assumptions about the relationship between the stock of money and economic activity, often with no econometric validity tests. In some of its variants, the size of the underground economy is estimated residually, which suggests vulnerability to the omitted variables problem.

For example, the Gutmann version relies on the assumption that the ratio of currency to demand deposits would have remained historically constant were it not for growth in the underground economy. To many observers, this has seemed an unreasonable *ad hoc* supposition, given the multitude of other factors that have influenced the choice between currency and demand deposits over time—among them, changing financial regulations, the growth of near banks, the introduction of credit and debit cards and changes in the cost and convenience of these cards over time, automatic teller machines, the arrival of the dollar coin, and a variety of other banking innovations.

The Feige method starts from Fisher's well-known payments-transactions identity (MV=PT).[20] If we assume that PT, the value of transactions, is strictly proportional to total factor income, and then attempt to directly measure changes in the stock of money and its velocity over time, we can draw inferences about the growth of the overall economy and, by implication, its underground component. Now assuming proportionality between the total value of monetary transactions and total factor income is a questionable, though not uncommon, practice; and the picture is further clouded by the fact that the total volume of financial and non-financial transactions has expanded enormously during the postwar period, spurred by vastly improved computation, communica-

---

20   Irving Fisher, *The Purchasing Power of Money*: New York, Macmillan, 1911. "M" is the stock of money, "V' is its velocity of circulation, "P" is the price level, and "T" is the volume of monetary transactions.

tions, and transportation technologies and the resulting market globalization.

Accordingly, the strict application of this approach has yielded estimates of the underground economy that are so big as to be easily recognized as grossly unreasonable. This has led practitioners to attempt to restrict the measure of transactions to exclude those involving income or asset transfers. It is unclear how the Fisher identity can be usefully interpreted when PT is defined in this limited way, since it is clearly impossible to similarly limit M, the money stock.[21] Other difficulties with this approach include the requirement for an independent time series measurement of velocity and the need for an estimate of the constant proportionality factor which, it is assumed, links the value of monetary transactions to total factor income.

The Tanzi approach contrasts with the Gutmann and Feige methods in that some of its underlying hypotheses are subjected to statistical testing and its parameters, rather than just assumed, are estimated econometrically.[22] An explicit hypothesis is developed that relates the size of the underground economy to the average tax rate. Interestingly, this method has consistently yielded smaller estimates of the underground economy.

Conclusions

Statistics Canada holds that the underground market economy, depending on how it is defined, probably accounts for between 1 and 5 percent

---

21   Moreover, it is very difficult empirically to partition transactions effectively into distinct financial and non-financial categories. Karoleff, Mirus, and Smith (1993) found it necessary to exclude all transactions cleared in the main financial centres of Toronto, Montreal, Vancouver, and Calgary from their calculations in order to get results they believed were credible. Leaving out urban areas that account for one third of the total population and close to half of domestic economic activity seems a drastic solution to the problem.

22   The method still requires an unverifiable "starting point" assumption: a value for the size of the underground economy in some base period. Also required is an assumption about the relative velocities of money in the above- and below-ground economies.

of GDP. By the narrowest definition—the portion of market-based production of legal goods and services that escapes detection in the official estimates of GDP due to the efforts of some businesses and households to keep their activities undetected—the underground economy is very unlikely to exceed 3 percent of measured GDP and is probably a lot smaller. It could conceivably account for 4 percent of GDP if we broadened the definition to include illegal production, or even as much as 5 percent if we included production activities unreported to Revenue Canada but captured by StatsCan. However, the size of the Canadian underground economy today could not possibly reach double digits as a percentage of GDP unless its definition was extended to encompass non-market production.

Because the underground economy is small in relation to the economy as a whole, then, the impact of its omission on measured GDP growth rates is quite small. This can be shown with an extreme example. If underground output represented 3 percent of the economy and was growing by 10 percent while the observed economy was declining by 2 percent, the overall "true" number would be -1.7 percent. Since there are so many basic factors influencing both—weather, political developments, social attitudes and trends, stock and bond market prices, and so on—it is difficult to imagine how a growth differential as large as this could occur.[23] If it did, however, the drop in real GDP would be overstated by only 0.3 percent at most.

Still, at 3 percent of GDP the underground economy would represent $21 billion and at 5 percent, $36 billion, significant amounts that imply substantial unpaid federal, provincial, and municipal taxes. By commodity or by industry, its relative impact would be far from uniform. The underground economy is certainly not a factor to be ignored by either statisticians or tax collectors.

---

23   Spiro (1993) estimates that the underground economy grew by 0.8 percent of GDP over the two-year period ending in 1992. If it was 3 percent of GDP in 1990, this would imply average annual growth of 14 percent when the observed economy was growing by just 0.7 and 1.9 percent in the two years (in nominal terms, unadjusted for inflation).

References

Barthelemy, Philippe, "The Macroeconomic Estimates of the Hidden Economy: A Critical Analysis," in *Review of Income and Wealth*, ser. 34, no. 2, June 1988, pp. 183-208.

Berger, Seymour, "The Unrecorded Economy: Concepts, Approach and Preliminary Estimates for Canada, 1981," in *Canadian Statistical Review*, Statistics Canada Catalogue 11-003E, April 1986.

Blades, Derek, "The Hidden Economy and the National Accounts," in United Nations Economic Commission for Europe, ed., *Guide-Book to Statistics on the Hidden Economy*: New York, 1992, pp. 3-20.

Cagan, P., "The Demand for Currency Relative to the Total Money Supply," in *Journal of Political Economy*, vol. 66, August 1958, pp. 303-328.

Carson, Carol, "The Underground Economy: An Introduction," in *Survey of Current Business*, vol. 64, nos 5 and 7, May and July 1984, pp. 21-37 and 106-118.

Chandler, William, "The Value of Household Work in Canada, 1992," in *National Income and Expenditure Accounts*, fourth quarter 1993, Statistics Canada Catalogue 13-001, April 1994, pp. xxxv-xlviii.

Denison, Edward F., "Is U.S. Growth Understated Because of the Underground Economy? Employment Ratios Suggest Not," in *Review of Income and Wealth*, ser. 28, no. 1, March 1982, pp. 1-16.

The Economist, "The Shadow Economy: Grossly Deceptive Product," September 19, 1987.

Éthier, Mireille, "The Underground Economy: A Review of the Economic Literature and New Estimates for Canada," in François Vaillancourt, ed., *Income Distribution and Economic Security in Canada*: Toronto, University of Toronto Press, 1985, pp. 77-109.

Feige, Edgar L., "How Big is the Irregular Economy?" in *Challenge*, vol. 22, November-December 1979, pp. 5-13.

————, ed., *The Underground Economies*: New York, Cambridge University Press, 1989.

Fortin, Bernard, Pierre Fréchette, and Joëlle Noreau, "Dimensions et caractéristiques des activités économiques non déclarées à l'impôt," Université Laval, Cahier 8702, Québec, 1987.

Gervais, Gylliane, *The Size of the Underground Economy: A Statistics Canada View*, Statistics Canada, Catalogue No. 13-603, no. 2, June 1994.

Gutmann, P.M., "The Subterranean Economy," in *Financial Analysts Journal*, vol. 33 (1977) pp. 24-27 and 34.

Karoleff, Vladimir, Rolf Mirus, and Roger S. Smith, "Canada's Underground Economy Revisited: Update and Critique," paper presented at the 49th congress of the International Institute of Public Finance, Berlin, August 1993.

Macafee, K., "A Glimpse of the Hidden Economy in the National Accounts," in *Economic Trends*, February 1980, pp. 81-87.

Mirus, Rolf, "The Invisible Economy: Its Dimensions and Implications," in George Lermer, ed., *Probing Leviathan, An Investigation of Government in the Economy*: Vancouver, The Fraser Institute, 1984.

Mirus, Rolf and Roger S. Smith, "Canada's Irregular Economy," in *Canadian Public Policy*, vol. 7, no. 3, Summer 1981, pp. 444-453.

———, "Canada's Underground Economy," in Feige, Edgar L., ed., *The Underground Economies*: New York, Cambridge University Press, 1989, pp. 267-280.

Paquet, Gilles, "The Underground Economy," in *Policy Options*, January/February 1989, pp. 3-6.

Spiro, Peter S., "Evidence of a Post-GST Increase in the Underground Economy," in *Canadian Tax Journal*, vol. 41, no. 2, 1993, pp. 247-258.

Statistics Canada, *A User Guide to the Canadian System of National Accounts*, Catalogue 13-589E, November 1989.

———, *Guide to the Income and Expenditure Accounts*, Catalogue 13-603E, November 1990.

Tanzi, Vito, "The Underground Economy in the United States: Estimates and Implications," in *Banco Nazionale del Lavoro Quarterly Review*, vol. 135 (1980) pp. 427-453.

United Nations Economic Commission for Europe, ed., *Guide-Book to Statistics on the Hidden Economy*, New York, 1992.

Taxes, Deficits, and the Underground Economy

Peter S. Spiro

Introduction

There has been a groundswell of concern about the underground economy in Canada, to an extent not found in other countries. In 1993, some 77 articles featured the underground economy in magazines and newspapers listed in the *Canadian Periodicals Index*, as compared with half a dozen in 1992.[1] There is a widespread belief with very few dissenting that the underground economy is a growing problem in Canada and has contributed to a worsening of government deficits.

We also have a higher degree of consensus about the factors underlying the growth of the underground economy than about most other issues in economic policy. There is virtual unanimity among policy analysts on the important relationship between tax rates and the under-

---

1   By contrast, the *US Business Periodicals* Index contained only three references to the subject, and of these, one was about Canada.

ground economy. In his 1994 pre-budget consultation document, Ontario's Minister of Finance stated:

> The Government of Ontario understands...the fatigue taxpayers are feeling, and that there are limits to how much revenue the tax system can deliver. The Government is also aware of the problem of the underground economy and how it means honest taxpayers have to pick up more than their fair share of the cost of public services.[2]

There also appears to be a rare degree of unanimity on the empirical proposition that the underground economy has grown substantially as a percentage of GDP since early 1991. One key piece of evidence for this is the large increase in cash in circulation relative to reported incomes. There is also a tremendous amount of anecdotal evidence and consumer survey data, which is probably why the issue has attracted such widespread popular attention. Even Statistics Canada's analysis of discrepancies in the GDP data supports the view that the underground economy began growing in 1991.[3]

Taxes are undeniably an important factor in the underground economy. Nevertheless, the connection is not as clear-cut or as easily quantifiable as many editorial writers have supposed. This article will marshal the relevant empirical literature to evaluate the likely contribution of various tax changes in the past few years to growth in the underground economy.

Effect of the GST

One hypothesis that has considerable support is that the introduction of the GST in 1991 sparked a substantial increase in the size of the underground economy in Canada. In an earlier article, this writer highlighted the increase in the ratio of cash in circulation to consumer expenditure that coincided with the coming of the GST. Even taking into account

2   Ontario Ministry of Finance, *Preparing for the Ontario Budget 1994, A Guide Book to Budget Consultations:* Toronto, Queen's Printer for Ontario, February 1994.

3   Gylliane Gervais, "The Size of the Underground Economy, "Statistics Canada Discussion Paper, February 1994, pp. 9 and 17.

such other factors as declining interest rates, the growth in cash was extraordinary. The article offered the conservative estimate that the underground economy had increased as of mid-1992 by an amount of about 0.8 percent of GDP.[4]

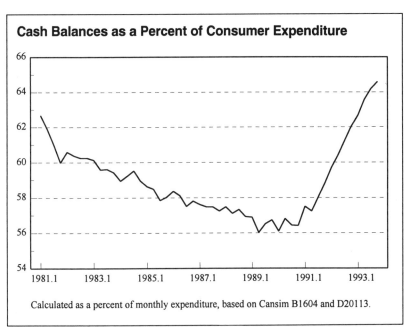

Cash Balances as a Percent of Consumer Expenditure

Calculated as a percent of monthly expenditure, based on Cansim B1604 and D20113.

Figure 1

There is a problem with interpreting these data due to the issue of velocity of circulation, and considerable judgement needs to be applied in imputing growth in the underground economy from growth in cash. Probably, the cash to expenditure ratio is higher in the underground economy than in the legal economy. Among other things, participants in the underground economy who do well and want to save some of their money cannot invest in mutual funds: they have to hoard it in the form of cash until they can find some way to "launder" it. Logically, some of this excess cash may have gone into safety deposit boxes rather

---

4   Peter S. Spiro, "Evidence of a Post-GST Increase in the Underground Economy," in *Canadian Tax Journal* 1993, vol. 41, no. 2, pp. 247-258.

than more expenditure.[5] Figure 1 updates the data and suggests growth in the underground economy of perhaps 2 percent of GDP from early 1991 to the end of 1993.[6]

Besides the introduction of the GST, 1991 also saw large tobacco tax increases that contributed to growing sales of contraband cigarettes. Eventually, Statistics Canada began to estimate contraband cigarette sales by assuming that increased cigarette exports were all spirited back into the country clandestinely. By this measure, contraband accounted for about 15 percent of total 1991 cigarette sales in Canada.[7] At a street price reported to be half the legal price, this traffic would have been worth about $700 to $800 million annually. Even so, however, it could account for only a relatively small fraction of the growth in the underground economy[8] as indicated by the growth in the currency ratio.

The GST was introduced in the midst of a severe recession, and this may also have had some effect on the amount of evasion. However, the recession is unlikely to have been an independent factor. There is no consensus in the literature as to whether a recession will spur growth in the underground economy. Some analysts point out that many of the services consumed in the underground economy are

---

5   The growth in the relative proportion of $1,000 bills supports the view that some hoarding has taken place, as these notes are rarely seen in circulation. These $1,000s, with their $100 counterparts, grew from 39.4 percent of total cash outstanding in 1990 to 43.8 percent in 1992 (*Bank of Canada Review*, Spring 1993, Table K1).

6   It should be noted that the growth in the cash expenditure ratio shown in Figure 1 was 14.5 percent from 1991 to 1993. The estimate that the underground economy has grown by only 2 percent thus makes considerable allowance for such factors as the declining velocity of cash. Econometric analysis that explains the derivation of this estimate is found in this author's article, "Estimating the Underground Economy: A Critical Evaluation of the Monetary Approach," *Canadian Tax Journal* 1994, vol. 42, no. 4, pp. 1059-1081.

7   Gylliane Gervais, op. cit., p. 37. This report indicates that StatsCan will add in these estimates of contraband sales when it revises its GDP figures.

8   Estimated to amount to $5.7 billion in consumer expenditures by Spiro, op. cit., p. 255.

discretionary and that the underground share will therefore decline in recessions. Others argue that people receiving unemployment benefits will be tempted to cheat by working in the underground economy.

One critic, Don McIver, has suggested that the growth in Canada's currency ratio was due to such financial factors as the falling inflation rate.[9] He pointed to a large increase in the US cash ratio beginning about 1990—an increase that appears, as documented in recent studies by that country's Federal Reserve Board,[10] to have been due to the growing use of US currency as a medium of exchange in eastern Europe. Examination of the cash ratio in the United Kingdom, which also experienced substantial reductions in its inflation and interest rates in the period 1991-1993, shows that the cash ratio there continued to decline.

It has also been claimed that recent growth in GST revenue is inconsistent with the tax evasion hypothesis. For example, one pro-GST editorial has suggested that those who claim "the GST was behind the growth in tax evasion...might like to explain why GST revenue grew *faster* than the economy last year."[11] In reality, the relationship between measured GDP and GST revenue growth in any particular year has no bearing on whether or not there is tax evasion. For one thing, large sectors of the economy, such as groceries and government-provided services, are exempt from the GST. The government sector grew much more slowly than GDP in the 1993/94 fiscal year, meaning that the part of GDP that carries the GST was growing faster than total GDP.[12] GST

---

9   "Underground Mining," in *Sunlife of Canada Analysis*, November 30, 1993.

10 Richard D. Porter, "Foreign Holdings of the U.S. Currency," Federal Reserve Board discussion paper, 1993. See also "More for Boris," in *The Economist*, November 27, 1993, p. 86.

11 "Meet the new tax, same as the old tax," in the *Globe and Mail*, March 14, 1994, p. A12.

12 There is also a technical reason why net GST revenue would grow faster on average than GDP with inflation between 0 and 3 percent. GST revenue shown here is net of the low-income tax credits, which are increased only to the extent that CPI inflation exceeds 3 percent and would thus tend to grow more slowly than GDP in a low-inflation environment.

Table 1: Federal Government GST Revenue

Fiscal year	Net GST revenue ($ billions)	Nominal GDP ($ billions)	GST as percentage of GDP	GST revenue shortfall ($ billions)
1991/92 budget	16.35	700	2.33	
1991/92 actual	15.17	680	2.23	0.7
1992/93 actual	14.9	688	2.16	1.2
1993/94 estimate	15.6	712	2.19	1.0

revenue grew about 4.7 percent while the estimated value of nominal GDP grew only 3.5 percent.

Table 1 looks at the history of GST revenue. The 1991/92 budget predicted GST revenue of $16.35 billion: the actual turned out to be much lower, partly because the GDP was below forecast. However, the GST collected was also smaller as a percentage of actual GDP than the budget had predicted. Even after adjusting for lower GDP growth than forecast, there was a $1 billion shortfall in fiscal 1993/94 relative to the initial GST revenue projection in the 1991/92 budget. This may actually be a useful lower bound estimate of the amount of evasion. Moreover, it is likely that GST-induced tax evasion has led to an underestimation of GDP itself, which would imply that the total amount of GST evaded is considerably more than $1 billion.

Effect of income tax rates

The question of the tax rate which maximizes revenues has been an important implicit question in the recent Canadian debate on taxes. Many critics of government policy have suggested that deficits would have been smaller had tax rates been lower.[13]

---

13   This is an oft-repeated assertion. However as Horry, Palda, and Walker point out in *Tax Facts 8* (The Fraser Institute, 1992, p.1), econometric studies suggest that "almost no country is at the point where an increase in tax rates will lead to less tax collected."

Defenders of the GST argue that high income tax rates spurred increased evasion, not the GST. For example, the *Globe and Mail* has opined that "the GST was said to be behind the growth in income tax evasion, as if 54 percent income tax rates had nothing to do with it."[14] It is true that there were also income tax rate increases in 1991 and we may legitimately ask what role they might have played in spurring the growth of the underground economy.

It should be noted that theoretical economic models do not state unambiguously that higher income tax rates lead to higher rates of evasion, particularly in systems with progressive rates. As with every other "price," there is both a substitution effect and an income effect. Higher tax rates do incite the temptation to cheat via the substitution effect, since the monetary gain increases. However, there is also the matter of risk aversion in the face of potential punishment and how the income effect interacts with it. For example, if higher-income people are more concerned about the risk of being caught and possibly going to jail and they are also the ones facing the highest tax rates, it is not obvious that higher tax rates do necessarily lead to higher rates of evasion.

International cross-section evidence on the relationship between taxation and the underground economy can be seen in Figure 2, which relies on admittedly crude estimates of the underground economy as a percentage of GDP in a dozen OECD countries.

It is interesting to note that taxes are not the only factor conditioning the underground economy: societal norms in each country are also important. Some countries have large underground economies in spite of relatively low tax rates. If the Mediterranean countries in Figure 2 are excluded, however, we can pick out a distinct trend towards larger underground economies in tandem with higher total taxes as a percentage of GDP. In this group of countries, the underground economy rises roughly 0.25 percentage points for each percent of increase in taxes.

Econometric estimates abound for most types of behaviour, but empirical studies of tax evasion are particularly difficult. The critical problem is to obtain reliable data on the amount of tax evasion taking place. However, some enterprising US researchers have managed to conduct studies that may be applicable to Canada. In fact, the best data

---

14   "Meet the new tax, same as the old tax," op.cit.

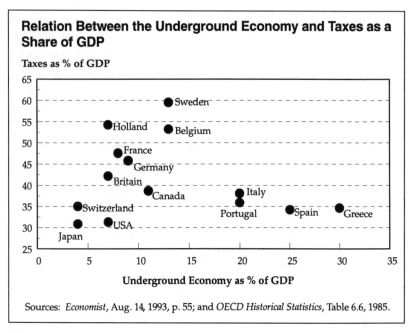

Relation Between the Underground Economy and Taxes as a Share of GDP

Sources: *Economist*, Aug. 14, 1993, p. 55; and *OECD Historical Statistics*, Table 6.6, 1985.

Figure 2

we have on tax evasion emanates from the United States. Once every 10 years, the US Internal Revenue Service (IRS) conducts audits of 50,000 randomly selected taxpayers to build a statistically valid tax evasion profile. The random nature of this procedure is important: ordinarily, tax audits concentrate on high income earners in expectation of higher returns in taxes recovered.

On one of these decennial occasions, Charles Clotfelter, with access to the individual data points of the IRS data set, conducted an econometric study on the effects the marginal tax rates of various individuals were liable to have on their rates of evasion.[15] Clotfelter found that marginal income tax rates did indeed influence evasion significantly. Clotfelter's preferred estimate implied that unreported income went up 0.2 percent for each percent of increase in the income tax rate.

---

15 Charles Clotfelter, "Tax Evasion and Tax Rates: An Analysis of Individual Returns," in *Review of Economics and Statistics*, August 1983.

A second US study used a more aggregate estimate of unreported income—the discrepancy between the national income estimates of personal income and the amount declared as income on tax returns submitted to the IRS. These researchers also found it "questionable whether the gain in revenue from reduced evasion would be large enough to offset the revenue loss due to lower tax rates."[16] Indeed, they found that the percentage of unreported income rises by only 0.05 percent for each percent of increase in the income tax rate.

Particularly at higher income levels, however, the presumption is that individuals do not resort to outright income tax evasion as much as to legal avoidance through tax reduction schemes. It is also assumed that higher tax rates will reduce work intensity and measured income and hence tax revenue. One study that attempted to take all these factors into account was done by the well-known supply-sider Lawrence Lindsay, who used a detailed microeconomic model of taxpayer behaviour to analyze the impacts of the US federal income tax cuts of 1981. He found that "at least one sixth, and probably one quarter, of the revenue loss ascribable to the 1981 tax law changes was recouped by changes in taxpayer behaviour over the period 1982-84."[17] It is interesting that Lindsay's upper limit estimate is not much larger than Clotfelter's reckoning that 20 percent of the revenue loss from a tax rate cut is recouped through increased compliance.

Some recent work by Martin Feldstein, an outlier relative to the studies mentioned so far, shows much stronger tax revenue increases from tax rate cuts. Feldstein has become a harsh critic of the Clinton administration's tax hikes for high earners, predicting virtually no net revenue increase for the US government.[18] He came to this conclusion

---

16 Stephen Crane and Farrokh Nourzad, "Inflation and Tax Evasion: An Empirical Analysis," in *Review of Economics and Statistics*, 1986, p. 221.

17 Lawrence Lindsay, "Individual Taxpayer Response to Tax Cuts 1982-1984 with Implications for the Revenue Maximizing Tax Rate," Harvard Institute of Economic Research Discussion Paper no. 1288, December 1986.

18 Martin Feldstein, "Clinton's Path to Wilder Deficits," in the *Wall Street Journal*, February 23, 1993; and "The Effect of Marginal Tax Rates on Taxable Income: A Panel Study of the 1986 Tax Reform Act," National Bureau of Economic Research Working Paper no. 4496, October 1993.

by following a set of 4,000 individual taxpayers through the years before and after the 1986 tax reform and observing that income taxes collected from the highest income segment actually rose in spite of tax rate cuts. Unfortunately, Feldstein fails to account for the fact that his period of study covers an economic boom in which incomes at the higher end— e.g., lawyers and corporate executives—ballooned with performance bonuses. The nature of the economic cycle was probably the main reason for the rise in reported income from top earners.

What does this imply for the Canadian situation in the early 1990s? In 1991, the average combined federal and provincial marginal tax rate for incomes between $28,000 and $55,000 rose to 40.82 percent from 40.3 percent the year before. For incomes above $55,000, the rate rose to 46.98 percent from 44.95 percent the year before. Compared to the pre-reform rates of 1987, the 1990 rates represented a reduction for high earners who had previously faced a top marginal rate of 51 percent. For middle-income earners, the marginal rate in 1987 had been only 37.5 percent. In 1992, income tax rates were almost unchanged, declining 0.15 percent for the upper group and rising 0.13 percent for the middle group.[19]

The evidence from the IRS studies of tax compliance suggests that the bulk of tax evasion occurs among independent business owners with relatively modest incomes. This would imply that the tax rate applicable to middle-income earners is the one to watch. Between 1990 and 1991, that rate increased by only 0.5 percent. According to Clotfelter, this would mean a 0.1 percent reduction in reported income that would have amounted to roughly $600 million in 1991. Personal tax increases, therefore, do not appear to be a large enough factor to explain much of the rise in underground economic activity indicated by cash balances in 1991 and 1992.

Psycho-social factors behind GST resentment

There is a reason beyond mere pedantry for trying to establish the GST's role in the underground economy solidly and beyond reasonable doubt.

19 These data are found in the 1990 to 1992 annual issues of the Canadian Tax Foundation's *National Finances*, in the table entitled "Combined Federal and Provincial Personal Income Tax Marginal Rates for Selected Fiscal Years."

If we feel convinced that the GST had a significant effect, we have acquired a significant lesson in the politics of tax design.

From a rational economist's viewpoint, the GST should not have had this effect. The federal finance department had even argued that the GST would have an opposite effect, actually reducing tax evasion. Gilles Paquet, among others, endorsed this view: "Since it would be a multi-stage tax, it would constitute, in all likelihood, a much better technique to catch cheaters."[20]

In contrast to this view, we have a persuasive theoretical analysis by Jonathan Kesselman concluding that "a change in the tax mix will have little or no impact on total evasion or on the distribution of real net incomes between evaders and non-evaders."[21] If Kesselman is correct, the GST would not have reduced evasion, but it should also not have contributed to a major increase in evasion.

The GST was imposed at the relatively low rate of 7 percent. It was replacing another tax, albeit a hidden one, and the Department of Finance was by and large correct in its claim that the switchover was revenue-neutral from the federal government's standpoint. Yet the GST overnight became the most unpopular tax imposed by a Canadian government in peacetime. *Globe and Mail* columnist Peter Cook commented that "the single most unpopular act of the late, unlamented Mulroney government was its introduction of the goods and services tax."[22] This was not just hindsight: during 1990, newspapers were full of headlines such as "Arguing the Case for a GST Revolt," "Two-thirds of Canadians still oppose tax," "GST 'last straw'," "Individuals Crushed by Tax While Companies Get off Lightly," and "A Shopping List for GST Haters."[23] When Prime Minister Mulroney took the unprecedented step

---

20 "The Underground Economy, " in *Policy Options*, February 1989, p. 5.

21 "Evasion Effects of Changing the Tax Mix," in *The Economic Record* 69, June 1993, pp. 131-148.

22 *Globe and Mail*, January 10, 1994.

23 Respectively: *Financial Post*, January 30; *Daily Commercial News*, January 15; *Financial Post*, July 3; *Financial Post*, July 27: and *Financial Times*, September 24.

of increasing the size of the Senate to force the GST legislation through, the cover of *Maclean's* magazine screamed with the two-inch bold headline, "HOW MUCH CAN CANADA TAKE?"[24]

So why did the GST cause such an outcry? Three broad lines of explanation can be suggested, and probably all have some merit: the visibility issue, perceived government overspending, and unfair taxation.

A GST defence popular with its supporters held that the general population in its ignorance could not be made to understand that the GST was just replacing another, less efficient tax. The old manufacturers' sales tax was invisible, while the GST was right up front. According to this argument, the mistake was making the GST visible, and no doubt a lot of Canadians agreed. Even before the reform proposal, however, large numbers of Canadians must have known about the existence of the MST and most of the rest must have been reached by the federal government's advertisements.

Part of the problem was that many of the pro-GST arguments emanating from the federal government consisted of half-truths. The GST may well have been revenue-neutral, but in that case why would it be expected to cause a substantial increase in the Consumer Price Index in the month it was introduced? The obvious answer is that the GST represented a major tax shift away from producers and onto consumers that has been estimated by Patrick Grady as representing $4.6 billion.[25] The GST also came in on top of a string of income tax reforms that had shifted a larger share of the total tax burden to middle income taxpayers.[26]

Who would have been the beneficiaries of this change? The federal government argued that it would make the country's exports more competitive and so create jobs for all Canadians. This claim was rendered ludicrous by events, as Bank of Canada policies led to a severely overvalued dollar, a plunge in Canadian competitiveness, and a massive hemorrhage

---

24   *Maclean's*, October 8, 1990.

25   "An Analysis of the Distributional Impact of the Goods and Services Tax," in *Canadian Tax Journal*, vol. 38, no. 3 (May-June 1990), pp. 632-643.

26   Patrick Grady, "The Burden of Federal Tax Increases Under the Conservatives," in *Canadian Business Economics*, vol. 1, no. 1 (Fall 1992).

of jobs. As things turned out, the switchover had no short-term beneficiaries. In other circumstances, the corporate sector would have bene-
fited early, especially in industries where Canadian exporters were
international price-takers. In the longer term, the benefits may well even
have been more widely dispersed, with workers gaining some real wage
increases. Even in the final general equilibrium, however, the return on
capital and hence the highest income groups in society would probably
have gained more than anyone else.[27]

A third anti-GST strand came from a general sense among Canadians
of being overtaxed by governments that were careless with the money they
received. The introduction of an additional layer of sales tax with large
administrative costs for both government and taxpayers particularly ran-
kled with people who were concerned about wasteful spending. By 1990,
the term "tax revolt" was often heard. Kevin Avram, president of the
Association of Saskatchewan Taxpayers, declared: "The root cause of the
tax revolt triggered by the goods and services tax is excessive government
spending."[28] Another activist foretold widespread civil disobedience because "the middle class has reached a level of taxation that is too high to
bear."[29] As already noted, these people were not speaking from ignorance.
In spite of the vaunted revenue-neutral nature of the GST, it was part of a
substantial increase in the tax burden on the middle class—the sort that
sparks increased evasion.[30]

---

27   This would generally be true if the international supply of equity capital to
     Canada is relatively inelastic with respect to the after-tax rate of return,
     which it seems to be. The vast bulk of international capital flows is in the
     form of interest-bearing securities, not equity. Taxes on profits fall more
     heavily on upper income groups. The Fraser Institute estimates that upper
     income groups pay 67 percent of taxes on profits. Canadians with incomes
     over $250,000 derive about 38 percent of their incomes from investments
     as against 14 percent for the average taxpayer (Department of National
     Revenue, *Taxation Statistics* 1993, Table 2).

28   "Forget tax reform, we need spending reform," in *Canadian Speeches*, No-
     vember 1990, p. 13.

29   *Maclean's*, October 8, 1990, p. 26.

30   Michael Spicer and Lee Becker, "Fiscal Equity and Tax Evasion: An Experi-
     mental Approach," in *National Tax Journal*, vol. 33, no. 2.

The federal government ought to have taken the tax revolt warnings seriously. In a decentralized economy, taxes rely substantially on voluntary compliance by citizens. If they find a particular tax very unfair, they will refuse to pay it, and this seems to have happened with the GST.

Had a referendum been held on the GST issue, there is no doubt that it would have been resoundingly rejected. This is not a hypothetical suggestion, since in Switzerland the recent introduction of a VAT was actually the subject of a series of referenda.

It is reasonable to assume that Switzerland will have less trouble with evasion. In a society where people realize that the tax is a result of expressed consensus rather than arbitrary decree, their consciences are more likely to propel them into compliance. Psychological studies of taxpayer behaviour have found that evasion increases when people can convince themselves that a tax is unfair. For their own self-esteem, most people like to think of themselves as honest. Indeed, society could not function at all were this not the case, as there are never enough policemen to watch everybody, or police to watch the policemen. However, once people see themselves as being cheated by government, they feel justified in "cheating back."

The GST started out with a huge strike against it. Even with the wave of public opposition, however, compliance could have been increased with stronger enforcement. Studies do find that penalties for evasion work as deterrents. Holger Wolf has constructed an analytic model of tax revolts which shows that the attractiveness of cheating for any individual increases with the awareness that others will be cheating along with him. He suggests that this kind of revolt could possibly be nipped in the bud by a few symbolic, high-profile prosecutions before it gets out of hand.[31]

The underground economy and government deficits

It has been suggested in these pages that the growth in the underground economy since 1991 may have been as much as 2 percent of GDP. That

---

31   "Anti-Tax Revolutions and Symbolic Prosecutions," National Bureau of Economic Research Working Paper no. 4337, April 1993.

would represent $14 billion in national income unreported for tax purposes. Based on typical tax rates, this implies a revenue loss of roughly $6 billion to all levels of government in Canada. A loss of this size would represent about 12 percent of the deficits incurred by all levels of government in 1993.

However, there is more than one type of connection between the underground economy and government deficits. Not only does the underground economy contribute to higher deficits, but high deficits may in turn further encourage people to participate in the underground economy. The accumulation of debt and the need to pay interest on that debt create a situation where tax rates are forced to increase without any corresponding increase in government services to the public.

Taxes as a percentage of GDP have been rising in Canada while government spending on current goods and services as a percentage of GDP has been on a declining trend since the early 1980s, interrupted by the recession. One of the main reasons for this is the growth of interest payments on the public debt, which is a particularly serious problem at the federal level but a growing problem in the 1990s for provincial governments as well. The growth of public-debt interest means that a large proportion of the taxes people are paying today goes to pay for services consumed in the past by people who may no longer be alive. Current taxpayers find it hard to derive pleasure from past deficits. Tax rates that increase without any offsetting benefits to taxpayers are going to be deeply resented, as psychological studies of tax evasion suggest.[32]

This is one reason why the Ricardian equivalence hypothesis, which claims that government deficits do not matter, cannot be correct. Proponents of Ricardian equivalence argue that individuals are forward-looking, anticipating the future tax burden resulting from higher government deficits, and will therefore increase their savings rates. Remarkably, the serious practical problems that arise with attempts to collect higher taxes seem to have eluded these theoreticians.[33]

---

32 Alm, Jackson and McKee, "Estimating the Determinants of Taxpayer Compliance with Experimental Data," in *National Tax Journal*, vol. 45, no. 1.

33 The issue is not addressed at all in the literature survey by John Seater, "Ricardian Equivalence," in *Journal of Economic Literature*, March 1993.

Continual growth in the proportion of GDP going to service the interest on the country's public debt requires either reduced government services or increased tax rates. Deficits should be considered a matter of great concern because of the increasing difficulty of paying the interest on a growing pool of public debt. This is a function both of the size of government deficits and of the real interest rate on the debt issued to finance these deficits. There is evidence that tight monetary policy in Canada over the past several years has exacerbated the problem by causing substantially higher real bond yields.[34]

Conclusions

This article has examined some possible factors behind the spurt of growth in the Canadian underground economy that began in 1991. The inescapable conclusion is that the GST was the primary catalyst triggering this growth.

While the GST was the culprit in this latest episode, other evidence supports the view that there was already a substantial underground economy in Canada before 1991. Econometric analysis from both Canada and the United States suggests that the large share of GDP taken by taxes in total (and in particular high rates of income tax) is the primary cause of the long-run growth in the underground economy.

---

34   Peter Spiro, "The Differential Between Canadian and US Long-Term Bond Yields," in *Canadian Business Economics*, Winter 1994.

Canadian Attitudes Towards Taxation

Bruce Flexman

Introduction

There is a great deal of controversy nowadays about the extent of Canada's underground economy and how we can measure it with any degree of accuracy. Some of the debate has focussed on the definition of this underground economy. Does it include only activities using illegal means to avoid paying tax? Or does it encompass activities in which individuals legally avoid taxes—for example, doing their own home repairs instead of hiring contractors. All things considered, it would seem that our definition of the underground economy should cover illegal practices only: it would be too difficult to separate self supply transactions undertaken for tax motives from those engaged in for other reasons.

The primary debate about the size of the underground economy in Canada, however, revolves around the methods used for arriving at estimates. Some commentators base their estimates on changes in the money supply.[1] Another approach measures reported and unreported activities in the Canadian economy sector by sector and attempts to estimate levels of underground activity within these sectors.[2] Smith and Revenue Canada favour a microeconomic approach: estimates of levels of evasion in particular industry sectors provide a more focussed approach for targeting future audit activity.

But does the size of the underground economy really matter? If 5 percent or 20 percent of the Canadian gross domestic product turns out to be underground, how does this information help us to reduce this economy? The fact is that taking the measure of the underground economy is an important first step in building appropriate public policy to deal with tax evasion or cheating. If no attempt is made to quantify our subject and establish whether it is growing or shrinking, it will be that much more difficult for us to make a rational allocation of public resources to deal with the matter. It would also be very hard to evaluate measures taken to combat tax evasion without some sense of their effectiveness.

Is there a simpler way to establish our measurement? Canadians' perceptions of the underground economy draw mainly on anecdotal evidence. With the introduction of the GST, it has become commonplace to hear open talk of paying cash for goods or services to avoid this tax. During 1993, we saw numerous reports about tobacco smugglers and the huge profits they were earning. One could not help noticing the news clips of people openly purchasing contraband cigarettes. The evening news showed us snowmobiles laden with smuggled cigarettes crossing the St. Lawrence in the winter darkness. These anecdotes colour our perception of the underground economy, but do they help us to measure it?

---

1   See the papers in this volume by Rolf Mirus and Roger S. Smith, Faculty of Business, University of Alberta, "Canada's Underground Economy: Measurement and Implications," and Peter Spiro, Ontario Ministry of Finance, "Taxes, Deficits, and the Underground Economy."

2   See the paper in this volume by Philip Smith of Statistics Canada, "Assessing the Size of the Underground Economy: The Statistics Canada Perspective."

Whatever the case, these perceptions of the size of the underground economy do have special significance. If people come to see tax cheating as acceptable, more of them may feel able to rationalize their own behaviour to evade taxes. Now our Canadian tax system is based on selfcompliance. Customs officers cannot check every vehicle crossing the border; Ottawa is not able to collect GST on every transaction and so has to enlist businesses to act as its agents. Taxpayers are responsible for preparing tax returns and reporting income, including income from such cash transactions as tips and gratuities and interest from foreign bank accounts. The government does not employ enough tax auditors to ensure that each return is checked in detail for compliance. A key ingredient of any tax system is the degree to which it encourages voluntary cooperation, and our Canadian system is still premised on a high degree of selfcompliance.

Does the anecdotal evidence suggest that this selfcompliance is being eroded? Are people losing faith in the basic fairness of their tax system? If there is an erosion of confidence, will this translate into a greater degree of evasion? A recent KPMG survey, outlined in greater detail below, captured the views of Canadians on these and other important questions about taxes and the underground economy.

Certainly one of the most important of these questions is whether or not popular perceptions of the underground economy actually affect the level of Canadian tax cheating. Much taxpayer compliance is motivated by the penalties and other deterrents for people caught evading taxes. For certain types of cheating such as paying cash for services or purchasing contraband alcohol or tobacco, however, the penalties may be so remote that taxpayers' behaviour will be based more on their perceptions of what is right than on the existence of deterrents.

Businesses feeling that their competitors are not complying may feel forced to enter the underground economy. For individuals, the perception that many others are not paying their share of taxes may be the only rationalization needed for failing to report certain types of income where the chances of getting caught seem very slim.

Again, Canadians' perceptions of the extent of the underground economy are important in measuring its impact. If the underground economy is perceived to be large and growing, it may become a self-fulfilling prophecy. Canadian perceptions are also important tools for determining the causes of the underground economy and suggesting courses of action for containing it. The objective must be to change public perceptions about the underground economy in order to promote voluntary compliance. If we are to accomplish this, we have to track changes in public perceptions to determine how views are changing and whether our various initiatives are actually working.

We begin with the methodology used in our survey. Our results are then reviewed as they relate to popular perceptions and factors that may contribute to these perceptions. We go on to analyze these results to identify certain taxpayer profiles. The paper concludes by discussing the implications of the survey results for future steps to deal with the underground economy.

Survey methodology

The KPMG survey of attitudes towards taxation was undertaken by Canadian Facts, the country's largest such company, for our Centre for

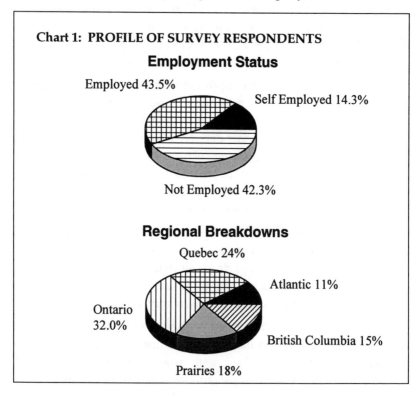

Chart 1: PROFILE OF SURVEY RESPONDENTS

Employment Status

Employed 43.5%

Self Employed 14.3%

Not Employed 42.3%

Regional Breakdowns

Quebec 24%

Atlantic 11%

Ontario 32.0%

British Columbia 15%

Prairies 18%

Government Foundation. The survey was national in scope, with respondents randomly chosen from different regions to ensure representativeness of the Canadian population. Some 1,025 Canadians were contacted by telephone during the week January 31 to February 5, 1994.

The survey identified respondents who were selfemployed. Chart 1 summarizes the profile of survey respondents with respect to employment status and regional locations. The survey also captured biographical information on respondents' ages, marital and employment status, education, language, and approximate incomes. Where appropriate, the survey questions were asked in different order to avoid any potential bias.

It should be pointed out that the survey was conducted during a period of heightened awareness of tobacco smuggling. It was on February 9, 1994, shortly after the survey, that the federal government announced a reduction of taxes on cigarettes to combat the high-profile smuggling problem.

Survey results

(a) Extent of evasion

Respondents were asked: "To what extent, if any, do you feel that people are evading some of their full share of taxes? Would you say it is happening...a lot, a fair amount, a little, hardly at all, or don't know?" Chart 2 outlines the survey results from this question for all Canadians. It is disturbing that 61 percent of survey respondents felt that there was a lot or a fair amount of evasion. However, it is not clear whether they were making any distinction between tax evasion and legal tax avoidance. There is also no indication as to whether people thought that "a lot" or "a fair amount" meant more than 10 percent, more than 30 percent, or some other figure.

Respondents were then asked whether they agreed a lot, agreed a little, disagreed a little, or disagreed a lot with certain statements about taxation in Canada. They were also given the option of having no opinion. Chart 3 shows the responses to the statement: "Most people are honest and pay all the taxes that they should." This answer provides background for the extent of perceived evasion. Some 38 percent of respondents disagreed either a little or a lot with this statement: this group apparently feels that most people are dishonest and do not pay

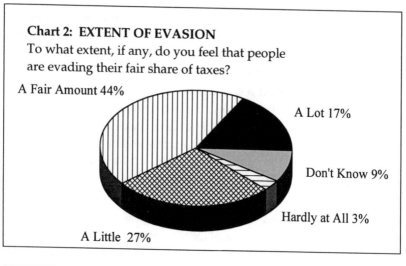

Chart 2: EXTENT OF EVASION
To what extent, if any, do you feel that people are evading their fair share of taxes?

A Fair Amount 44%

A Lot 17%

Don't Know 9%

Hardly at All 3%

A Little 27%

Chart 3: LEVEL OF HONESTY
Most people are honest and pay all the taxes they should

Agree a Little 26%

Agree a Lot 31%

No Opinion 5%

Disagree a Little 19%

Disagree a Lot 19%

all the taxes they should. Respondents from Quebec and young people perceived higher levels of tax cheating among Canadians. Older taxpayers and respondents from British Columbia perceived lower levels than the average.

Many taxpayers are complying out of fear of being caught for tax evasion. Respondents were asked their degree of agreement with the following statement: "Most people would cheat on their taxes if they knew they would get away with it." Not surprisingly, 72 percent agreed

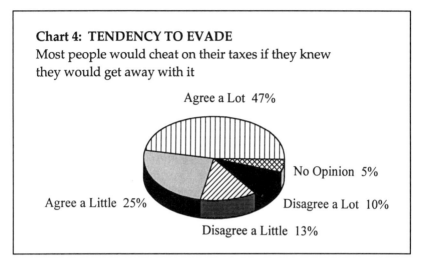

Chart 4: TENDENCY TO EVADE
Most people would cheat on their taxes if they knew they would get away with it

Agree a Lot 47%

No Opinion 5%

Agree a Little 25%

Disagree a Lot 10%

Disagree a Little 13%

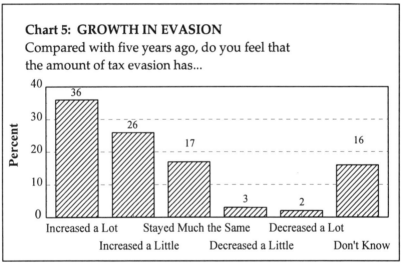

Chart 5: GROWTH IN EVASION
Compared with five years ago, do you feel that the amount of tax evasion has...

that with no risk of being caught, most Canadians would not be self-complying. Chart 4 summarizes these responses. The equivalent figure for respondents aged 18 to 24 was 85 percent as against 58 percent for senior citizens aged 65 and over.

(b) Evasion growth

Survey respondents were asked to compare what they perceived as the current level of evasion with their perceptions of five years before, and indicate whether they thought it had changed. As can be seen in Chart 5,

62 percent of respondents felt that the amount of tax evasion had increased either a little or a lot in the previous five years. This result reflects a heightened awareness of tax evasion. Only 5 percent of respondents felt there had been a decrease in tax evasion.

(c) Evasion preferences

Respondents were asked to comment on the level of certain types of tax evasion by others and state whether they would engage in them if they believed they would not be caught. The four ways of evading tax presented to respondents were as follows:

(i)   not reporting some income on the income tax return;

(ii) purchasing liquor or cigarettes that had been smuggled into Canada;

(iii) avoiding the GST by having work done for cash; and

(iv) not declaring goods bought abroad when returning to Canada.

Chart 6 summarizes respondents' perceptions of the ways taxes were being evaded by other Canadians. The responses indicate that Canadians feel a significant proportion of the population are evading

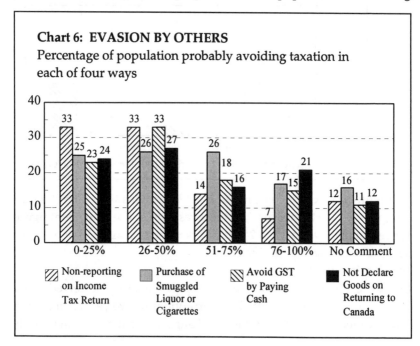

Chart 6: EVASION BY OTHERS
Percentage of population probably avoiding taxation in each of four ways

taxes, at least occasionally, in the ways outlined by the survey question. Clearly, income tax evasion by not reporting amounts on the personal return is seen as the least prevalent of these practices. This result is not surprising, given that there is less latitude for many Canadians to misreport income for tax purposes when information slips for such common income sources as wages and interest are provided to the government.

Quebec respondents perceived higher levels of evasion than respondents in other provinces for smuggled liquor and cigarettes. Respondents from Ontario indicated the highest levels of evasion for cross-border shoppers and persons paying cash to avoid the GST.

Disturbingly, perceived levels of evasion by others differ with the respondents' ages. Younger respondents perceived much higher levels of tax evasion in the four scenarios presented.

Respondents also answered a hypothetical question on their own propensities for tax cheating. Survey respondents were asked if they had an opportunity during the next year and believed they would not be caught, they would engage in the following:

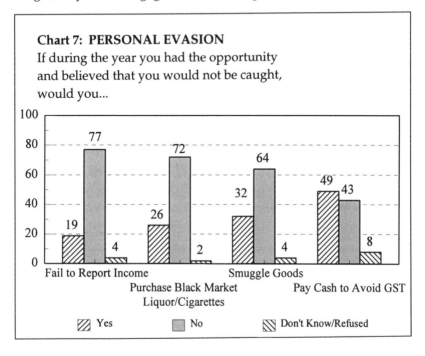

Chart 7: PERSONAL EVASION
If during the year you had the opportunity and believed that you would not be caught, would you...

(i) not reporting income on their income tax returns;

(ii) purchasing, for themselves or others, liquor or cigarettes that had been smuggled into Canada;

(iii) avoiding the GST by having work done for cash; or

(iv) not declaring goods bought abroad when returning to Canada.

Chart 7 summarizes the national responses to this question. The results suggest that Canadians are prepared to avoid paying the GST but less inclined to fail to report income for tax purposes. Interestingly enough, very few respondents refused to reply to this question. It seems probable that failure to report income on a tax return is perceived as involving a higher risk of reprisal even though the question started with the premise that respondents believed they would not be caught: for some taxpayers, moreover, having to sign the tax return before filing may help to make failure to report income a disturbing prospect.

The high levels of respondents prepared to avoid GST can be attributed, at least in part, to the unpopularity of this tax. Consumers may also feel that there is nothing illegal about paying cash to avoid GST since it is difficult for the government to prove intent.

Given the seriousness of tobacco smuggling in Quebec during 1993, Quebec respondents showed a much higher inclination to purchase smuggled cigarettes or alcohol. The responses show consistent differences in inclination to cheat based on respondents' ages. Younger respondents were much more prepared to evade tax than older taxpayers were in any of the scenarios presented. Chart 8 outlines these results.

(d) Evasion acceptability

The final question of our underground economy survey dealt with the issue of the acceptability of evading income tax or GST as follows:

> "Earlier on we talked about the evasion of taxes and the extent to which some people might cheat to avoid paying tax. In your view, is the evasion of income tax by other people something that is
>
> - totally acceptable to you
> - mildly acceptable to you
> - mildly unacceptable to you
> - totally unacceptable to you
> - don't know?"

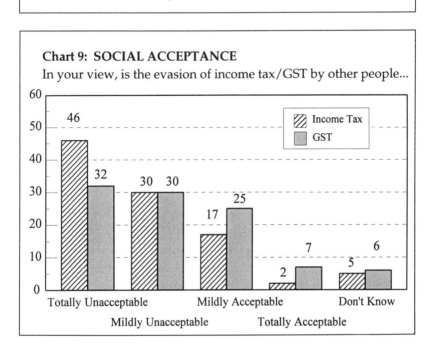

Chart 8: EVASION BY OTHERS

If during the year you have the opportunity
and believed you would not be caught,
would you . . . .

18-24 Years: Non-report 24, Purchase Smuggled 40, Avoid GST 39, Not Declare 52
25-34 Years: Non-report 23, Purchase Smuggled 31, Avoid GST 32, Not Declare 52
35-49 Years: Non-report 20, Purchase Smuggled 27, Avoid GST 33, Not Declare 52
50-64 Years: Non-report 18, Purchase Smuggled 20, Avoid GST 26, Not Declare 51
65+ Years: Non-report 8, Purchase Smuggled 8, Avoid GST 12, Not Declare 33

- Non-report on Income Tax Return
- Purchase Smuggled Liquor or Cigarettes
- Avoid GST by Paying Cash
- Not Declare Goods on Returning to Canada

Chart 9: SOCIAL ACCEPTANCE

In your view, is the evasion of income tax/GST by other people...

Income Tax / GST

Totally Unacceptable: Income Tax 46, GST 32
Mildly Unacceptable: Income Tax 30, GST 30
Mildly Acceptable: Income Tax 17, GST 25
Totally Acceptable: Income Tax 2, GST 7
Don't Know: Income Tax 5, GST 6

In an attempt to remove any order bias in responses, about half of respondents had the alternatives reversed, starting with "don't know" through to "totally acceptable to you." Once again, respondents indicated greater respect for the income tax system than for the GST. Of some concern is the fact that 19 percent of respondents were either mildly or totally accepting of income tax evasion and 32 percent were mildly or totally accepting of GST evasion by other people. See Chart 9 for the responses to this question.

Consistent with earlier findings, older respondents, particularly senior citizens, found income tax or GST evasion more unacceptable than younger respondents did. Although the majority of Canadians find evasion unacceptable, it is both surprising and disturbing that significant numbers find evasion socially acceptable. Apparently, morality has been eroded where taxes are concerned—a situation partly attributable to the effects of the GST.

Survey results: other factors influencing the underground economy

A number of factors may affect a person's inclination to participate in the underground economy to avoid taxes. To the extent that the tax system is considered fair, it is reasonable to assume that more individuals will be inclined to comply voluntarily. If people feel that their tax dollars are not being used wisely, some may see evasion as the only way to control government expenditures. Perceived level of enforcement may be a strong deterrent for prospective tax evaders. Finally, certain design features of the tax system may spur a willingness to evade. Here, we will deal with the survey responses on factors that may influence the size of the underground economy.

(e) Fairness

Respondents were asked whether they agreed a lot, agreed a little, disagreed a little, or disagreed a lot with the following statement: "The present tax system is basically unfair to average Canadians."

Some 74 percent of respondents agreed with this statement either a little or a lot. Quebec respondents were particularly strong in their agreement: 84 percent agreed. Chart 10 summarizes the responses.

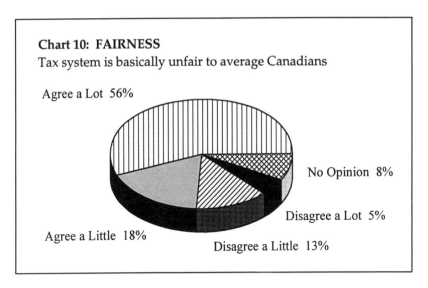

Chart 10: FAIRNESS
Tax system is basically unfair to average Canadians

Agree a Lot 56%
No Opinion 8%
Disagree a Lot 5%
Agree a Little 18%
Disagree a Little 13%

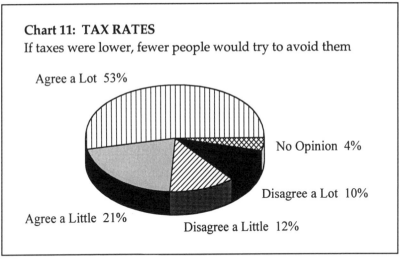

Chart 11: TAX RATES
If taxes were lower, fewer people would try to avoid them

Agree a Lot 53%
No Opinion 4%
Disagree a Lot 10%
Agree a Little 21%
Disagree a Little 12%

One would expect taxpayers to complain about the fairness of the tax system. We recognize that it would be more meaningful to track perceptions of taxing fairness over a period of time and measure any significant change. We encourage governments to initiate such tracking.

Chart 11 shows approximately three quarters of respondents agreeing that fewer people would try to avoid taxes if they were lower. In Quebec, 87 percent of respondents agreed. Responses may reflect the

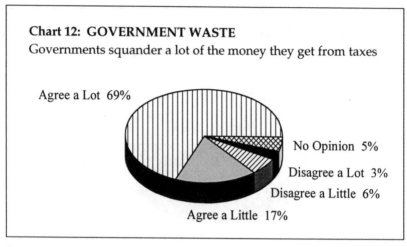

Chart 12: GOVERNMENT WASTE
Governments squander a lot of the money they get from taxes

Agree a Lot 69%

No Opinion 5%

Disagree a Lot 3%

Disagree a Little 6%

Agree a Little 17%

fact that tobacco smuggling was out of control at the time of the survey, particularly in Quebec.

(f) Fair value for taxes

The survey revealed that 86 percent of respondents felt their governments at all levels were wasting much of the money they raised in taxes. This attitude may be fuelling the growth of the underground economy. Chart 12 summarizes the responses.

A similar question asked survey respondents whether they felt Canadians were getting good value for the taxes they paid to their

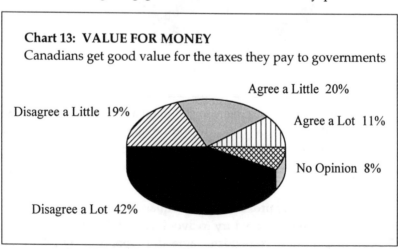

Chart 13: VALUE FOR MONEY
Canadians get good value for the taxes they pay to governments

Agree a Little 20%

Disagree a Little 19%

Agree a Lot 11%

No Opinion 8%

Disagree a Lot 42%

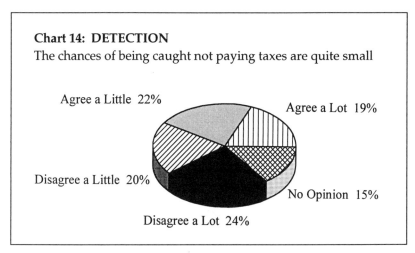

Chart 14: DETECTION
The chances of being caught not paying taxes are quite small

Agree a Little 22%

Agree a Lot 19%

Disagree a Little 20%

No Opinion 15%

Disagree a Lot 24%

governments. The survey results suggest that 31 percent of Canadians felt they were receiving value, while 61 percent disagreed to some extent. With ever-increasing government expenditures being used to service interest on debt accumulated from past deficits, it is not surprising that Canadians feel they are getting less value for the taxes they pay.

(g) Enforcement

Levels of tax evasion reflect perceptions of perpetrators' chances of being caught. A tax administration that is visible in its efforts to catch and prosecute tax evaders sends a strong message to other taxpayers that the system is being operated effectively and that tax evaders run a significant risk of being caught. Respondents were almost evenly divided on whether they thought their chances of being caught for tax evasion were small. The question did not explore what types of tax evasion were more likely to escape detection. Chart 14 summarizes our survey results for this question.

Canadians appear to be prepared to accept stronger medicine to deal with tax evasion and, by implication, the underground economy. Charts 15 and 16 indicate strong support for increased efforts by Revenue Canada to catch evaders and stiffer penalties for these offenders. Since most survey respondents would not have had much information about current levels of enforcement and penalties assessed to tax evaders, these responses are based on perceptions.

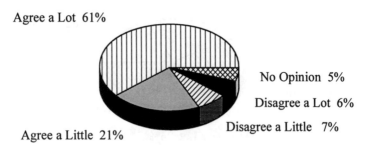

Chart 15: ENFORCEMENT
Revenue Canada should increase its efforts to catch
people who cheat on their taxes

Agree a Lot 61%

No Opinion 5%

Disagree a Lot 6%

Disagree a Little 7%

Agree a Little 21%

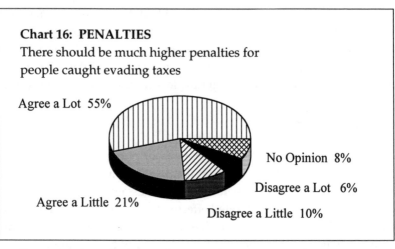

Chart 16: PENALTIES
There should be much higher penalties for
people caught evading taxes

Agree a Lot 55%

No Opinion 8%

Disagree a Lot 6%

Agree a Little 21%

Disagree a Little 10%

Revenue Canada has only recently reintroduced its practice of publicizing taxpayers who are prosecuted and convicted for income tax evasion. Interestingly, the survey indicates a general concern among Canadians about the level of taxation and the use of their tax dollars, with significant numbers prepared to evade tax by different means and yet overwhelmingly supportive of increased enforcement and penalties. In the early 1980s, Revenue Canada was maligned for what was then seen as heavyhanded enforcement, and the department reacted with reduced publicity of these activities. However, this survey indicated public acceptance of more visible signs that Revenue Canada is main-

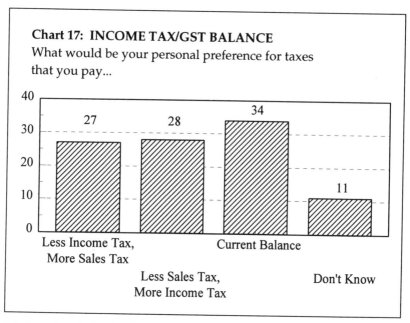

Chart 17: INCOME TAX/GST BALANCE
What would be your personal preference for taxes that you pay...

taining a level playing field by ensuring that tax evaders are caught and penalized.

(h) Tax policy

At the time our survey was conducted, the government had just asked the House of Commons Standing Committee on Finance to recommend an alternative to replace the GST. The survey contained two questions dealing with tax policy and GST replacement. The first asked whether the mix of sales and income taxes should be revised: it was phrased as follows:

"As you know, governments raise money in two main ways. One way is to tax income, and the other is to tax purchases through a provincial sales tax or the GST. If we accept that the money has to be raised by taxation, which would be your personal preference for taxes that you pay?

- Less income and more tax on your purchases;
- Less tax on purchases and more income tax;
- The present balance between income tax and tax on purchases, or
- Don't know?"

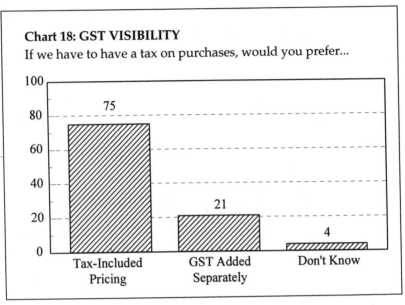

Chart 18: GST VISIBILITY
If we have to have a tax on purchases, would you prefer...

No clear consensus emerged from the survey results. More than a third of respondents felt that the current balance was appropriate, while the remaining respondents expressing opinions were split almost evenly on whether there should be more income tax or more sales tax. As one would expect, higher-income respondents favoured more sales tax, while the less educated, unemployed, or part-time workers favoured more income taxes.

The second question asked whether any sales tax replacing the GST should be visible—calculated separately—or folded into the sales price. The question was phrased as follows:

"The main taxes on purchases are provincial sales tax and the GST. If a new tax on purchases was introduced as a replacement for GST, it could be one where the tax was included in the price you saw in the store, or one where the tax was added to the price at the cash register. If we have to have a tax on purchases, would you prefer:

- A tax that is already included in the final price you see;
- A tax that is added separately when you pay, or
- Don't know?"

Chart 18 shows that Canadians overwhelmingly favour tax-included pricing. Respondents apparently felt that loss of tax visibility outweighed the inconvenience of having to deal with tax-extra pricing.

Taxpayer profiles

The survey on Canadian attitudes towards taxation contained 10 statements with which respondents were asked to indicate their degree of agreement or disagreement. An analysis of these belief statements identified three underlying factors: attitudes towards government and taxes, attitudes towards enforcement, and attitudes towards tax evasion. Using these three factors, the analysis segmented the population into the following four groups:

(a) Model Citizens

Model Citizens tended to believe that Canadians received good value for their taxes, the present system was fair, Revenue Canada should increase its enforcement activities, and that people are not foolish to pay all their taxes. Model Citizens were likely to be higher-income individuals or graduates. This group represented 22 percent of the survey population.

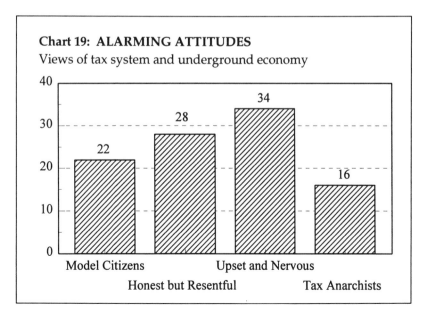

Chart 19: ALARMING ATTITUDES
Views of tax system and underground economy

(b) Honest but Resentful

People in the Honest but Resentful segment felt that the most people were honest and would not cheat. However, they believed that the system was unfair, taxes were squandered, and good value was not being received for taxes paid. Some 28 percent of the population fell into this segment.

(c) Upset and Envious

The Upset and Envious segment believed that taxes were unfair, wasted, and provided little value to taxpayers. They felt that most people avoided paying their full tax bill and wanted to see stronger action against cheaters. At 34 percent, this was the largest segment.

(d) Tax Anarchists

The Tax Anarchists were very similar to the Upset and Envious category under the headings of fairness, waste, and value for taxes. However, the Tax Anarchists believed that people were foolish to pay all their taxes and opposed Revenue Canada taking more enforcement initiatives or increasing penalties. This group represented 16 percent of the survey population. Not surprisingly, a high percentage of Tax Anarchists were self-employed.

Conclusions

Our survey provided a snapshot of Canadian attitudes towards taxation at a particular point in time. Such taxpayer attitudes should be considered by governments when formulating tax policy and evaluating measures to combat the underground economy. While that economy may be very difficult to quantify, the same cannot be said, fortunately, of taxpayer attitudes, so critical for a tax system that relies on selfcompliance.

A number of conclusions emerge from the survey results. First, any assault on the underground economy will be hampered by Canadian attitudes to government use of their tax dollars. Some 86 percent of Canadians believe that governments squander a lot of the money they collect in taxes. Less than one quarter of Canadians could be categorized as "model citizens." Half of our respondents were categorized as "upset and envious" or "tax anarchists."

Governments at all levels are facing a dilemma in this regard. The reality is that Canadians will necessarily receive less value for their tax dollars as more and more of government revenues are required to service the national debt and governments have to slash their operating deficits. Until governments are able to get their fiscal house in order, Canadian taxpayers will feel cheated of their tax dollars. This will only make the underground economy tougher to combat.

Canadians believe that evasion is growing and widespread—a view that is particularly prevalent among younger Canadians. The political opposition to the GST and the visibility of this tax have led to a perception of increased underground activity. While the GST was introduced as a more effective tax for dealing with the underground economy, it would appear that Canadians believe the opposite and are inclined to try avoiding the GST. Canadians have overwhelmingly indicated a preference for a less visible tax included in the base price of goods and services. This may encourage the government to mandate tax-included pricing for a GST replacement tax.

According to the survey, younger people are more inclined to evade taxes and see evasion as more widespread. Does this mean that younger people are more inclined to evade taxes because of their youth or that we have hatched more tax cheaters in the younger generation who will retain their cheating propensities as they age? If the latter is true, it is a very disturbing trend, especially given the fact that younger generations will inevitably inherit the problems of dealing with a sizeable national debt.

The survey found Canadians ready to accept tougher enforcement by Revenue Canada. But are they? A fiercer Revenue Canada will not necessarily attack tax cheaters only: all taxpayers may come under close scrutiny. This type of initiative might backfire if innocent taxpayers felt that Revenue Canada had become heavyhanded with taxpayers generally.

The experience of the early 1980s demonstrated the risks of aggressive enforcement. During this period, Revenue Canada made concerted efforts to unearth billions of dollars in uncollected taxes, and efforts by the department's auditors were highlighted and publicized. Public reaction was mobilized, and the Conservatives in Opposition were quick to call for curbing Revenue Canada's powers.

The same Conservatives then came to power on a platform that included taxpayers' rights, and Revenue Canada was duly curtailed.

Now the department may be just as effective in enforcing the tax laws as it ever was, but Canadians appear to think otherwise. It is therefore important that Revenue Canada be more visible in its enforcement activities and ensure that clear cases of tax evasion are publicized and penalized.

Our survey indicated a surprisingly high social acceptance of tax evasion. Perhaps the political drama of the passage of the GST legislation had placed stress on respect for our tax laws. Whatever the cause, the survey showed that a significant number of Canadians find it acceptable to cheat on their taxes. Most importantly, the view is more prevalent among young people. This is the most disturbing conclusion to emerge from the survey. Where a certain level of compliance with the tax system is voluntary, any erosion of taxpayer morality will lead to a growing underground economy.

The attitudes of Canadians told us that our tax system was in trouble. While the survey reports perceptions and not actual levels of evasion, these perceptions may become realities if governments fail to come up with an effective response. Governments will have to adopt a strategic approach to the underground economy: the option of raising taxes to offset tax revenues lost underground is no longer viable.

A key element of this strategic approach must be to monitor taxpayer attitudes with a view to influencing them over time. While tax administration has historically focussed on the appropriate mix of enforcement and service to taxpayers, it must also nurture taxpayer morality as an investment in improved future compliance within the Canadian tax system.

Revenue Canada: A Sectoral Approach to Measuring the Underground Economy

Tim Gahagan

The matter of the underground economy is approached here from a tax practitioner's perspective. We will briefly examine some estimates of the size of the underground economy, dealing with their advantages and disadvantages and, in particular, their usefulness for detecting underreported or unreported income or sales.

There is a need in this area for the kinds of analysis and estimates that might be more helpful for tax compliance. While aggregate estimates are interesting and important from a broad public policy perspective, they do not have a level of precision or provide the detailed analysis required to identify specific sectors or areas where tax compliance might be an issue. They also do not deal with questions of behaviour and factors which affect it.

Size of the underground economy

Most, if not all, estimates of the underground economy are aggregate measures developed by looking at the economy as a whole. The difficulty, of course, is that one is trying to measure activity which is unmeasured or unreported. Because of this, assumptions have to be made that are open to a great deal of debate.

The following difficulties arise with aggregate measures:

- there is no one accepted methodology and, depending on assumptions, even the same approach can result in widely differing estimates;
- aggregate measures provide little insight or precision about specific areas where underground activity may be occurring;
- the wide variations exemplify the challenges and difficulties that characterize aggregate measurements collectively.

We will briefly review the major methods used, the first being the group using monetary aggregates. Tracking the velocity of cash and reported transactions, this approach infers the size of the underground by the traces they leave. The argument is that a shift in cash balances and cash in circulation suggests greater cash transactions. This involves assumptions about the velocity of money and the medium of exchange—cash, cheque, or barter. Of course, many factors might affect cash relative to total money supply, and estimates of the size of the underground economy using this approach also depend on the choice of base year for comparison.

A second method is to compare the national income measure with national expenditures and infer that the difference is a measure of hidden activity. This method yields estimates of perhaps 4 percent of GDP for the underground economy. The observed differences may reflect a range of factors. The study entitled "The Size of the Underground Economy: A Statistics Canada View", points out these issues.

A third method compares employment statistics. In Canada, this has been done by comparing the *Labour Force Survey* with the *Survey of Employment, Payroll and Hours*. Such comparisons reveal a growing variation between these surveys since 1991, but the reasons for this remain unclear. Some have argued that it reflects differences in methodology and coverage, particularly of the service sector. In any event, estimating the size of the underground economy requires knowledge of worker productivity in the informal economy, and such estimates are not readily available to give us an appropriate measurement.

A fourth approach is to use household surveys, extrapolate to the total population, and compare the results with other aggregate measures such as the national accounts. This approach may have problems of non-response and survey response bias—most people will not want to talk about activities they are not reporting.

Now these approaches yield a wide range of estimates of the size of the underground economy, ranging from a low of about 3 percent to in excess of 20 percent of GDP—discrepancies that have been the subject of much debate. Might it not be possible to reduce the range of estimates by concluding agreements on the methodologies and assumptions to be used? In the absence of consensus, we can only anticipate continued wide variations in estimates and thus unclear consequences for public policy.

From the standpoint of improving tax compliance, we might draw the following conclusions:

- first, none of these measures provides specific estimates of unreported or underreported income or sales;
- secondly, more precision is needed with respect to sectors and areas where non-reporting and underreporting may be problems;
- thirdly, less aggregate and more micro analysis might yield higher returns and improved explanations of the reasons and consequences of underground activity.

Sector-specific studies

From a tax practitioner's perspective, sector-specific or micro analysis may be more useful and hold more promise in terms of the quest for the underground economy. Sector studies such as one by the Canadian Homebuilders Association, which has estimated that up to 55 percent of home renovation activity is done "under the table," provide indicators of the seriousness of unreported income and sales in specific areas of the economy. Another example is the Quebec construction industry survey revealing that 25 million hours went unreported in 1991 at a cost of approximately $420 million. This type of detail is needed if we are to gain a better appreciation of the underground economy and formulate appropriate responses to its presence.

A related approach is to survey businesses and individuals. These can help identify areas of non-compliance and the characteristics of non-compliant individuals. For example, a survey by the Canadian Federation of Independent Business found that 25 percent of 11,000 small-business respondents felt that they were facing unfair competition from the underground economy. A further example is the KPMG Peat, Marwick, Thorne survey which found that 19 percent of taxpayers would evade income taxes given the opportunity and a low likelihood of being caught. KPMG also found a significant number who viewed tax evasion as socially acceptable.

Unfortunately, no prior survey benchmark is available to determine whether or not tax evasion is actually on the rise. However, the kinds of surveys mentioned above can provide useful insights into the extent of tax evasion, the characteristics of people who are not reporting, and the reasons behind the practice. Studies along these lines are at least somewhat effective at identifying underground activity and unreported or underreported income.

The approaches Revenue Canada uses for identifying possible problem areas include:

- historical analysis of compliance and trends,
- matching of information,
- using other sources of data,
- international exchange of information, and
- working cooperatively with the provinces.

These approaches, supplemented by sector-specific studies, can enable us to identify areas where underreported and unreported activities occur. As a result, Revenue Canada has now targeted its efforts to sectors where cash transactions are prevalent—construction, jewellery, restaurant/hospitality services, home renovations, car repairs, and other services. With the Matching Program, Revenue Canada is identifying non-registrants and non-filers and working with the provinces, industry associations, and other experts to improve our ability to identify specific sectors and their characteristics.

This may not be public attention-grabbing work, but it is what is needed to identify underreported and unreported income. It is not only advantageous but the only feasible way to proceed.

Conclusion

Aggregate estimates are interesting, but if they are to be helpful in broad policy terms, their methodological range and differences have to be narrowed. Even then, aggregate measurements may not be as helpful as sector-specific or micro studies that can yield the greater precision needed to guide action and allow us to understand what is going on.

Revenue Canada must, in its attention to underreported and unreported income and sales, be able to rely on much sharper analyses such as sector and compliance studies to best direct its enforcement activities.

A Provincial Perspective on Revenue Forecasting[1]

Lois McNabb

Our purpose here is to look at various factors that affect the accuracy of government revenue forecasts. Beginning with an overview of provincial revenue sources and the environment of revenue growth and forecast performance, we will go on to look at the accuracy of revenue forecasts in BC budgets and some evidence that the size of the underground economy is increasing.

Provincial revenue sources

Like most Canadian provinces, British Columbia levies a broad range of taxes that include personal income tax, corporation income and corporation capital taxes, a sales tax called the social service tax, property tax, and taxes on hotel accommodations, insurance premiums, and transfers of real property.

---

1   Based on information available to April 15, 1994.

The province also collects royalties on the sale of natural resources and levies fees, licences, and fines. It receives transfers from the federal government to cover some of the costs of health care, postsecondary education, and social assistance: part of this revenue is received as income tax receipts and part through cash payments. Finally, the province collects revenue from government enterprises that include provincial liquor stores, the lottery corporation, and the power utility.

As shown in the 1994 provincial budget, revenue in 1994/95 was expected to total $18.7 billion. Of this total forecast, 62.6 percent was expected to come from taxation, 12.5 percent from federal government transfers, 9.7 percent from natural resources, 9.6 percent from other sources including fees, licences, and investment income, and 5.6 percent from provincial Crown corporations and enterprises (see Chart 1).

Ten years previously, BC's revenue profile had been somewhat different. The main differences were in taxation revenue and federal contributions, which then comprised respectively 57 and 21 percent of the 1984/85 total.

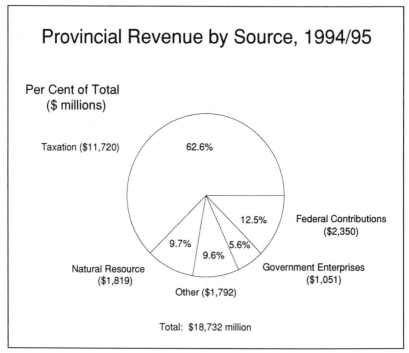

Chart 1

Factors affecting provincial revenue growth and forecast performance

A number of factors affect the growth of provincial revenue and our ability to forecast it. These include:

- the stage of the economic cycle;
- structural changes in the economy and differences in the provincial economy from the rest of Canada;
- commodity prices and exchange rates;
- the quality and timeliness of provincial economic data;
- changes to the tax structure and revenue elasticity;
- federal offloading; and
- the underground economy, including the effects of higher taxes, cross-border shopping, and tax collection programs.

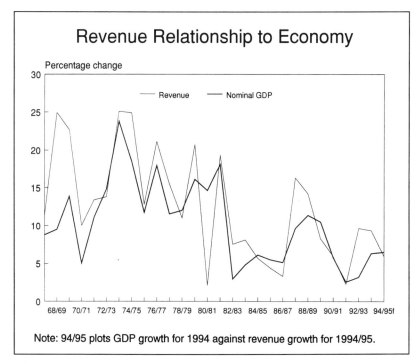

Note: 94/95 plots GDP growth for 1994 against revenue growth for 1994/95.

Chart 2

Stage of the economic cycle

The following chart shows the relationship between nominal gross domestic product (GDP) growth and overall growth in provincial government revenue. Revenue growth rates reflect the impact of changes in tax rates, which contributed to higher revenue growth than GDP growth in 1987/88 and 1988/89 and again in 1992/93 and 1993/94.

The stages of the British Columbia business cycle affect revenue collection. One way of looking at this is to measure the elasticity or responsiveness of revenue to the economic cycle, calculated as the ratio of the revenue growth rate to the growth rate of nominal GDP. Revenue elasticity may vary considerably, reflecting lags in the tax system and the varying sensitivities of individual revenue sources over the economic cycle. In general, revenue elasticity tends to be higher when the economy is picking up. Conversely, it will tend to be lower when the economy is in recession (see Chart 3).

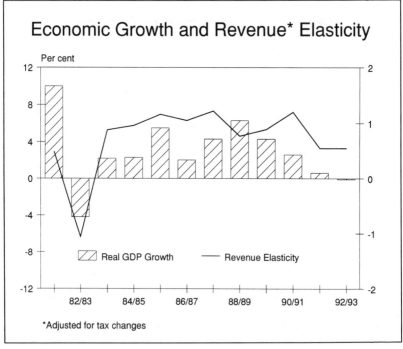

Chart 3

In the early 1980s, British Columbia experienced its worst recession in half a century. In 1982/83, real GDP shrank 4.2 percent, nominal GDP increased 3 percent and revenue, adjusted for tax changes, fell 7.5 percent. The elasticity of total revenue, adjusted for tax changes and relative to GDP, was -1.06.

Difficult economic circumstances may encourage tax evasion, resulting in lower provincial revenues. For example, the unemployed may not report income because they might thereby forfeit unemployment insurance or income assistance benefits.

Structural changes

The shift to services

British Columbia's economy, originally resource-based, has matured to a broader, service-based structure. Although resource extraction and processing are still important, substantial diversification has occurred

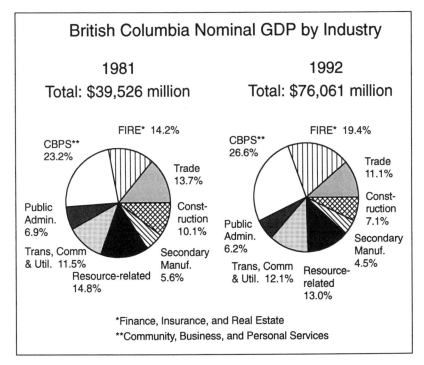

British Columbia Nominal GDP by Industry

1981 — Total: $39,526 million
1992 — Total: $76,061 million

1981:
CBPS** 23.2%
FIRE* 14.2%
Trade 13.7%
Construction 10.1%
Secondary Manuf. 5.6%
Resource-related 14.8%
Trans, Comm & Util. 11.5%
Public Admin. 6.9%

1992:
CBPS** 26.6%
FIRE* 19.4%
Trade 11.1%
Construction 7.1%
Secondary Manuf. 4.5%
Resource-related 13.0%
Trans, Comm & Util. 12.1%
Public Admin. 6.2%

*Finance, Insurance, and Real Estate
**Community, Business, and Personal Services

Chart 4

in markets and types of products—the service sector and secondary manufacturing. The province has been successful in finding new markets for its traditional products, while the service sector has now expanded beyond support to resource industries.

Chart 4 shows that in 1981, the service-producing sector (shaded areas) generated about 69 percent of total nominal output. By 1992, the service share of total nominal output had increased to 75 percent. Similarly, the service-producing industries' share of total employment increased from 70 percent in 1981 to 76 percent in 1992.

The growing importance of service industries may lead to slower growth in government revenues because in British Columbia, most services are not taxed, although the sales tax now applies to some labour and legal services.

Self-employment

Self-employed people represent a growing share of the British Columbia workforce. In 1981, just under 14 percent of the province's workforce was self-employed: by 1993, this percentage had risen to 18.

Between 1981 and 1993, the number of self-employed residents of British Columbia more than doubled. During the same period, the number of self-employed persons in Canada as a whole increased by only one fifth (see Chart 5). British Columbia has a higher proportion of self-employed people than the rest of the country.

The chart shows cyclical behaviour in the self-employed share of the workforce. The percentage of self-employed falls when economic growth is peaking and increases when economic growth slows down.

Self-employment may affect provincial revenue growth and forecasts in two ways. First, self-employed people are able to write off many of their expenses for income tax purposes and must provide for their own retirement income. Secondly, in a period of rapid growth in self-employment relative to paid employment, traditional relationships between government revenue and employment may break down: self-employed people initially generate less income than those in paid employment.

Commodity prices and exchange rates

Many British Columbian export commodities are priced in US dollars. The value of the Canadian dollar thus has a direct impact on the prices

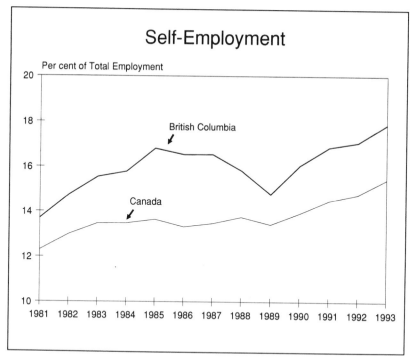

Chart 5

BC exporters receive. For example, as the value of the Canadian dollar appreciates, given no change in US-dollar lumber prices, lumber producers would get less for their product. Conversely, as the Canadian dollar depreciates, lumber exporters receive more.

The BC Council of Forest Industries estimates that every one-cent drop in our dollar over a period of one year adds $130 million to the value of forest product exports.[2] How much of this added value translates into government revenue will depend on the exporters' behaviour. Part of the additional income may feed through to corporate profits and thus into corporate income tax. If, on the other hand, some of the additional income goes to wage increases, the province's personal income tax revenue will rise. Higher Canadian-dollar prices will also affect the stumpage rates charged on timber harvested on Crown land.

---

2   "Forest industry stands to log huge benefit from export as dollar dips," in the *Vancouver Sun*, April 7, 1994.

Because lumber prices can be volatile, revenue results vary significantly from budget forecasts even when our forecasts of volumes harvested are correct.

Quality and timeliness of provincial economic data

Forecasting government revenue is made more difficult by the lack of timely provincial economic data. The lags for such important economic data as nominal gross domestic product (GDP), personal income, and investment are longer than for the same data at the national level. These data are subject to revision over a five-year period and estimates can change quite significantly, particularly at turning points.

Initial estimates of provincial wages and salaries, for example, are made with survey information. More refined estimates are produced about three years later, when information on personal income tax collections becomes available. By then, of course, the more accurate information is of little use in forecasting.[3]

Changes in tax structure and revenue elasticity

Over the last decade, a number of changes in British Columbia's tax structure have affected the elasticity of government revenue. These include:

- The transfer of responsibility for school property taxes from local school boards to the provincial government. Business property taxes have been a provincial source since 1982/83 and residential taxes since 1990/91. This revenue source is stable and relatively unaffected by economic cycles.
- The property transfer tax on real-estate transactions was introduced in 1987/88. This tax can be as volatile as property markets.
- The provincial stumpage system was modified in October 1987, when the Comparative Value Pricing (CVP) System replaced the Rothery Pricing System. The CVP System determines stump-

---

3   Statistics Canada has since begun using administrative records to improve the quality and timeliness of provincial wage and salary data.

age based on the relative value of timber (i.e., high stumpage rates on high-quality timber; low rates on poor-quality timber). The Rothery system determined stumpage on a residual basis—the residual difference between selling prices and company operating costs. The changeover to CVP has mitigated the extreme sensitivity of provincial revenue to lumber price fluctuations: stumpage rates now change on the same percentage basis as lumber prices. Before, when stumpage rates were high and prices fell, stumpage absorbed most of the fall: now, stumpage is no longer the last claim on resource revenues and tends to be less volatile as a source of income than it used to be under the Rothery System. Changes announced in April 1994 increased revenue from stumpage by making the system more sensitive to price changes above US $250 per thousand board feet.

- The 1991 increase in the contribution limits for registered retirement savings plans (RRSPs) caused a significant increase in contributions by higher-income people and contributed to a slowdown in the growth of income tax revenue.

Elastic revenue sources include provincial income taxes and the social service tax. Less elastic or inelastic sources include the corporation capital tax that was reintroduced in 1992, tobacco and liquor taxes, and federal government contributions.

Federal offloading

Since 1982/83, the federal government has made successive changes that have reduced the rate of growth of federal transfers relative to the original formulas. The most significant reductions occurred in the 1990 federal budget, which froze the per-capita entitlement for Established Programs Financing contributions and placed a 5 percent cap on the growth of social assistance transfers under the Canada Assistance Plan.

Over the last decade, the federal government has provided a smaller and smaller share of the provincial costs of programs, and growth in federal transfers has become less sensitive to the economic cycle. As a result, federal cash transfers fell from 21 percent of revenue in 1984/85 to 12.5 per cent in 1994/95.

In addition to previous cutbacks to provincial transfers, the 1994 federal budget announced a unilateral freeze on Canada Assistance Plan transfers for the 1995/96 fiscal year, pending a planned reform of social security programs scheduled for 1996/97. The federal government has also declared its intention of saving $1.5 billion annually in transfer payments to all provinces, beginning in 1996/97.

The underground economy

Many commentators have suggested that the failure of governments to meet revenue targets is evidence of a growing underground economy. However, the underground economy is only one possible reason for a slowdown in the growth of government revenues. In fact, judging by British Columbia's experience relative to the rest of Canada, underperforming revenue forecasts likely have more to do with cyclical and structural developments than with the underground economy.

Three factors that may encourage underground activity are public resistance to higher taxes, cross-border shopping, and federal tax collection efforts.

Resistance to higher taxes

Although it is difficult to determine the point at which higher taxes will trigger a decline in tax revenue, anecdotal evidence and public opinion surveys suggest that further significant increases in some taxes may not be viable either economically or politically. Taxpayers tend to be increasingly skeptical and intolerant of tax increases when the benefits of government programs are remote and they perceive waste and inefficiency in public administration. This state of mind can lead to a drop in voluntary tax compliance.

One reason for the hostility may be a deterioration in the public finances. As Don Drummond has noted,[4] from 1975/76 to 1986/87 Canadians received $1.12 worth of services for every dollar they paid in federal taxes. Based on federal budget data for 1994/95, however, Canadians now receive 99 cents in program spending for every dollar

---

4   See Don Drummond, "Five Questions about the Underground Economy," a paper presented to the Fraser Institute Conference on the Impact of the Underground Economy, April 21-22, 1994.

of federal taxes. With debt-servicing costs eating up a quarter of the expenditure budget, a federal move to balance the national budget through spending cuts would leave Canadians with only 75 cents' worth of services for every dollar of tax they paid.

The introduction of the goods and services tax (GST) in 1991 may have triggered a sharp increase in various kinds of tax evasion. This was the first general tax applied to services in Canada, and it offered greater opportunities for cheating, as there is often no evidence that services were performed.

A recent survey by the KPMG Centre for Government Foundation showed that while only 19 percent of Canadians would cheat on an income tax return if they believed they would not be caught, 49 percent would pay cash to avoid the GST. Forty-four percent of British Columbians said they would not pay the GST if they thought they would not be caught.[5] Clearly, the British Columbia government will be affected by cheating on the GST if federal and provincial taxes are not paid on income arising from these transactions.

A second area of evasion is tobacco taxes. High tobacco taxes have created a huge black market in smuggled tobacco products, and in response the federal government and some provinces have lowered their taxes.

Rising income tax rates mean greater incentives for taxpayers to evade taxes, use tax avoidance schemes, or shelter income through tax-sheltered investments like RRSPs, thus contributing to slower growth in income tax revenue. Higher tax rates also affect personal decisions about work and leisure: people may not work as hard because the extra income after tax is too little to compensate them for lost leisure.

Cross-border shopping

In British Columbia as in the rest of Canada, most people live within a hundred miles of the United States border. High taxes may well boost cross-border shopping activity. However, the exchange rate also plays a significant role in decisions to buy south of the line. The purchases of

---

5   "Hostility to GST high, survey finds," in the *Globe and Mail*, March 25, 1994, p. B3. For more on the KPMG survey, see the paper by Bruce Flexman, "Canadian Attitudes Towards Taxation," elsewhere in this volume.

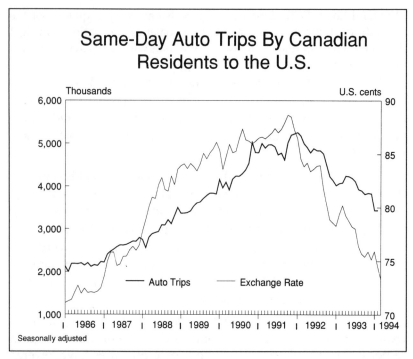

Same-Day Auto Trips By Canadian Residents to the U.S.

Thousands

U.S. cents

— Auto Trips   — Exchange Rate

| 1986 | 1987 | 1988 | 1989 | 1990 | 1991 | 1992 | 1993 | 1994

Seasonally adjusted

Chart 6

choice are generally goods that are heavily taxed in Canada—gasoline, tobacco, alcohol—or high-priced due to government supply restrictions, for example on dairy and poultry products, or import tariffs affecting such items as shoes and clothing.

From 1990 to 1992, cross-border shopping was a major public issue in British Columbia. As proxied by the number of same-day auto trips to the US, the level of cross-border shopping increased substantially between 1986 and 1991 (see Chart 6). At the same time, the value of the Canadian dollar was appreciating relative to the US dollar, and Canadian prices tended to be higher anyway because of our smaller market and a multi-layered distribution system that increased margins between the manufacturer and the retailer.[6]

6   See Ernst & Young, *Responding to Cross Border Shopping: A Study of the Competitiveness of Distribution Channels in Canada:* Report to the National Task Force on Cross Border Shopping, 1992.

In the period 1991 to early 1994, however, the number of same-day trips to the US fell by 19.1 percent. Not coincidentally, the value of the Canadian dollar against its US counterpart fell 12.3 percent between January 1991 and December 1993. The increase in the prices of foreign goods resulting from the depreciation of the Canadian dollar appears to have more than offset the rise in general prices resulting from the implementation of the GST. Canadian retailing has also become more competitive.

The loss in tax revenue from cross-border shopping was less than some suggest because many of the items that were cheaper in the US—food and children's clothing, for example—are not subject to provincial sales taxes in BC. This suggests that the main tax losses were in taxes on fuel, tobacco, and alcoholic beverages.[7]

Federal tax collection efforts

Most provinces, including British Columbia, have tax collection agreements authorizing the federal government to collect personal and corporate income taxes on their behalf. Revenue Canada also collects provincial alcohol and tobacco taxes at the border on behalf of British Columbia.

While the tax collection agreements reduce administrative costs for British Columbia and taxpayers have to file only one income tax return, they do mean that British Columbia relies on the federal government to collect over 30 percent of the province's revenue. Thus, the federal government's tax collection and auditing efforts can have a large effect on provincial revenue.

From 1986 to 1991, data show a downward trend in personal income tax auditing by Revenue Canada. After that time, the tax department announced that it was intensifying its auditing thrust, although the British Columbia government continues to monitor the level of enforcement by Revenue Canada.

However, Revenue Canada did form special audit teams to focus on industries with low levels of compliance—construction, jewellery,

---

7   Revenue Canada now collects provincial tax on tobacco and alcoholic beverages.

hospitality, home renovation, car repair, and other service industries. The income tax and excise portions of Revenue Canada were combined, and the department is increasing the number of joint GST/income tax audits to cross-reference files and improve the identification of those not reporting income.

British Columbia's experience

Forecasting

Between 1982/83 and 1993/94, provincial government revenue was, on average, $93 million higher than budget forecasts. The actual results varied from $802 million under budget in 1982/83 to $939 million over budget in 1988/89.

The average absolute change—ignoring whether the change was positive or negative—between a budget revenue forecast and actual results over the years 1982-1994 was $408 million or 4.1 percent of the forecast. By the early 1990's, however, revenue forecasting accuracy was improving to average less than 2 per cent of actual revenue.[8] While changes in the fiscal balance can result from changes in either revenue or expenditure forecasts, revenue remains the most important source of error. In fact, in 10 of the 12 years 1982-1994, revenue changes explained most changes in the fiscal balance from budget forecast to year end—a situation that reflects the greater sensitivity of revenue to the economic cycle, but also the greater degree of government discretion and control over spending during the year.

In seven of those years, revenue was higher than budget. Between 1987/88 and 1989/90, revenue was much higher than expected due to unexpectedly strong growth in the economy and policy changes affecting revenue. When an economy is strengthening, it is difficult to forecast the magnitude of the improvement. When the economy is weakening, revenue growth tends to fall more quickly.

Finally, it is difficult to forecast exactly when the economy will reach such turning points or how sharp the turns will be. In 1988, for example,

---

8   More recent information shows revenue 3.0 percent above budget in 1993/94, 4.3 percent above budget in 1994/95 and 1.7 percent below budget in 1995/96 (preliminary numbers).

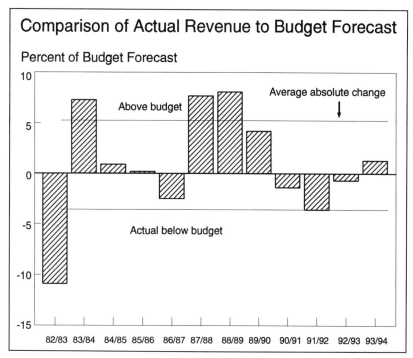

Comparison of Actual Revenue to Budget Forecast

Percent of Budget Forecast

Above budget

Average absolute change

Actual below budget

82/83 83/84 84/85 85/86 86/87 87/88 88/89 89/90 90/91 91/92 92/93 93/94

Chart 7

the provincial economy grew by 11.4 percent in nominal terms, significantly more than the original budget estimate of 6.9 percent, and thus contributed to a sharp revenue increase in 1988/89. Other factors contributing to revenue were mid-year policy changes such as the new stumpage system in 1987/88 and one-time asset sales as part of privatization initiatives.

Tobacco tax

When a taxpayer perceives that gains from tax evasion outweigh any associated risks and costs, this creates an incentive for underground activity. In Canada, high tobacco taxes in recent years have tilted the balance between the risks and benefits of evading taxes and led to widespread non-compliance.

As already noted, higher tobacco taxes created a huge black market in untaxed tobacco. The most serious problems occurred in Quebec and Ontario, where most of the contraband tobacco products were exported tax-free to the United States before being smuggled back into Canada. Following federal and provincial tax increases in 1991, the domestic sales of Canadian cigarettes declined by 14 percent in that year and 11 percent in 1992—far exceeding the historical 4 percent annual rate of decline in tobacco consumption. In British Columbia, taxable consumption declined 10 percent in 1991/92 and 6.5 percent in 1992/93 as compared with an average annual drop of 3.8 percent between 1986/87 and 1991/92.

Although the situation in British Columbia does not appear to have been as critical as it was in Quebec and Ontario, provincial finance ministry records suggest that about $75 million was lost to illegal activities in 1993/94, when tobacco tax receipts totalled $478 million. Estimated annual losses were about $450 million for Quebec and more than $1 billion for the federal government before these taxes were reduced in February 1994.

In an effort to combat tobacco smuggling, the federal government and five provinces—Quebec, Ontario, New Brunswick, Nova Scotia, and Prince Edward Island—reduced their tax rates to bring the price of a carton of cigarettes down to the $23 to $35 range. In British Columbia, the retail selling price of a carton of cigarettes was then about $46— roughly 50 percent above the selling price in 1989. Federal and provincial taxes accounted for about 78 percent of this price—$14 in federal taxes and duties and $22 in provincial levies.

Lower taxes in central and eastern Canada threatened to turn an international smuggling problem into an interprovincial one, creating new enforcement problems. However, British Columbia worked in cooperation with the other western provinces and northern territories to enforce current tax rates and ensure that smuggling did not increase. British Columbia's actions included requesting federal legislation to tighten the regulation of the interprovincial transportation of tobacco and working closely with Revenue Canada and the Royal Canadian Mounted Police on smuggling and the underground economy. The province has also considered the expansion of the tobacco marking program under which, since December 1993, manufacturers have been including a green tear strip in their cigarette packaging to certify that taxes were paid and the cigarettes were acquired through a legitimate wholesaler.[9]

British Columbia's tobacco enforcement efforts appear to be taking hold. Statistics on provincial tobacco sales from manufacturers to wholesalers indicate that the level of legitimate cigarettes entering the province has not decreased since the federal government and some eastern provinces lowered their tobacco rates. Meanwhile, the provincial enforcement drive had enjoyed such results as the seizure of a tractor-trailer carrying 50,000 cartons with a street value of $1 million.

Personal income tax

Personal income tax is the most important source of BC government revenue, generating an estimated $4.8 billion or one quarter of all revenue in 1994/95. Since 1984/85, personal income taxes have grown relatively faster than other revenue sources, reflecting increases in the tax rate, growth in personal incomes, and the effects of de-indexing deductions combined with the progressiveness of the tax system. Over the 10 years leading up to 1994/95, personal income tax revenues grew at an average annual rate of 10 percent as compared with 7 percent growth in personal incomes.

As a result of recession, however, personal income tax revenue growth slowed sharply in 1991 and 1992. In 1992/93, the government experienced an unexpected shortfall of almost 15 percent in personal income tax revenue due to unexpectedly low assessments for 1991 and downward revisions to the federal estimate of payments for 1992. A detailed analysis of tax-return data from Revenue Canada showed that these unexpectedly weak assessments were largely due to the effects of the recession, which prompted a structural shift in the workforce from full- to part-time employment and a decline in paid-employment hours worked that was a sign of more self-employment. A decline in interest rates has also contributed to a sharp drop in the investment component of assessed income.

---

9   This program was expanded in September 1994 and March 1995 and now applies to all loose tobacco, pre-proportioned tobacco sticks and tobacco products sold tax-exempt to Status Indians.

British Columbia's high marginal tax rate may be providing an incentive for tax avoidance and evasion activities which include exploiting legal tax shelters such as RRSPs, underreporting income, and allocating taxable income to a lower-tax-rate province. Certainly, some policy analysts and business groups have expressed concern that recent increases in marginal tax rates (see Chart 8) will encourage high-income earners to locate elsewhere and take their tax payments with them. No estimate is available of the revenue loss to the province from such activities, however, and they do not appear to explain the slowdown in personal incomes in recent years.

Advice for government revenue forecasters

Despite all our best efforts, revenue forecasting remains very much an art rather than a science. The writer's own experience suggests four pieces of advice for other forecasters:

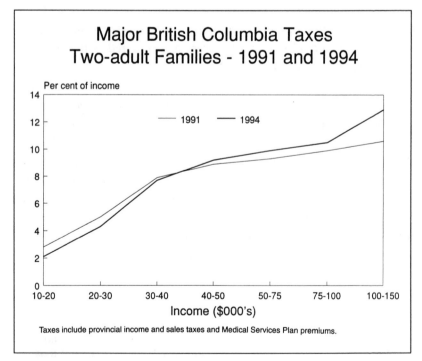

Chart 8

- *Be conservative*: the consequences of overestimating revenue are much more serious than the consequences of coming in too low. This is because the public and the media focus on the deficit/surplus as the main fiscal policy indicator. A revenue shortfall will be seen as evidence of "incompetence" on the government's part, even though the deterioration in the fiscal balance may be out of the government's control. It is also much easier for a government to decide what to do with revenue windfalls than it is to figure out what expenditures to cut after ministry budgets have been set.

- *Do sensitivity analysis*: numerous factors can affect the accuracy of a revenue forecast. Even if your forecasts for GDP and employment turn out to be correct, revenue may not come in as expected. As pointed out in an article about forecasting by US state governments, getting to within 2 per cent on a revenue forecast is a good performance in stable times.[10] Politicians need to be reminded about a forecast's level of uncertainty so that they are aware of its upper and lower risks. Based on our BC forecasting experience, we assume a 3 percent band around the revenue forecast at the beginning of the fiscal year.

- *Seek new sources of information*: look for additional sources of economic data that may help your revenue forecast. For example, in recent years we have used information on full-time/part-time work, paid employment, and total paid hours worked in the province to help determine what will happen to personal income tax revenue. We have also collected more regional data for early signals of problems in the economy or with particular revenue sources.

- *Obtain an independent check on the forecast*: to avoid the danger of overlooking factors that might seriously affect the forecast, have it reviewed by someone from outside. In 1984, the State of Washington established its Economic and Revenue Forecast Council to provide an objective revenue forecast for both the executive and the legislative branches of government.

---

10   "Cracks in the Crystal Ball," in *Governing*, December 1991, pp. 29-32.

References

British Columbia, Ministry of Finance and Corporate Relations, *1993 British Columbia Economic and Statistical Review*: Victoria, 1993 and subsequent editions.

British Columbia, Ministry of Finance and Corporate Relations, *Budget 94*: Victoria, 1994 and subsequent editions.

Drummond, Don, "Five Questions About the Underground Economy," paper presented to the Fraser Institute Conference on the Impact of the Underground Economy, April 21-22, 1994.

Ernst & Young, *Responding to Cross Border Shopping. A Study of the Competitiveness of Distribution Channels in Canada*: Report to the National Task Force on Cross Border Shopping, March 31, 1992.

Olberding, Douglas J., *Revenue Forecasting and Estimating in the Midwest*: A Report of the Midwestern Legislative Conference of the Council of State Governments, Lombard, Illinois, October 1992.

Shanahan, Eileen, "Cracks in the Crystal Ball," in *Governing*: Washington, DC, December 1991.

Section 2:
Law Enforcement Perspectives on the
Global Underground Economy

The Illicit Underground Substance Economy: An RCMP Perspective

Tim G. Killam

As the officer in charge of the proceeds of crime program at RCMP Headquarters in Ottawa, this writer finds it appropriate that these proceeds should be used to counteract the underground economy. At the same time, it is recognized that conventional drug and customs enforcement—seizing the commodity and laying substantive criminal charges—is also effective against the illicit drug, alcohol, and tobacco economy.

Background—proceeds of crime

The profits available from the traffic in illicit drugs represent a double-edged threat to the success of conventional enforcement measures: on the one hand, the potential for profit is a motivating factor for entrants into the drug trade; on the other, a criminal organization with accumulated financial resources is able to finance sophisticated import and distribution networks as well as to absorb periodic enforcement actions.

Accordingly, the RCMP has been involved since 1981 in attacking the profits derived from the drug trade.

In that year, the force created anti-drug profiteering sections to work hand in hand with existing drug units across the country. The main difficulty with this type of enforcement at the time was that the only legislative instrument available to police was the section of the *Criminal Code* entitled "Possession of property obtained by crime" (now s. 354), which contained no provision for the seizure of real property or such intangibles as bank accounts.

In January 1989, proceeds of crime legislation was finally enacted in Canada. It created the dual offences of possessing and laundering crime proceeds for numerous "designated drug offences" as well as "enterprise crime offences." The 1989 law contained the provisions previously lacking for the restraint and seizure of property. Alcohol and tobacco smuggling were added as relevant offences under proceeds of crime legislation in September 1993.

One of the more significant developments in enforcement efforts to reclaim the profits of drug crime occurred in April 1992, when the solicitor general of Canada announced a $33 million grant for a five-year pilot of "integrated anti-drug profiteering units" (IADPUs). The objective of the IADPU initiative was to fight money laundering and organized drug trafficking by targeting the proceeds of drug kingpins. The purpose of the IADPUs located in Montreal, Toronto, and Vancouver was to conduct a true test of the effectiveness of our proceeds of crime legislation under conditions of adequate funding and resources. The IADPUs were to lead a coordinated approach, working with members of municipal and provincial police agencies and full-time justice department lawyers on site in existing RCMP anti-drug profiteering facilities. The funding also allowed for on-site Revenue Canada/Customs intelligence officers and full-time forensic accountants. The goal of the initiative was to provide "critical mass" to allow IADPU investigators ready access to the considerable legal, customs, and forensic resources the funding from Canada's Drug Strategy could provide.

In March 1994, the RCMP made submissions to Treasury Board for the funding of 348 positions for customs enforcement, 248 positions for customs smuggling enforcement, particularly of alcohol and tobacco, and a further 100 positions solely for customs proceeds enforcement.

Most of the resources were concentrated in Ontario and Qu⟋
ing the origin of the initiative, which was principally mot⟋.
rampant tobacco smuggling then openly occurring throughout the cou⟋.
try, but especially in the centre.

Finally, in April 1994 the Force expanded its anti-drug profiteering sections throughout Canada by forming proceeds of crime sections responsible, not only for drug proceeds investigations, but also for customs, excise, and enterprise crime proceeds of crime investigations. This put the total complement of proceeds of crime investigators in Canada at approximately 225.

Drugs

The RCMP has enjoyed considerable success with its drug proceeds of crime investigations. Between 1989 and 1993 inclusively, its ADP investigators seized over $107 million in assets, approximately $25 million of which was forfeited back to the Government of Canada. During the same period, nearly $14 million in fines in lieu of forfeiture was received into government coffers. ADP sections also made referrals to other jurisdictions totalling over $70 million, some of which was shared back with Canada upon forfeiture in that foreign jurisdiction.

The value of the drug trade in Canada has been estimated at $10 billion annually with a corresponding figure of approximately $300 billion for the United States. The estimates for Canada could very well be understated. These figures are extrapolated from bits of evidence like the following. On February 22, 1994, 5.4 metric tonnes of cocaine were seized off the coast of Nova Scotia, thus eliminating approximately 11 million gram doses. This seizure alone significantly affected health care costs, family violence, property crimes, and quality of life. Assuming that the cocaine was all destined for Canada, primarily the Quebec/Ontario market, we could reasonably expect that it would be diluted or "cut" at least once, thus making the total amount available for sale 10.8 metric tonnes. If sold for $25,000/kg, an extremely conservative estimate of the value of this shipment of cocaine would be $270 million (10,800 kg x $25K). The value of this same shipment if all sold in one-gram doses at $150, a low street price, would be $1 billion, $650 million.

To carry the analogy farther, if we estimate that enforcement officials intercept less than 10 percent of all drugs, and even if this seizure of 11,000 kgs of cocaine was the only drug seizure for 1994, taking the worth of the cocaine at street value, namely $1 billion, $650 million, multiplied by 10 this would equal $16 billion, $500 million. Looking at this 1994 seizure and comparing the figures for all other drugs seized in Canada between 1988 and 1993 inclusively, the inescapable conclusion is surely that the annual underground drug economy in Canada is massive and probably underestimated at $10 billion.

Customs—alcohol and tobacco

As already stated, until September 1993 it was not an offence to possess or launder profits from smuggling tobacco and alcohol. Now the resources are in place under the umbrella of the RCMP proceeds of crime units to attack the profits from alcohol and tobacco smuggling. Police had also gained the complementary authority to lay charges and seize, restrain, and forfeit assets under the *Criminal Code* proceeds of crime provisions with regard to alcohol and tobacco smuggling. The force was now strategically positioned to attack this area of the underground economy.

To illustrate, we estimated that each member of the former anti-drug profiteering sections (presently proceeds of crime sections) who worked daily with the proceeds of crime legislation generated approximately $400,000 in revenue per year. With the additional 100 members enforcing proceeds of crime legislation under the Customs and Excise alcohol and tobacco program, revenues in the vicinity of $40 million per year could reasonably be anticipated.

The potential could be even greater when one considers reports like the one in 1994 about a single financial institution in the US which over a 15-month period had handled US $250 million in alleged tobacco smuggling profits destined for Canada. Forfeitures of assets in this type of range would make a noticeable dent in the underground economy as well as produce significant savings for the Government of Canada.

Some idea of the scope of the smuggling problem in the early 1990s is in order, even though that crisis, sustained by high Canadian taxes, later subsided somewhat. During 1992 alone, 3,179 persons were charged with customs and excise offences: this figure increased to 3,389 in 1993.

In 1992, there were 505 liquor seizures with a retail value of $4.2 million, while in 1993 the figure rose to 631 liquor seizures having a retail value of $11.3 million. When it came to tobacco, the increases were more drastic: 3,461 tobacco seizures in 1992 with a retail value of $31.4 million, and 5,291 tobacco seizures in 1993 worth $53.5 million on the retail market.

In 1994, drastic cuts in federal and provincial tobacco taxes had the desired effect of curbing the smuggling frenzy. This indicates, if proof were needed, that smuggling organizations are adaptable and will switch to the commodity with the highest profit margin. Over the long haul, though, experience suggests that the most effective way to combat this kind of crime is to hit the offenders in their pocketbooks. The formation of customs and excise proceeds of crime investigative units has already gone a long way towards achieving these objectives.

The Underground Economy in the US: Some Criminal Justice and Legal Perspectives

Bruce Zagaris

Introduction

Globalization is exercising a dramatic impact on the US underground economy. Increasingly, this new perspective is enabling people who are active in this economy to exploit lacunae and differences in law among countries and successfully conduct their crimes undetected. By looking at selected areas of the underground economy and such activities as tax crime, contraband, trade crime, bribery, the smuggling of illegal aliens, and money laundering, we can distinguish some criminal justice and legal perspectives on trends in the US underground economy in an international context.

The underground economy, defined as all off-the-books and unregulated activity, is growing in the US, especially in cities with large immigrant populations like Los Angeles, Miami, and New York.[1] The ability to instantaneously transport people, capital, and ideas makes residents of the remotest parts of the world aware of opportunities in the rest of the world. Access to technology anywhere enables people to create and implement quiet and unobserved ways of amassing wealth, which is the prime function of the underground economy.

The "gray area phenomenon," which denotes the inability of sovereigns to control the conduct of non-state actors and non-governmental processes and organizations in certain areas within their borders, has shifted power from legitimate governments to new, half-political, half-criminal powers. The gray area phenomenon has added an increasingly important political dimension to the underground economy and the need to design mechanisms to control these groups.

The explosion of free trade and economic integration throughout the world and especially in this hemisphere facilitates the international activities of the underground economy and requires more strategic global law enforcement policies to combat them. Unfortunately, our political leaders and academicians have not yet summoned the vision to even conceptualize a comprehensive strategy, let alone start recommending, negotiating, and implementing one. Criminal justice, international law, and international organization theory must be more creatively utilized if the US, other governments, and the world community generally are to contain and control the rising power of traditional and new forms of organized crime and other emanations of the underground economy.

We will begin here by tracing some of the underground economic sectors that are impacted by globalization and then canvass some of the international trends that will enable the world community to design and implement mechanisms to combat this economy. We will also be laying stress on the growing costs of the politicians' failure to act.

---

1 For background on the growth of the role of immigrants in the US underground economy, see Deborah Sontag, "Emigres in New York: Work Off the Books," in the *New York Times*, June 13, 1993, p. 1.

Sectors of the underground economy

Underground immigrants

Refugees symptomize the sickness of our times. As 1993 began, the numbers of people forced to leave their countries for fear of persecution and violence had risen to a total of 18.2 million, based on an average of nearly 10,000 new refugees a day.[2] "Non-refoulement" is the guarantee under international law that people shall not be forced to return to countries where their lives or freedom would be endangered because of "race, religion, nationality, membership of a particular social group or political opinion."

Non-refoulement can be implemented only through cooperation with governments, although extending protection under the terms of international agreements remains a non-political, humanitarian act. Since the climate of receptivity for refugees has cooled in many asylum countries, however, and since refugees are part of a complex stream of migration and often mingled with people who only need humanitarian aid, the US and other nations have refused to extend the principle of non-refoulement or begun limiting the principle's beneficiaries by characterizing them as economic refugees or illegal immigrants.[3]

The profits from smuggling aliens, since the going price is said to be between US $25,000 and $40,000, and the opportunity to use the smuggled aliens, whose families are normally able to pay only a small part of the smuggling cost, provide a powerful economic incentive to conduct this activity. Smuggled immigrants are forced to work seven days for meagre pay, endure dangerous conditions doing legitimate work, if they are fortunate, in such places as restaurants and garment factories. In many cases, smuggled immigrants are forced to engage in such criminal activities as drug and arms trafficking, smurfing—a form of money laundering—and prostitution.

In New York, law enforcement officials have determined that criminality among immigrants falls into patterns. Immigrant women from

---

2   United Nations High Commission for Refugees, *The State of the World's Refugees. The Challenge of Protection*, 1 (1993).

3   Ibid. at 5-10.

⌐atin America and Korea often work as prostitutes. Dominicans ply cocaine on the streets. Chinese and, to a lesser extent, Sicilians control the heroin trade. Nigerians engage in smuggling and fraud. The Russian mob operates bureaucracy schemes from Medicare fraud to evading taxes on oil distribution. Chinese operate gambling houses and smuggle other Chinese to the US.[4]

Actually, the immigrant underground in New York City is mostly above ground. Its sidewalks bustle with at least 10,000 illegal vendors hawking handbags, perfume, and ties from briefcases and folding tables, the contemporary pushcarts: undercutting legitimate merchants, this group has sparked the most furious political controversy. On corners in Brooklyn and Queens, immigrant labourers gather daily to wait for construction and gardening work. In storefronts and basements, Chinese and Hispanic immigrants work at sewing machines, hot presses, and workbenches while sweatshops and illegal industrial homework, virtually nonexistent twenty years ago, continue to grow.

The New York mentality seems to support or at least tolerate the underground economy, preferring the pioneer discount environment. Increasingly, union-dominated industries like construction and apparel manufacturing are using immigrant subcontractors and workers to reduce labour costs. Illegal industrial homework such as sewing, knitting, and assembling goods for manufacturers has become a $1 billion industry. In the last few years apparel sweatshops, which numbered about 200 in the early 1970s, have grown to some 3,500 to 5,000. By the Census Bureau's conservative estimate, 400,000 illegal immigrants live in New York City—5 percent of the city's population—and 25,000 more arrive every year.

An important element of the underground economy is the law that criminalizes certain behaviour and forces immigrants underground. For instance, the *Immigration Reform and Control Act* of 1986, which was designed to curb the flow of illegals, has also had the effect of making these immigrants, often in collusion with other persons, engage in fraud to furnish the documents employers are supposed to demand before hiring.

Perhaps most significantly, while international law obligates the US to permit political asylees and refugees to reside there during periods

---

4   Ian Fisher, "A Window on Immigrant Crime in Jackson Heights: Drugs, Dirty Money and Prostitution," in the *New York Times*, June 17, 1993, p. B1.

of turmoil, the US government's application of its own law to such various groups as persons fleeing the Central American conflicts in El Salvador, Guatemala, and Honduras, and the violence in Haiti, is in contrast with its application of the same law to persons fleeing Cuba and Nicaragua during the war with the contras. These last groups were treated quite favourably and obtained asylum status with greater ease, thereby giving credence to charges that the US violates the international legal principle of non-discrimination when applying its laws and regulations to persons moving across its borders.[5]

Similarly, the arrest of undocumented juveniles on the US-Mexican border and their detention for months and even years makes criminals of thousands of refugees while they are deprived of the minimum freedoms of education, counsel, medical attention, and so forth. Other refugees have to remain underground to avoid detection and detention.[6]

As long as the comparative quality of life is perceived as being substantially better in the US than in other source countries, the incentives for illegal migration will be present. The problems of illegal migration and the immigrant underground are unique in the US, given its enormous border area, high quality of life, and tradition of civil liberties.

Controls on illegal migration and the immigrant underground have in part emulated western Europe: imposing more enforcement requirements on transportation companies,[7] attempting to expedite

---

5   *The Movement of Persons Across Borders*, Louis B. Sohn and Thomas Buergnethal, eds, 17 (1992).

6   For background, see, e.g., "Brutality Unchecked: Human Rights Abuses Along the Border with Mexico" (Americas Watch, May 1992); "Sealing Our Borders: The Human Tool" (American Friends Service Committee, February 1992); "US Congress Moves Towards the Establishment of Immigration Enforcement Review Commission Act for Monitoring Alleged Human Rights Abuses of the Border Patrol," in 10 *Int'l Enforcement L. Rep.* 391 (October 1993).

7   See, e.g., "European Ministers Agree on Enforcement and Criminal Action on Illegal Migration," in 9 *Int'l Enforcement L. Rep.* 71 (February 1993: article on an agreement among 35 European countries to make transportation carriers liable to fines under new rules on the movement of illegal aliens); "Canada Proposes Law to Increase Penalization of Maritime Industry in Effort to Prevent Stowaways," in 9 *Int'l Enforcement L. Rep.* 70 (February 1993).

and deny frivolous asylum claims,[8] and limiting employment and welfare benefits for illegal immigrants.

An important arm of European policy for controlling illegal immigration has been agreements with source and transit countries whereby the latter will receive the migrants in return for technical and financial assistance and economic programs.[9] France and many other European countries require people to carry identity cards: national police can ask anyone for proof of identity and immediately imprison persons who are unable to produce it. The enforcement of immigration controls through identity checks often results in the questioning of persons who appear foreign by their dress or actions. Illegal aliens and organized crime are countering these developments by the more sophisticated manufacture and use of fraudulent travel documents.[10]

While the North American Free Trade Agreement does not specifically have as its intent to curb the flow of illegal migrants, many US policy makers have cited NAFTA as helping to provide more economic opportunities in Mexico and thereby dampening the migrants' motivation.[11] These policy makers might consider more specific arrangements with other countries in the region that have traditionally furnished the bulk of the migrant flow.[12] Certainly, the end or at least substantial

---

8   See, e.g., "German Court Denies Ghanian Citizen Asylum Indicating Strict Enforcement of New Asylum Law," in 9 *Int'l Enforcement L. Rep.* 281 (July 1993).

9   See, e.g., "Germany and Poland Conclude Migration Enforcement Cooperation Agreement," in 9 *Int'l Enforcement L. Rep.* 204 (May 1993); Bertold Baer, "German-Bulgarian Cooperation against Illegal Migration Emulates Other German Agreements," in 8 *Int'l Enforcement L. Rep.* 414 (October 1992).

10   "Fraud in Travel Documents is Facilitated by Technological and Political Developments," in 8 *Int'l Enforcement L. Rep.* 174 (May 1992: discusses the use of electronic imaging and colour copies in the production of false passports and visas).

11   See Philip L. Martin, *Trade and Migration: NAFTA and Agriculture* (1993).

12   See the recommendations in *Unauthorized Migration: An Economic Development Response*: Report of the Commission for the Study of International Migration and Cooperative Economic Development, July 1990.

lessening of violence and civil war in Central America, comb
emerging democracy and free trade in that region, has assisteu
reducing migration throughout the Americas.

The European Union countries are frustrating the problem of illegal migration regionally with a series of mechanisms that include the new European Police (EUROPOL), an intelligence system to watch illegal migrants, and the harmonization of policies on visas and other matters of immigration law. The transnational nature of illegal migration requires a more international and regional approach by the US as well.

Contraband

The most controversial contraband traffic in the US today is in illicit drugs and psychotropic substances. Most experts are agreed that the demand and the enormous profits generated by interdiction policies and overcriminalization continue to motivate the large industry that includes peasants who grow coca and poppy plants and such intermediaries as refiners, transporters, wholesale and street peddlers, money launderers, security guards, and so forth.

At one level, the world community has a comprehensive program to control illicit drug trafficking that targets four major areas: preventing and reducing the demand, controlling the supply, suppressing the traffic, and treating and rehabilitating the users. Much criticism has been directed at the failure of the US to devote enough resources to address the first and last of these targets: demand and user treatment. We in the US are actually repeating mistakes made back when the offending substance was alcohol. Some of the very changes in attitude from tolerance to intolerance that occurred in the decades leading up to national Prohibition in 1920 and the backlash against Prohibition that began after 1933 and ended with repeal are being echoed now.[13] Like Prohibition, the Draconian US anti-drug laws incarcerate and criminalize large numbers of people and fuel the rise of diverse organized crime groups, many of which have grown and diversified over the years.

---

13   For an overview of US drug control policy, see David F. Musto, "Patterns in US Drug Abuse and Response," in *Drug Policy in the Americas*, Peter H. Smith, ed., 1992, pp. 29-44.

During the Reagan Administration's "War on Drugs," the militarization of the conflict involved enlisting the armed forces in interdiction.[14]

The Clinton administration has shifted the emphasis slightly from interdiction to demand reduction and treatment, although it has also shifted a lot of resources into law enforcement and tougher sentencing. While education has already influenced well-educated middle-and upper-class Americans to decrease drug use, it has not been as successful with the underclass and less educated. For the latter Americans, drug use and trafficking are ways of life and an economic alternative to the dearth of opportunities in their lives. These groups are prone simultaneously to a host of societal problems that include family breakups; violence at home, school, and on television; and poor role models, minimal educational opportunities, dilapidated housing, and insufficient medical care. Meanwhile, the drug component of the US underground economy is fortified by the intersection of drug and arms trafficking, growing gun violence, and the wholesale incarceration of Afro-Americans. Rather than augmenting resources to solve their problems (e.g., drug prevention), the national, state, and local governments have generally cut such resources and continue to beef up prosecutions and sentences meted out to traffickers and even users.

As a result, foreign leaders such as the highly respected Colombian attorney general Gustavo de Greiff have explicitly advised the industrialized countries and particularly the US to provide more support to treatment, especially for the heavy users, mainly in the underclass, who consume the bulk of narcotics in the US. There are also calls for a more active government role in education, more controls on the trading of chemicals produced in industrialized countries that are needed for processing narcotics; more efficient means of obtaining judicial evidence against persons involved in the business, and more open sharing of evidence with courts in producing and consuming countries.[15]

---

14 Bruce M. Bagley, " Myths of Militarization: Enlisting Armed forces in the War on Drugs," in *Drug Policy in the Americas*, op. cit., pp. 129-50. For background on the initial rationale for the militarization of the war on drugs, see Donald J. Mabry, "Narcotics and National Security," in *The Latin American Narcotics Trade and US National Security*, Donald J. Mabry, ed., 1989, pp. 3-10.

Despite the bankruptcy of its drug control policies, the US continues to repeat its mistakes. The various legalization options deserve at least a thorough debate in a country that prides itself on its openness. One of the difficulties with US drug policy, especially as regards decriminalization, is that the current debate is muddled on both the popular and the scholarly planes. Such basic legalization details as which drugs should be covered and how regulation would replace prohibition are rarely set forth, which leaves both sides arguing in the dark. The debate often blurs even the basic distinction between the effects of drugs and the effects of drug control policies.[16]

US influence in regional and even international drug policy due to its big-power status and anti-drug spending ensures that its bankrupt policy will continue worldwide. Increasingly, however, the European Union is seriously debating legalization while the Inter-American Drug Abuse Control Commission, pressed by governments such as Mexico's and Canada's, is supporting increased attention to the issues of demand, treatment, and alternative economic development in the supply countries.

Tax crimes

As the US federal and state governments recently raised their rates of tax and interest and penalties for non-payment of tax on top of the base broadening of prior years, there is evidence of growing non-compliance and associated criminal activity. Some types of non-compliance and evasion differ between the federal and state levels.

In California, tax evasion and its related underground activity are reportedly growing fast. Some of the reasons are acceptance of fraud and tax evasion as ways of doing business; lack of support for an efficient and aggressive educational system by Californian taxing authorities; the absence of police powers under current prosecution programs; inade-

---

15   Gustavo de Greiff, "The Coke King Compromise," in the *Washington Post*, March 13, 1994, p. C1.

16   Mark A.R. Kleiman and Aaron Saiger, "Taxes, Regulations, and Prohibitions: Reformulating the Legalization Debate," in *Drug Policy in the Americas*, op. cit., p. 223.

quate criminal and civil penalties to curb tax fraud; and a lack of comprehensive tax legislation to restrict criminal activities.[17]

One example of a revision in law that could halt the theft of hundreds of millions of dollars a year, at 17 cents a gallon, is California's fuel vendor tax. The current law imposes the fuel vendor tax at the distributor level: some distributors collect the tax and never remit it to the state. Legislative proposals would impose the tax at the manufacturing level to drastically reduce the loss of tax revenue.

Fuel tax evasion is estimated to cost the State of California $50 million a year in lost revenue. Diesel fuel is an attractive target for evasion because 40 percent of its retail price consists in state and federal taxes. Potential profits from not paying tax on a truckload of black-market diesel can run as high as $3,450 as compared with a normal return for honest businesses of $75 to $375 on a truckload of taxed fuel. Where the tax is actually collected, some fly-by-night wholesalers simply disappear with their saddlebags full while others keep and use the money for six to nine months before finally remitting it to the state.[18] Diesel tax collection, meanwhile, is further complicated by the existence of approximately 91,000 businesses or individuals registered as diesel taxpayers, including 655 wholesalers, 3,062 retail service stations, and 17,000 interstate truckers. However, the state has only 24 terminals.[19]

Federal and state governments lose up to $1 billion annually from these evasions, though the *Omnibus Budget Reconciliation Act* of 1993 tightened enforcement by mandating collection at refinery terminals starting January 1, 1994. Some California legislators have proposed that the State of California harmonize its law with the federal law.

Another California compliance problem has involved unitary tax, especially as it concerns foreign-based multinationals. Unitary tax is a method of assessing tax on the international income of multinational corporations doing business in a state. The most prominent piece of

---

17 For background, see Bill Stall and Ralph Frammolino, "California Taxes," in the *Los Angeles Times*, October 26, 1993, p. 6B.

18 "State Developments, California," in *Daily Report for Executives*, October 22, 1993, 203 d77.

19 Ibid.

litigation here has been the *Barclays Bank* case which challenges the unitary tax laws of California and is now pending in the US Supreme Court.

Meanwhile, tax evasion also continues at the US federal level. To understand the new pressures favouring evasion at the national level, we have to recall that the top rates of direct taxes on personal and corporate incomes were lowered decisively under the Reagan reforms but that many tax concessions were simultaneously cut back or eliminated. In fact, tax rates could be reduced without massive loss of revenue only by widening the tax base and closing tax loopholes. The goal was to produce a simpler tax system and one that would not allow inflation to automatically push taxpayers into higher tax brackets even though their real incomes were not rising.[20]

The initial tax reform proposals argued that the magic of lowering marginal tax rates would create such a surge of private enterprise that the resultant rise in economic activity and incomes would trickle down and produce as much revenue, if not more. An international ramification of the Reagan administration's tax reforms was the lowering of tax rates in a number of other countries as part of a necessary process of tax harmonization. Many policy makers recognized that the growing integration of the world economy, facilitated by ongoing revolutions in telecommunications and information technology, did not allow countries the luxury of maintaining radically different direct tax levels. Taxpayers, especially corporations operating transnationally, could arbitrage across separate tax jurisdictions to secure the best tax treatment and overall economic result.

Indeed, the movement even spread to developing countries, in part through the advocacy of "supply-side" economics by international financial instructions, which often made lowering direct tax rates an ingredient of their recipes for structural adjustment. Their influence assisted in lowering rates and simplifying tax arrangements generally in countries as diverse as Mexico, Ghana, India, and Morocco.

---

20 Aziz Ali Mohammed, "This Year's Tax Fashion: More Pain for Everyone; For East and West, The Bill is Due, and Getting Larger," in *World Paper*, September 1993 (Lexis-Nexis).

Meanwhile, the US tax reform wave crested and has undergone change during the Clinton administration, which has raised tax rates for individuals and corporations while continuing to reduce or eliminate tax deductions. Several factors have helped to stymie the drive for lower taxes. The first is the failure of the reforms to prevent a large revenue loss and consequent massive bulges in budget deficits and the associated burden of public-debt servicing. A second factor was the discovery that the lower levels of government—states, counties, and municipalities—were having to either impose higher taxes within their jurisdictions or else curtail essential public services in the face of reduced financial assistance from the federal level. In particular, the "balanced budget" constraint in the US applies extensively at sub-national levels to restrict available services and even the means of raising money. With direct tax rates frozen or rising sluggishly, an unfortunate recourse was had to higher indirect taxes on sales, which were generally perceived as regressive and tending to abet inequalities in society.

Politically, the US has been targeting more tax revenue from multinational enterprises, which have been reputed not to pay their fair share of profits, either shifting their money to related enterprises in low-tax countries or arbitrarily saddling their US enterprises with the costs of their international operations, thereby reducing net US income and taxes owing in the US.

The result has been a series of laws and regulations in the transfer pricing area. These laws and regulations have dramatically increased the amount of record keeping and reporting the multinationals have to do, with requirements for maintaining very detailed records on how transfer pricing is figured, simultaneous filing of income tax returns, and the appointment of agents in the US where none already exist and who are able to receive summonses. All these new requirements are accompanied by severe economic penalties and loss of procedural rights for taxpayers failing to comply. Simultaneously, the procedural rights of the Internal Revenue Service have been substantially improved so that tax authorities are now able to demand information at a much earlier stage, extend the statute of limitations, prevent the introduction of foreign documents not made available to them immediately during an examination, and completely disregard records where the taxpayer has not furnished such information at the proper time.

In addition, the US tax authorities have concluded tax information exchange and related mutual assistance agreements with their foreign counterparts so that tax agents can obtain and verify information and documents concerning the multinationals quickly and directly.

Another taxpayer stratum affected by the tax compliance drive is the high net-worth US individual. Because US tax residents, i.e. US citizens or persons who are either permanent residents or present in the US for approximately 183 days during the year, must pay tax on their worldwide income, regardless of its source, more individuals are expatriating—formally surrendering their citizenship or permanent residency to avoid paying tax on their worldwide income.[21] In 1993, 306 persons expatriated, up from 157 in 1992.[22] These expatriates are motivated by more than the desire to minimize taxes. Many Americans are already living overseas and therefore have less contact and derive little or no benefit from Medicare, welfare, and the various services and benefits US tax residents actually living in the US receive. Sometimes, in fact, while people are travelling or living overseas, US citizenship can have adverse consequences. The US does have an anti-expatriation tax that enables the IRS to keep imposing income tax for ten years on persons leaving to avoid tax, but prosecutions have been few since proving tax-motivated intent is difficult.

Tax evasion is also connected with the larger problem of unrecorded transactions in the underground economy. Much of this economy involves activities that are illegal, such as trading in narcotics and arms and smuggling prohibited goods across national frontiers. The increasing sophistication and worldwide reach of these underground enterprises produce vast losses of tax revenue while forcing the state to spend heavily on prevention.[23]

---

21   For background on the tax expatriate trend in the US and elsewhere, see Marshall J. Langer, *The Tax Exile Report* (2nd ed., 1993).

22   "Americans Are Taking Capital Abroad to Avoid Taxes," in *Tax Notes*, March 7, 1994, p. 1307, citing an article by Bridgid McMenamin in *Forbes*, February 28, 1994, p. 55.

23   Stall and Frammolino, op. cit.

Another type of US underground activity spawned by tax evasion has been work by undocumented domestic workers, babysitters, gardeners, labourers, and so on. The requirement that employers pay taxes and file various returns on any worker receiving more than $50 in a quarter has generated widespread non-compliance. Under the US tax code, every employer required to withhold tax on wages is liable for payment of such tax whether it is collected or not. Any responsible person, typically a corporate officer or employee who wilfully fails to withhold, account for, or pay tax withholdings to the government is liable to a penalty equal to 100 percent of such tax.[24] Civil and criminal penalties can be imposed if an employer wilfully fails to furnish or furnishes a false or fraudulent withholding statement to an employee.[25]

Failure to report and pay such taxes came to the public's attention at the start of the Clinton administration when it was found that the first two nominees for Attorney General, Zoe Baird and Kimba Wood, had failed on both counts. Ms. Baird had to withdraw and Woods's candidacy was withdrawn before it was submitted.[26] More recently, William Kennedy, a White House counsel and former law partner of Hillary Clinton, was also disciplined for failing to pay and report such taxes. These cases have become known collectively as "Nanny-gate." The sheer numbers of similar cases have resulted in proposed legislation (S 1231) to raise the threshold at which social security taxes must be paid for domestic workers to $620 annually, along with the national average wage.

The IRS has been working on various ways of targeting potential groups for audit through computerized mechanisms to detect various patterns and types of taxpayers who are not reporting transactions or otherwise evading taxes. The agency is also tackling non-compliance by expanding its Market Segment Specialization Program (MSSP) into dozens of new areas ranging from entertainment, mining, and construc-

---

24   *Internal Revenue Code*, 6672.

25   *Internal Revenue Code*, 6674 and 7204.

26   For background, see Martha F. Davis, "Podium: No Papers, No Rights, No Safety," in the *National L.J.*, February 22, 1993, p. 16.

tion to seafood purchasers, art dealers, bail bondsmen, and citrus growers. Concurrently, the IRS is developing comprehensive guides to avoid the use of manpower to conduct audits in nearly 90 industries. The Market Segment Program pinpoints both large industry segments and narrower subgroups.[27]

Criminal prosecution of foreign nationals

A major problem contributing to the growth of the US underground economy has been rapid expansion in the extraterritorial application of criminal sanctions under US export legislation and the prosecution of foreign nationals using questionable law enforcement practices.[28] The criminalization of the purchase of non-arms goods and services because they will eventually reach embargoed countries such as Cuba, Iran, Iraq, and Libya has resulted in Byzantine laws and regulations that the two agencies responsible for them disagree about and enforce differently.

Most enforcement actions are instigated and driven by undercover informants who have usually been convicted of crimes and whose freedom depends on their "cooperation," meaning that unless they set up and help prosecute other individuals they will remain under US correctional supervision. Some informants are also given economic incentives that require them to help with arrests and successful prosecutions before they can receive all of their compensation. Accordingly, their interest lies in securing convictions rather than fairness and the integrity of the justice system.

The perception of fairness in the investigation of these cases has been compromised by the use of undercover sting operations in which the US Customs Service, working with informants, banks, and other

---

27 Rita L. Zeidner, "IRS Targets 90 Markets in Market Segment Specialization Program," in 62 *Tax Notes*, February 28, 1994, p. 1105.

28 For additional discussion of this issue, see Bruce Zagaris, "Can the World Ride the Bucking Bronco or Can an American Sheriff Only Find Happiness in a Warm Gun?": unpublished paper delivered to the DC Bar Association program on "The Expanding Extraterritorial Application of US Export Law: Regulation of Foreign Transactions and Criminal Prosecution of Foreign Nationals," April 4, 1994.

agencies, arranges transactions and makes payments for purposes of entrapment. In at least eight cases during the early '90s, sting operations resulted in the arrest and prosecution of foreign individuals who had no prior criminal records. These cases follow several standard scenarios. Most of the subjects were lured into leaving their own countries under false pretences of engaging in business transactions only to be seized. In one case, a Cypriot national was arrested in a private plane after he had visited the Bahamas so that the US government could circumvent its extradition treaties with the Bahamas and Cyprus, bringing diplomatic protests from both governments.[29]

Another pattern has been for the foreign individuals, although successful businessmen with no criminal records whatsoever, to be denied bail and spend anywhere from three to 18 months in jail. When incarceration is combined with threats to bring additional criminal charges, foreign defendants usually plead guilty. Most cases that have gone to trial ended in speedy acquittal, sometimes even before the defence rose to present its case.

The US government's *modus operandi* in these cases has spawned a new sector of the underground economy. Overcriminalization, lack of jurisdictional restraint, and heavy-handed tactics have led to refusal by the Canadian government to even hold a hearing on one US extradition request, at least four civil lawsuits in the US, Canada, and Egypt, and the Inter-American Commission on Human Rights. The use of under-cover sting operations against former high-level Polish officials and intensive media coverage of their trials resulted in the staging of anti-American demonstrations in Warsaw just before the Polish elections in September 1993 that helped to shift the parliamentary balance towards the socialists.[30]

---

29 For a discussion of the Cypriot case, see "US Customs Agents' 'Sting' of Cypriot in the Bahamas and Costa Rican Court's Invalidation of US Extradition Treaty Put Pressure on US Extradition Policy," in 9 *Int'l Enforcement L. Rep.* 58 (February 1993).

30 John J. Fialka, "Customs Service's 'Stings' to Curtail Arms Sales Draw Blood (Its Own) as Cases Collapse in Court," in the *Wall Street Journal*, March 18, 1994, p. A12.

This unilateral, overzealous use of economic sanctions against a multitude of countries has made criminals out of many unknowing persons and driven underground many more. Only by exercising restraint in applying its extraterritorial jurisdiction, limiting the scope of investigations, selecting cases carefully, respecting the sovereignty of other countries, and paying attention to international human rights law, including the rule of law in the apprehension and pre-trial treatment of foreigners and fairness throughout the entire criminal justice process as it is applied to foreigners, will the US be able to limit the growing detrimental effects of the enforcement of its international export control policy from both a diplomatic and a criminal justice perspective. Because these cases involve large foreign and international legal components, the failure to cooperate closely with foreign governments will continue to have adverse short- and long-term consequences.

Money laundering

One very important component of the underground economy is money laundering, an essential support service that enables criminals to enjoy the fruits of their crimes. The very nature of money laundering precludes US or international law enforcement agencies from knowing the actual amounts being put through the wash, but estimates in 1993 ran as high as $100 billion in the US and $300 billion worldwide.

Money laundering is a diverse and complex process. It involves three independent steps that may coincide: placement, as bulk cash proceeds are physically placed; layering, as the proceeds of criminal activity are separated from their origins by layers of complex financial transactions; and integration, when an apparently legitimate explanation and cover are provided for illicit proceeds which by this stage have been transformed into legitimate assets.[31]

Drug smuggling generates an enormous amount of income that attracts organized criminals and affords them great power. The civilian and military employees of the former Panamanian government of General Noriega are alleged to have amassed more than $300 million between

---

31 For background on money laundering and its phases, see Office of the Comptroller of the Currency, *Money Laundering: A Banker's Guide to Avoiding Problems*, 1-2 (June 1993).

1985 and 1990 through their association with Chinese criminal smuggling organizations.[32] The methods of drug smuggling and its huge profits readily mesh in with such other organized criminal activities as alien smuggling. For instance, a recent study of Asian organized crime in the US reported that two thirds of the Chinese gangs were involved in both heroin and human contraband.[33]

The unprecedented amounts of cash and cash equivalents derived from narcotics will fuel generalized corruption as exemplified by the Bank of Credit and Commerce International (BCCI) and the rise of the new cocaine cartels. Recent technological advances and the rise of free trade are enabling organized crime groups to launch new criminal activities such as credit card fraud and move illegal goods, capital, and persons more easily within free trade areas where barriers have been removed without a complementary strengthening of law enforcement mechanisms.

The "global village" phenomenon that facilitates the movement of persons, funds, and commodities will continue to provide opportunities for new financial manipulations including secret and illegal control of banks, non-bank financial institutions, and other business organizations that have the ability to move money. We will also be seeing the use of new money laundering strategies such as illegal letters of credit, prime bank instrument fraud, phoney loans, and fraudulent stock transactions, all making international systems increasingly vulnerable to manipulation. All these developments put pressure on governments, international governmental organizations, and non-governmental organizations to strengthen anti-laundering and other measures for dismantling criminal organizations while not moving so fast that legitimate commerce, travel, and money movement are unreasonably constrained.

Organized crime groups and the gray area phenomenon undermine the economic base of the world and many of the world community's crucial political alliances. For instance, US economic interests at home

---

32 *Time*, May 14, 1990, p. 70.

33 "A Guerilla War on Alien Smuggling: Agenda for Action by the First Chinese Alien Smuggling Conference," cable report from the US Consulate General, Hong Kong [Hong Kong 011714], November 3, 1992.

and abroad suffer as the "bad guys" weaken international banking, undercut the export base of the US and other countries, and exacerbate the balance of payments problem as they shift US capital to illicit organizations.

The kind of money these criminals control buys them access to the highest echelons of executive power. They can also influence the judiciary in the prosecution and adjudication of criminal cases. The sub-regime of regulating international money movement is gathering a momentum of its own and expanding beyond mere narcotics trafficking.[34]

Asset forfeiture laws are being ratified in several countries as a means of developing a set of rules by which governments and international organizations can cooperate in countering this massive criminal activity. Here, we will review some initiatives to regulate international money movement and criminalize a vital component of the underground economy.

Indeed, the US was among the first states to enact anti-laundering legislation.[35] However, the most important anti-laundering law work has been done through intergovernmental organizations (IGOs). The United Nations, especially the United Nations Drug Program, Interpol, the Financial Action Task Force (FATF) of the G-7 Economic Summit, and the G-10 Committee of Central Bankers have all directed the application of anti-laundering laws. At the regional level, the European Union, the Council of Europe and its Laundering Convention, the Organization of American States, and the regional FATF branches have done important work. These IGOs have helped negotiate conventions, secure passage of model laws, regulations, and principles; they have assisted in training, auditing compliance with international conventions, and preparing and disseminating bulletins to notify law enforcement officials about new techniques and problems.

---

34 For more discussion of international anti-laundering regulation from a US perspective, see Bruce Zagaris, "Dollar Diplomacy: International Enforcement of Money Movement and Related Matters —A United States Perspective," in 22 *Geo. Wash. J. of Int'l L. & Economics*, pp. 465-552 (1989)

35 For background on US anti-laundering laws, see Bruce Zagaris, "Dollar Diplomacy," op. cit., p. 465.

Several international conventions oblige states to criminalize money laundering. What differs among countries is the norm of conduct required to criminalize participation in laundering. Some countries require the transgressor to understand or at least have knowledge of the crime, but some treaties and laws criminalize conduct that is merely negligent or careless. In all cases, there must be agreement to lift or override the right to financial secrecy. International conventions require governments to override secrecy rights whenever a government makes a request for evidence in connection with a criminal proceeding.

Anti-laundering laws accomplish their goals in part by creating an audit trail throughout the world as banks, financial institutions, and non-financial institutions are required to "know their customer," which means that they must obtain written identification from the customer and verify and record such information. A related aspect of the "know your customer" principle is the currency transaction report which obliges covered persons to transmit customer information to the competent authorities. Another principle is the duty of covered persons to identify and report "suspicious transactions." These obligations mark an attempt to privatize anti-laundering enforcement. Covered persons commit a crime themselves by failing to perform them. Even so, the private sector has complained of the burden of distinguishing legitimate from suspicious international dealings.

Another anti-laundering principle requires governments to trace, freeze, seize, confiscate, and ultimately forfeit illicit assets from crime.[36] The novelty of this principle and the legal and cultural differences among legal systems have impeded its uniform application. Some asset forfeiture laws include only criminal activity, while others will consider civil and administrative actions. Many countries cooperate with asset forfeiture provisions only when laws are derived from the penal code and some confine application to the proceeds and instrumentalities of crime.[37]

---

36   For additional background, see Bruce Zagaris, "Constructing a Financial Enforcement Regime to Reallocate Assets from the 'Bad Guys' to the 'Good Guys,'" in *Gray Area Phenomena Confronting the New World Disorder*, Max G. Manwaring, ed., pp. 93-108 (1993).

37   For more background on the international aspects of asset forfeiture, see Bruce Zagaris and Elizabeth Kingma, "Asset Forfeiture: International and

Governments and international organizations are still struggling to achieve a proper balance between individual and property rights and the need for intrusive procedures to privatize law enforcement. The need to avoid undue interference with normal commerce and overburdening the private sector with costly administrative work must also be balanced against the privatization of enforcement.

The gray area phenomenon

The "gray area phenomenon" (GAP) has complicated and exacerbated the problems of the underground economy in the US. Exemplifying the growing role of international influences and the need for international solutions, the GAP is defined as the existence of threats to the stability of nation states by non-state actors and non-governmental processes and organizations.[38] It inhabits large regions or urban areas where control is in the hands of new half-political, half-criminal powers rather than legitimate governments.[39] The GAP exists in many parts of Andean countries controlled by narco-traffickers and/or terrorists. It exists in many parts of Afghanistan, especially its border with Pakistan. Throughout Russia and many post-Soviet countries, real control rests with the mafia.

In the US, the GAP exists where chunks of inner cities are controlled by gangs, narcotics traffickers, and ethnic organized crime. In Miami, for example, several apparent political assassinations of Haitian leaders have occurred in daylight after the funerals of Haitian political leaders who had themselves been assassinated.

A proposed strategy and theory of engagement for the GAP applies the paradigm that endeavours to understand and operate

---

Foreign Laws," in 5 *Emory J. Int'l Law*, 446 (1991).

38   Edward G. Corr, introduction to *Gray Area Phenomena*, op cit., p. xiii, quoting Peter Lupsha, "The Gray Area Phenomenon: New Threats and Policy Dilemmas," unpublished paper presented at the High Intensity Crime/Low Intensity Conflict Conference, Chicago, Illinois, September 27-30, 1992, pp. 22-23.

39   Ibid., referring to Xavier Raufer, "Gray Areas: A New Security Threat," in *Political Warfare* (Spring 1992).

successfully in "uncomfortable" low-intensity conflict (LIC) situations. In such conflicts, the adversaries' strength depends largely on the existence of "gray areas" where governments cannot govern. The paradigm for coping with these phenomena is based on the underlying premise that the outcome of such conflict is not primarily determined through the skilful manipulation of violence by the police and military. Rather, a holistic approach is required so that the outcome will be determined by (1) the legitimacy of the government, (2) unity of effort, (3) the type and consistency of support for the targeted government, (4) the ability to reduce outside aid to the insurgents or traffickers, (5) intelligence (or action against subversion), and (6) the discipline and capabilities of the government forces.[40]

Although the GAP is particularly problematical for many of the weaker nation states caught in the spiral of international disorder, the US is also vulnerable. The large and relatively well-off US market acts as a magnet for criminals dealing in illegal aliens, narcotics, arms, stolen art, plutonium, and prostitutes. And once they have made money, the US economy remains a magnet for laundering it.

Part of the problem of the current world order and a contributing factor to the US underground economy emanates from gray areas out of states' control. Some destructive groups in the mostly non-industrialized, non-democratic Southern world oppose all things Northern and have embarked on a fundamentalist *jihad* against "McWorld," a term for integrationist modern society. The new "bad guys" include terrorists, insurgents, drug traffickers, rogue states, neo-Luddite ecoterrorists, xenophobes, and fundamentalists.[41] Although the US will need diverse responses to effectively neutralize the new "bad guys," clearly the lacunae in the international economic and legal systems, combined with the big, porous US border and the ease with which the new technology can instantaneously transfer information, money, people,

---

40 Stephen Sloan, introduction to *Low-Intensity Conflict: Old Threats in a New World*, Edwin G. Corr and Stephen Sloan, eds, p. 12 (1992).

41 For background, see Scott B. MacDonald, "The New 'Bad Guys': Exploring the Parameters of the Violent New World Order," in *Gray Area Phenomena*, op. cit., pp. 33-62.

and goods, leave the US and its neighbours increasingly vulnerable and require a much bolder response than hitherto.

Until now, the bulk of resources to combat the new "bad guys" has come from unilateral US programs. To the extent that the US participates in multilateral programs, these programs tend to be concentrated on a highly specific dimension of a problem. For example, most US resources for international criminal cooperation in this hemisphere are directed to the drug area, where the US has provided significant financing for the operations of the Inter-American Drug Abuse Control Commission of the Organization of American States and the International Drug Enforcement Conference (IDEC), an initiative to institutionalize regional cooperation by high-level drug law enforcement officials from Western Hemisphere countries.

IDEC was first convened in 1983 as an outgrowth of the International Drug Enforcement Alumni Association (IDEA), a group of Drug Enforcement Administration (DEA) international training courses. Its principal objective is to share drug-related intelligence and develop an operational strategy that can be used against international drug traffickers. The DEA's Administrator is the permanent co-president of the conference. IDEC funding comes largely from the DEA and International Narcotics Matters, US Department of State.

Another regional anti-drug initiative is the Joint Intelligence Coordination Center (JICC), a generic term that describes an individual centre. When a JICC is connected with the El Paso Intelligence Center (EPIC), it becomes part of the Sentry network. The JICC/Sentry program is a successful and cost-effective mechanism in the arena of counter-narcotics information gathering. It provides information about movements of private aircraft and vessels and persons suspected of involvement in narcotics trafficking to law enforcement agencies involved in counter-narcotics activities.

An integrated approach to the underground economy

Some global interactions are initiated and sustained entirely or almost entirely by nation states. Other interactions, such as those initiated by organized criminal groups, involve private persons. One prerequisite for successfully combatting organized criminals is to view the law enforcement community as an actor in a world politics paradigm and contrast it with the state-centric paradigm in which only nation states have significantly more active roles.

If the US and other nation states are to succeed in their campaigns against the underground economy, countries confronting problems of traditional and emerging new criminal groups must become more sensitive to a paradigm in which organizations other than nation states are accorded power. A successful effort will entail a more innovative use of existing and new bilateral and multilateral mechanisms as well as more uniformity in national actions so that law enforcement officials can be as mobile and efficient as organized criminals. Already, law enforcement officials suffer from their lack of the close-knit family ties that facilitate the operations of criminal groups.

A fully supported "international regime" for anti-laundering and financial enforcement would permit national governments as well as intergovernmental organizations (IGOs), international non-governmental organizations (INGOs), and non-governmental organizations (NGOs) to make more effective use of limited resources. "International regime" is a specialized term that originated with international organization theory in the early 1970s[42] to cover phenomena that involve mostly governmental actors but affect non-governmental actors in such diverse areas as international trade,[43] money, and oceans.[44] A regime may be formal—for example, the General Agreement on Tariffs and

---

42 For an early discussion of "international regimes," see Robert Keohane and Joseph Nye, "Transnational Relations and World Politics," in *International Organization* 25, no. 3 (1971), later enlarged and published as a book by Harvard University Press in 1972.

43 For a discussion of international regimes and international trade, see Jack A. Finlayson and Mark. W. Zacher, "The GATT and the regulation of trade barriers: regime dynamics and functions," in *International Regimes*, Stephen D. Krasner, ed., pp. 274-314.

44 See, e.g., Robert Keohane and Joseph Nye, *Power and Independence*, 1977, pp. 63-164.

Trade[45] —or informal, the regime being merely inferred from the actions of the states involved.[46]

The purpose of international regimes is to regulate and control certain transnational relations and activities by devising appropriate procedures, rules, and institutions. In fact, international regimes have been defined as "norms, rules, and procedures agreed to in order to regulate an issue area." Participants in international regimes will benefit through explicit or tacit cooperation based on such shared concerns as reducing narcotics supply and demand, reducing the power of organized criminal groups, combatting money laundering, and so forth. Since international regimes incarnate specific objectives, they are considered to be more fluid in nature and more likely to undergo evolutionary changes than regular intergovernmental organizations (IGOs).

Unilateralism is inadequate in the post-Cold War world. In response to changed circumstances, the Bush administration diverged from its predecessor's unilateralism and increasingly emphasized collective strategies and problem solving as its term progressed. The Clinton administration appears to be pursuing a systematic strategy that has been called "assertive multilateralism."[47]

The US has the resources in both the private and public sectors to exercise leadership in conceptualizing, proposing, and implementing institutions and structures that are capable of overcoming the power of organized criminal groups—both the old-line traditional groups and the newer groups in narcotics and arms trafficking. Rather than trying to impose policies on other countries, the US should first try to develop a multilateral consensus and then assume the leadership without which

---

45 Finlayson and Zacher, op. cit.

46 An example of an informal regime in international criminal cooperation would be the deportation of certain individuals wanted for crimes and the permission of neighbouring countries to allow "hot pursuit" on their territory. Such informal cooperation has occurred among the Benelux countries and between the US and Mexico and their border states (e.g., Sonora and Arizona).

47 Viron P. Vaky, "The Organization of American States and Multilateralism in the Americas," in *The Future of the Organization of American States* 7 (1993).

regional organizations will not be able to handle problems like the underground economy.

The role of the Organization of American States in promoting cooperative enforcement in the region should be accentuated. Traditionally, the Inter-American Juridical Committee has helped with the preparation of international criminal cooperation conventions. In 1985, the Inter-American Drug Abuse Control Commission (CICAD) was established and has succeeded in providing training for officials, securing the passage of model anti-laundering legislation, and providing other cooperative mechanisms.

International criminal cooperation within the OAS has a long and successful history that has included uniform legislation and conventions for cooperation in broad as well as technical crime matters. To provide stronger regional cooperation against crime and technical assistance to the smaller and weaker countries, the region should have a regional mechanism, the Americas Committee on Crime Problems (ACCP). Similar to the European Committee on Crime Problems under the aegis of the Council of Europe, the ACCP would be established by the OAS justice ministers with a small secretariat. Initially, OAS member states would voluntarily second officials as staff. The ACCP would deal with a vast array of crime problems that affect the Americas, proposing draft conventions and uniform legislation, helping with uniform data, providing technical assistance, and generally supporting the efforts of national governments and other international organizations like Interpol and the UN. The ACCP would also mobilize and cooperate with international non-governmental organizations such as the International Penal Law Association and the Association of Chiefs of Police, and national non-governmental organizations such as judicial, police, criminal justice, bar, banking, and accounting organizations.

The US, other governments, INGOs, and NGOs should actively explore and stimulate the design and establishment of mechanisms and institutions to combat in more comprehensive and integrated ways the growing underground economy and organized crime on both the world and regional levels while the opportunity still exists.

Understanding the Mafia: The Business of Organized Crime

John Burton

Introduction

There has been a long debate, dating back into the 19th Century, about the exact nature of the Mafia. How is it organized? What is the extent of organization involved—for example, in terms of geography, vertical integration, horizontal collusion...? And what business or businesses are so organized? Here, we will be looking at such questions from the perspective of business economics and strategic management analysis.

We will confine our attention specifically to criminal enterprises that go under the general label of the "Mafia" or "Cosa Nostra" ("Our Affair") in North America and Italy—specifically, Sicily. The Mafia/Cosa Nostra, of course, represent particular branded versions of a more general species of organized criminal enterprise that includes the Yakuza in Japan, the Triads in the Chinese diaspora, yardie gangs in Jamaica and the UK, the so-called cocaine cartels of Colombia, and other Italian crime organizations such as the Camorra of Naples. All of these criminal enterprises share certain similarities, but they also exhibit differences. For brevity's sake we have stuck to the manifestation of organized crime that we think we all know from the "Godfather" films and other popular entertainments.

In the sections that follow, we will first develop two highly opposed "polar" views of the nature of the Mafia as a business enterprise that have emerged over recent decades. A third section presents Gambetta's recent and important analysis of the Mafia. The paper then proceeds with some personal reflections drawing specifically on strategic management analysis and business economics. This alternative perspective takes issue with some parts of Gambetta's analysis, but only marginally, as its primary purpose is to make a positive addition to his analytical framework. A final section offers some concluding thoughts on this long debate about the nature of the Mafia business organization.

There is a fundamental disagreement among various authorities about the degree of organization—local/national/international—of the Cosa Nostra that extends to alternative diagnoses of what their business is fundamentally about. We will call these two poles of thinking about the Mafia the "octopus view" and the "disorganized crime" hypothesis.

The octopus view

This view emanates from various sources all of which concur in the proposition that the contemporary Mafia exhibits a high degree of national—indeed, in some versions, international—coordination. It came into prominence in the US in the early 1950s as a result of the work of a Senate committee on interstate crime chaired by Senator Kefauver. The Kefauver Committee concluded that there was an octopus-like coordination of such crime in America under the aegis of the Mafia:

> There is a nationwide crime syndicate known as the Mafia, whose tentacles are found in many large cities. It has international ramifications which appear most clearly in connection with the narcotics traffic.... Its leaders are usually found in

control in the most lucrative rackets in our cities. There are indications of a centralized direction and control of these rackets.[1]

Such conclusions were reaffirmed by the McClellan Committee of the US Congress in 1962[2] and then again by the 1967 President's Commission on Law Enforcement. The latter likened the Mafia to big businesses in the formal economy:

> Organized crime...involves thousands of criminals working with structures as complex as those of any large corporations.... The actions are not impulsive but rather the result of intricate conspiracies carried out over many years and aimed at gaining control over whole fields of activity to amass huge profits.[3]

This depiction makes the US Mafia sound like a multidivisional corporation complete with a long-range strategic plan and market share goals for each division. Yet others have taken the view that the Mafia is not mainly a national crime syndicate—the Kefauver position—but rather a global business organization. For example, Judge Giusto Sciacchitano of the anti-Mafia pool in Sicily which undertook the "maxi trial" of 464 alleged *mafiosi* in Palermo during 1984-1987 has concluded that the Mafia is

> global, unitary, rigidly regimented and vertically structured, governed from the top down by a *cupola* with absolute powers.... It is only now that we can see this globality, but it is always there.[4]

---

1   US Senate Special Committee to Investigate Crime in Interstate Commerce (the Kefauver Committee), 82nd Congress, Third Progress Report: Washington, DC, Government Printing Office, 1951, p. 147.

2   *Gambling and Organized Crime*: Washington, DC, US Congress, 1962.

3   President's Commission on Law Enforcement and the Administration of Justice, *Task Force Report: Organized Crime*: Washington, DC, US Government Printing Office, 1967, p. 1.

4   Quoted from an interview reported in Sterling (1990), p. 282. The book is a highly readable account of the "octopus" Mafia view.

With this vision of the Mafia in mind, let us now turn to the opposite pole of thought, which I have labelled the "disorganized crime hypothesis."

The disorganized crime hypothesis

Although the conventional wisdom in postwar American law enforcement circles has inclined strongly to the octopus view of the Cosa Nostra, this position has not been without its detractors, even including a few within those very circles. Indeed, it is reported that no less a figure than J. Edgar Hoover would hear no talk of the existence of a national crime syndicate and that the FBI under his direction was prevented from even looking for one![5]

When economists first started to apply their analytical tools to the study of crime in the late 1960s and early 1970s, however, the tendency was to accept the orthodox "octopus" view espoused by earlier inquiries into these matters (e.g., Schelling, 1967; Buchanan, 1973). Schelling's theoretical analysis of organized crime in particular was based on a view of the Mafia consistent with the octopus idea: a centralized, monopolistic organization operating in both illegal markets (e.g., gambling, narcotics) and the business of extortion.

A defect of these initial theoretical forays was that, like the governmental inquiries they followed, they lacked a solid basis in terms of serious management and economic research into the realities of organized crime as a business.

It does not need to be stressed that there are "certain problems" with undertaking such empirical research in this particular business arena. In the early 1980s, however, a detailed empirical study of certain organized crime activities was conducted by an economist named Reuter (1983). This study of the operations of the numbers, illicit bookmaking, and loan sharking businesses in New York City marked an important step in throwing considerable doubt on conventional wisdom about the business of the Cosa Nostra.

Surprisingly, Reuter was unable to find evidence in these three settings that could sustain the contention that markets were being monopolized or centrally controlled as argued in the octopus view. He was led to conclude that, while there are doubtless incentives to create a dominant group in any setting where violence is involved, there are a

5   Sterling (1990), p. 237.

number of other economic factors that tend to undermine monopolies in the underworld economy and keep them local, fragmented, and underintegrated as compared with legitimate industries. This is one facet of the disorganized crime hypothesis—the contention that supposedly very organized crime activities are actually typified by fragmentation as compared with their "above-ground" counterparts.[6]

Reuter did not deny that the Mafia had a monopoly face, though in a business area that conventional wisdom had largely ignored:

> The evidence supports a claim that the Mafia has a monopoly on dispute settlement services [for illicit enterprises]. No person who is not a Mafia member may sell such services in New York City.[7]

We will return to this matter in our discussion of Gambetta's analysis. It must suffice to note at this point that by the end of the 1980s a considerable rift of opinion had opened up concerning the nature of organized crime. On the one hand, there were those who portrayed the Mafia as a national or international regime directed like a global business in the formal economy. At the other extreme were those who dismissed this view as primarily a product of sensationalism on the part of politicians, prosecutors, the press, and empire-building law enforcement bureaucrats.[8]

The Mafia as the industry of private protection

Gambetta's 1993 contribution to Mafia studies is fascinating and important on a number of counts.[9]

---

6   An important precursor of the same general position, but from a more sociological perspective, who concluded that the Mafia was a largely non-organized entity was Hess (1973).

7   Reuter (1983), p. 171.

8   E.g., Woodiwiss (1993).

9   As the title of his book implies, Gambetta concentrates on the Sicilian Mafia, but it also contains many comparisons with both the American Cosa Nostra and other mainland Italian equivalents of Sicilian crime firms.

First, it stands as the most extensive and scholarly inquiry to date into the business organization and structuring of Sicilian Mafia activities including, for example, detailed case analysis of Mafia operations in the Palermo wholesale fish, fruit, and vegetable markets and public construction projects in the *Mezzogiorno*.

Secondly, although a sociologist by profession, Gambetta was led to conclude from his researches that in order to understand the Mafia it is necessary to adopt a thoroughgoing industrial economics approach to the entity, which he defines as "a specific economic enterprise, an industry which produces, promotes, and sells private protection."[10]

His analysis follows Reuter's in placing the enforcement of agreements and dispute resolution, conducted in environments where trust is "scarce and fragile," at centre stage for an understanding of the Mafia's essential nature. That is, he views the private protection services offered by Mafia families as genuine services responding to real demand, rather than as a phoney product covering up barefaced extortion, as Schelling did.[11]

Justice cannot be done here to Gambetta's lucid and subtle dissection of the workings of both protection firms ("families") and the private protection industry in Sicily. Drawing heavily on *mafiosi* testimony to judicial investigators, we will concentrate on his findings that are of crucial relevance to the opposing views already presented. These, in summary, are as follows.

The Mafia is not a centrally controlled industry, but rather a brand name for licensed operators in the private protection industry.

- This industry is made up of many individual separate firms that numbered 105 in Sicily as a whole—18 in Palermo alone—in the late 1980s.
- Membership in each protection firm is small, typically smaller than 100, and may be as small as two persons.

---

10 Gambetta (1993), p. 1.

11 Gambetta is not claiming that recourse to the Mafia is an optimal means of settling market transactions, only that it is a rational device in the absence of clear criminal and civil laws—as in western Sicily between 1812 and 1860 with the abolition of feudal law.

- Since the late 1950s there have been attempts to form tentative provincial cartels composed of three geographically contiguous "families" apiece, coordinated by the *commissione (or cupola).*[12]
- The primary purpose of the *commissione* was to regulate the use of violence within families—and only subsequently between them.
- Interloper and breakaway protection firms do exist, and their number may have risen sharply in the late 1980s, even though established firms are clearly "not easily displaced" by those seeking to pirate their protection business.[13]
- Mafia families in Sicily and North America are separate and independent: linkages do exist, but they are weak.

The mass of evidence accumulated by Gambetta constitutes a clear refutation of the alarming view of the Mafia as a centrally coordinated global octopus organization. Rather, the Sicilian Mafia presents a picture of a rather fragmented and not entirely stable industry. Tentative attempts to create localized territorial market-sharing agreements have been made since the end of the 1950s, but even these rather loose arrangements sometimes break down—for example, as a result of the so-called "first Mafia war" of 1961-1963 that led to their suspension until the end of the 1960s.

Just to judge from the numbers of small firms in the Sicilian protection industry, as Gambetta concludes (p. 104):

> The possibility that the Mafia in Sicily would ever become a single centralized protection monopoly covering the entire region (let alone other parts of the world) is negated by this simple evidence alone.

Superficially, the opportunities for effective market centralization of protection services in the US are rosier than in Sicily, as the number of "families" is much smaller—24 in America as a whole, five of them

---

12 There may have also been an attempt to establish a mechanism for "family" coordination above the provincial level towards the end of the 1970s with the formation of a tentative *commissione interprovinciale*. It is not clear whether this ever worked.

13 Gambetta (1993), p. 255.

located in New York—and their territorial jurisdictions are larger. However, this would be to ignore the competition in this market, actual and potential, from youth gangs, biker gangs, prison-based gangs like the Black Guerrillas and Nuestra Familia, and others who might have the capability to service a demand for protection from illicit businesses.

The Mafia family as a firm: a strategic management perspective

At the same time, Gambetta's powerful study has strongly promoted the idea of understanding the Mafia in business and industrial terms. This approach raises a number of issues. Our purpose in this section is to address some of these, drawing on the standard framework of strategic management analysis used for companies operating in the above-ground economy.

Core competencies and the Mafia firm

Hamel and Prahalad (1990) argue that successful firms in the formal economy are typically based on a small set of core competencies from which they develop an evolving array of products over time. Now Gambetta's analysis might seem to suggest that he views the Mafia as a single-product enterprise founded on a single core competency—an acquired reputation in the protection business:

> Mafiosi are first and foremost entrepreneurs in one particular commodity—protection—and this is what distinguishes them from simply criminals, simply entrepreneurs, or criminal entrepreneurs."[14]

As Gambetta's description of the resources involved in the successful Mafia firm makes clear, however, other core competencies involved typically include intelligence gathering, capacity for violence, and the ability to operate clandestine networks and dealings. This array of competencies has applications in criminal business activities other than private protection. We should expect the dynamic Mafia firm to develop and diversify into such other business arenas in response to its percep-

---

14   Gambetta (1993), p. 19.

tion of the relative risks and returns in both their core product area and these alternative lines of business. In short, while the Mafia's quintessence *qua* Mafia may be protection, a durably successful enterprise of this kind is likely to end up in a much broader array of business activities. Henry Ford may have hit his stride with the Model T, but Ford today is a multinational engaged in a wide array of differing product and geographical markets.

Industry threats and opportunities in the underworld economy

This point is reinforced when we consider the fact that the Mafia firm, no less than its above-ground counterpart, has to deal with changing patterns of consumer demand, varying stages in the industrial cycle, and alterations in the regulatory framework. The dynamic criminal enterprise needs to vary its activities to reflect this varying pattern of threats and opportunities.

The US Mafia responded with alacrity to the opportunities for considerable profits from bootlegging that surfaced with the 1919 passage of the *Volstead Act*. Similarly, the 1933 repeal of Prohibition sent these crime firms in search of new activities, notably, as it turned out, prostitution and labour racketeering.[15]

As Gambetta himself points out, there are great difficulties with bequeathing and/or selling the property rights in a Mafia-type protection firm, not least because its corporate renown heavily depends on that of its owner-manager, the "capo" or "don."[16] Moreover, in both the US and Sicily the private protection business would seem to be in the maturity phase of its industrial cycle, while simultaneously in both settings there would appear to be increasing competition from non-Mafia interloper gangs.[17]

---

15 Tyler (1962), p. 152; Rubin (1973), p. 165.

16 Gambetta (1993), pp. 58-65.

17 Reuter (1983), Gambetta (1993).

For all of the foregoing reasons, I would anticipate that successful Mafia enterprises would be unlikely to survive in the long run as purely Mafia firms in Gambetta's sense of producing a single product—protection—in one market. The strategic management perspective we are using here suggests that, to the contrary, we should expect to see these criminal firms embark on deliberate diversification strategies of both the related and unrelated variety. The specific diversification profile that emerges over time will, of course, reflect the complex of threats and opportunities, risks and returns perceived in various possible avenues of development.

Recent diversification strategies of the Sicilian Mafia

This general point emerges clearly in the diversification strategies chosen by Sicilian Mafia firms in recent decades—a matter about which much is now known as a result of the Mafia prosecutions that have been going on since the early 1980s.

In the 1950s and 1960s, Sicilian Mafiosi were involved in the illicit drug trade, though only to a relatively minor extent. The estimated five-fold growth in narcotics demand in the period 1970-1985 offered them a new avenue for profitable diversification, with the consequence that

> in the late 1970s...the Sicilian Mafia became a major force in the world heroin trade. By the early 1980s, its families were supplying an estimated 80 percent of the market in New York, using morphine base from Asia treated in clandestine laboratories in and around Palermo.[18]

Arlacchi (1986) estimated that the net profit of only four Palermo families from this trade in the single year 1982 was in the order of US $750 million. However, this spate of "narcodollars" is probably subsiding: police in both the US and Italy estimate that the Sicilian Mafia has lost market share in the global heroin trade to new entrants and may

---

18   *The Economist* (1993), p. 22.

now being supplying only 5 percent of the US illicit market in this commodity.

An alternative diversification path has apparently come to the rescue, however. Italian government and European Commission hand-outs to southern Italy have grown enormously, and so has Mafia involvement in rigged tendering for the resulting public contracts. Some claim that this is now the Sicilian Mafia's single largest source of funds.[19] So it appears that the Mafia is not simply, as commonly claimed, "a state within the state": it is also now a "redistributive state within the redistributive state"!

Conclusion: towards a "networking" view of organized crime

Law enforcement, government, and academic circles have long pondered the nature of organized crime. Essentially—drawing on Williamson's (1975) terminology—debate has revolved around whether organized crime is best understood as a hierarchical system of coordination or an arena of fragmented market relations: the octopus view vs the disorganized crime view.

We will speculate that depicting the issue in terms of opposites has detracked the debate on Mafia business organization. Strategic management analysis of legitimate business has revealed the existence of a large volume of business arrangements between the polar extremes of marketplaces and hierarchies: "networks," as Thorelli calls them.[20] These collaborative arrangements do not easily fit into the orthodox markets/hierarchies framework now dominant in the social sciences and industrial organization theory. Classic examples of such collaborative business relationships include the *kieretsu* of Japan; formal joint venture franchising agreements; coproduction arrangements, and coordinated

---

19   Ibid., p. 26.

20   There are some complexities in Thorelli's analysis that need not detain us here; for a critique and alternative diagnosis of collaborative business arrangements, see Burton (1994).

supply-chain ties built on long-standing relationships between firms and their suppliers—e.g., the Benetton-supplier network in Italy.

The strategic management analyst would see that much of the "organization" in organized crime is best understood in terms of this networking mode of business rather than the markets/hierarchies paradigm. Gambetta's remark that "Mafiosi pursue lifelong contracts and establish organic bonds with their customers"[21] depicts a style of firm-customer relationships that typifies networking. Similarly, the linkages between the Sicilian and American Mafia fall very much into the category of informal, collaborative business arrangements based on relational exchange, trust, and personal contact.

There is much evidence that the use of collaborative business arrangements has expanded greatly in the above-ground economy over the past decade, particularly among international industries. It is interesting to note that some authorities now detect the same trend developing in global organized crime, with evidence, for example, of growing links between the Triads, the Mafia, and Colombian cartels.[22] This does not mean, however, that the octopus view of worldwide organized crime as the underworld equivalent of a corporate transnational behemoth in the formal world economy is the reality after all. Rather, the octopus becomes an image of the networking model that has always, it is argued here, pervaded the real business of organized crime.

---

21 Gambetta (1993), p. 56.

22 See "Worldwide Cooperation Among Organized Crime Elements Growing,", in *Atlantic Outlook*, no. 57, November 5, 1993: London, US Embassy, US Information Service.

References

Arlacchi, P. (1988), *Mafia Business*, M. Ryle, trans.: Oxford, Oxford University Press.

Buchanan, J.M. (1973), "A Defense of Organized Crime?" in S. Rottenberg, ed., *The Economics of Crime and Punishment*: Washington, DC, American Enterprise Institute, 1973, pp. 119-132.

Burton, J. (1994), *Collaboration vs Competition?*: Birmingham, UK, University of Birmingham, Department of Commerce.

The Economist (1993), "The Sicilian Mafia: A State within the State," April 24, 1993, pp. 21-26.

Gambetta, D. (1993), *The Sicilian Mafia: The Business of Private Protection*: Cambridge, Harvard University Press.

Hamel, G. and Prahalad, C.K. (1990), "The Core Competencies of the Corporation," in *Harvard Business Review*, May-June, pp. 79-91.

Hess, H. (1973), *Mafia and Mafiosi: The Structures of Power*: Lexington, Mass., Lexington Books.

Reuter, P. (1983), *Disorganized Crime: The Economics of the Visible Hand*: Cambridge, MIT Press.

Rubin, P.H. (1973), "The Economic Theory of the Criminal Firm," in S. Rottenberg, ed., *The Economics of Crime and Punishment*: Washington, DC. American Enterprise Institute, 1973, pp. 155-166.

Schelling, T.C. (1967), "Economics and Criminal Enterprise," in *The Public Interest*, no. 7 (Spring).

Sterling, C. (1990), *Octopus: The Long Reach of the International Sicilian Mafia*: New York, Simon and Schuster.

Thorelli, H.B. (1986), "Networks: Between Markets and Hierarchies," in *Strategic Management Journal*, vol. 7, pp. 37-51.

Tyler, G. (1962), *Organized Crime in America*: Ann Arbor, University of Michigan Press.

Williamson, O.E. (1975), *Markets and Hierarchies*: New York, The Free Press.

Woodiwiss, M. (1933), "Crime's Global Reach," in F. Pearce and M. Woodiwiss, eds, *Global Crime Connections: Dynamics and Control*: London, Macmillan, pp. 1-31.

Section 3:
International Experience with the
Underground Economy

Revised Estimates of the Underground Economy: Implications of US Currency Held Abroad

Edgar L. Feige[1]

A number of important public policy decisions now call for analytical and empirical knowledge of the nature, size, growth, causes, and consequences of the "underground economy." Our purpose here is to

1   The writer wishes to acknowledge the cooperation of FinCEN, the Financial Crimes Enforcement Network of the Department of the Treasury, and the Board of Governors of the Federal Reserve System in providing data and research support for various aspects of this study. I am also grateful for the continuing dialogue and cooperation I have received from Richard Porter on all aspects of my work. The views expressed are those of the author and do not represent the views of FinCEN or the Board of Governors of the Federal Reserve or its staff.

clarify the meaning of underground activity, update various discrepancy and fiscal estimates of its size and growth, and examine the empirical implications of new evidence on the growing use of US currency throughout the world for monetary estimates of the underground economy within the US itself.

The popular term "underground economy" is inexact, encompassing a wide range of economic activities including the production and distribution of illegal goods and services as well as legal activities whose concealment from or misrepresentation to government authorities involves tax evasion or benefit fraud. Given the diversity of hidden activities, it becomes necessary to develop a taxonomy of "underground economies" that identifies specific types of underground behaviours and suggests appropriate methods for estimating their prevalence.

The general penchant for hiding underground economic activities often precludes direct observation of their occurrence and leaves us to use indirect measures to detect the footprints of hidden activities in the sands of the observable economic continuum. Currency, as an anonymous medium of exchange, is viewed as the preferred means of payment in transactions that economic actors are trying to conceal. This makes cash stocks and flows a natural starting point in our search for the underground economy. The total amount of currency in circulation[2] is one of the best-measured macroeconomic indicators, since the production and distribution of currency by governments is strictly monitored and carefully recorded.

However, our knowledge is meagre when it comes to the location and circulation of the public's US currency holdings. Without reliable estimates of the varying amounts of US currency circulating overseas, we have no way of determining the size of the domestic money supply

---

2   "Currency in circulation" refers in the US context to the amount of the national currency held outside the Treasury and Federal Reserve. Except for small amounts of currency that may have inadvertently been lost or destroyed by the public (Laurent, 1974), currency in circulation includes the holdings of financial intermediaries and the public. Reliable data on financial intermediary holdings of vault cash are readily available, and it is therefore possible to obtain accurate estimates of the total stock of currency outside the banking system. For a complete description of the cash payments system, see Feige (1994b).

or its change over time. Our intention here is to demonstrate alternative ways of estimating the amount of US currency held domestically and overseas and present some temporal estimates of net US currency outflows. New estimates of domestic US currency holdings will then be used to reestimate the size and growth of the domestic US underground economy.

A puzzling macroeconomic anomaly is the huge amount of US currency outstanding—$390 billion—and its surprisingly persistent growth. Despite widespread predictions of the advent of the cashless society and decades of cash-saving financial innovation, per-capita holdings of United States currency increased from $160 in 1961 to $1,450 by the end of 1994. Adjusting for inflation, real per-capita currency increased by 70 percent and the proportion of the M1 money supply composed of currency rose from 20 percent to 30 percent. More than 60 percent of the outstanding stock of currency is now in the form of $100 bills.[3]

The suggestion that the average American family of four now holds $5,800 in currency, of which $3,480 is in the form of $100 bills, appears implausible. The number of notes in circulation is no less surprising than their value. There are presently some 17 billion common denomination notes in circulation. On a per-capita basis, this implies that each person holds, on average, 63 notes of which 9 are in the form of $100 bills. Adult US residents admit to holding only 12 percent of the nation's currency in circulation outside the banking system (Avery et al. 1986,1987). Allowing for US business holdings of currency, the whereabouts of more than 80 percent of the nation's currency supply is presently unknown.

These anomalous findings give rise to the "currency enigma" (Feige, 1990b, 1994a) which consists of a stock and a flow component. Our inability to identify the holders and locations of a large fraction of the US currency stock gives rise to a $300 billion "missing currency" problem (Sprenkel, 1993). This missing stock of currency is used as both a store of value and a means of payment for goods and services. If half of the missing currency were hoarded and the other half turned over at the rate

---

3   Surprisingly large per-capita currency holdings are not limited to the United States. In 1993, per-capita currency holdings in Switzerland, Japan and Germany amounted to (expressed in US dollars) $3,060, $2,944 and $1,579 respectively.

estimated for domestic currency use, this missing currency would generate a flow of "missing payments" roughly equal to the United States' GDP.

Two complementary hypotheses are put forward as possible explanations for the currency enigma. Some fraction of the missing currency may in fact be held by US households for conducting unreported transactions in the US underground economy. A considerably larger portion of the missing currency is more likely to be held abroad in the form of co-circulating currency. US dollars will be a co-circulating currency when they are routinely used by foreigners to effect payments in their own countries. Co-circulating currency (Krueger and Ha, 1995) is also used as a store of value and, in some instances, a unit of account. We will examine the extent to which the currency enigma can be resolved by appeal to both the underground economy hypothesis and the "world dollarization" hypothesis.

We begin with a taxonomic framework for defining different types of underground activity, review alternative methods of estimation, and update available estimates of various "underground economies" in the United States. Our second section presents direct estimates of US currency inflows and outflows derived from Currency and Monetary Instrument Reports (CMIRs) collected by the US Customs Service. Section 3 presents evidence on foreign US currency holdings derived from indirect methods that include a monetary demography model (MDM) and a note ratio model (NRM). Section 4 combines direct and indirect methods to obtain a factor model composite measure of overseas currency flows. To anticipate the results, direct measures of overseas holdings suggest that no more than 25 percent of US currency is presently held abroad: indirect methods yield a wide range of estimates of between 30 and 70 percent held abroad, and the composite estimate is roughly 40 percent. A final section looks at the implications of overseas currency holdings for the measurement of the domestic underground economy.

Defining and measuring underground economies

The early literature on the underground economy lacked an accepted taxonomy for classifying various underground activities. These activities were variously described as subterranean, irregular, informal, hidden, grey, shadow, clandestine, parallel, and black, but these modifiers were rarely augmented by explicit definitions to support analytical and empirical investigation. It is now well understood that there exists a variety of underground economies spanning both planned and market economies, be they developed or developing. Agents engaged in underground activities circumvent, escape, or are excluded from the institutional system of rules, rights, regulations, and enforcement penalties that govern formal agents engaged in production and exchange. Different types of underground activities are distinguished by the particular institutional rules they violate. With this criterion, we can identify four specific types of "underground" economic activity: illegal, unreported, unrecorded, and informal. The metric for measuring the dimension of each underground activity is the aggregate income generated by that activity. Table 1 presents a taxonomy of underground economies.

The *illegal* economy consists in the income generated by economic activities pursued in violation of legal statutes defining the scope of legitimate forms of commerce. The most notable illegal activities are the production and distribution of prohibited substances (drugs, for example) and such services as prostitution, pornography, and black-market currency exchange. Estimates of income produced from illegal activities are typically derived from crime-related statistics and range from $70 to $100 billion. In 1982, unreported income from drugs and gambling was estimated at roughly $26 billion (Abt Associates, 1984), and the 1990 retail value of drugs sold in the US has been estimated at around $40 billion.[4]

The *unreported* economy consists in economic activities that circumvent or evade fiscal rules as set out in the tax code. A summary measure of the unreported economy is the amount of unreported income—namely, the amount of income that should legally be reported to the tax authorities but is not. Since illegal income is taxable, the unreported economy includes both legal and illegal source income that is not properly reported. A complementary measure of the unreported economy is the "gross tax gap," the difference between the amount of tax revenues legally due the fiscal authority and the amount of tax revenues paid voluntarily. Since the "net tax gap" represents the difference be-

---

4   "What Americans Users Spend on Illegal Drugs": US Office of National Drug Control Policy, Technical Paper, June 1991, p. 5. Reuter (1996) describes the limitations of estimates of the size of the illegal economy.

TABLE 1

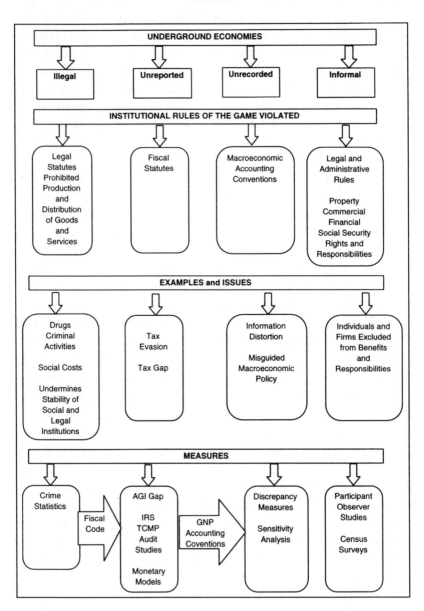

tween the amount of revenue due and the amount actually collected, the difference between the gross and net represents the revenues collected as a direct result of enforcement activities. Benefit fraud, false claims to benefits (welfare or unemployment payments) or subsidies to which the claimants are not legally entitled, should be formally included in "tax gap" measures.

The *unrecorded* economy consists in those economic activities circumventing the institutional conventions that define the reporting requirements of government statistical agencies. A summary measure of the unrecorded economy is the amount of unrecorded income—namely, the amount of income that should, under existing rules and conventions, be recorded in national accounting systems such as National Income and Product Accounts but is not. Unrecorded income represents a discrepancy between total income or output and the actual amount of income or output captured or enumerated by the statistical accounting system designed to measure economic activity. Since national accounting conventions differ with respect to the inclusion of illegal incomes, unrecorded income may or may not include components from the illegal sector.

The *informal* economy encompasses economic activities that circumvent the costs and are excluded from the benefits and rights of property relationships, commercial licensing, labour contracts, torts, financial credit, and social security systems. A summary measure of the informal economy is the income generated by economic agents operating informally.

Estimating the size of these various underground economies remains an inexact science at best. However, more precise definition of alternative underground economies has reduced the tendency to compare disparate measures, while improvements in tax compliance and monetary methodologies are narrowing the range of comparable estimates.

Updated estimates of unreported income in the US

Since underground economic activity typically exposes the participant to a risk of penalties if discovered, anyone engaged in such activity has an incentive to conceal that involvement. This propensity for secrecy creates special problems for the social scientist attempting to observe and quantify underground behaviours. Direct and indirect measures of various types of underground activity have been proposed, and each has well-known limitations (Feige, 1989).

Earlier empirical efforts to measure the extent and proliferation of these activities had revealed underground economies that were large enough to be economically significant and expanding considerably in the latter 1960s and through much of the 1970s. Costly regulation, rising tax rates, and a growing distrust of government were cited as the primary causes of increased underground activity. The conservative politics of the 1980s sought to reverse these trends by reducing government regulation, lessening the tax burden, and restoring a greater sense of trust and confidence in government by overhauling the tax system and reducing what were perceived as wasteful government expenditures. What we want to know is whether these efforts had any real effect on cutting the size and growth rate of the underground economy.

Various macroeconomic measures have been advanced as possible indicators of underground activity. These include the adjusted gross income (AGI) gap discrepancy measure produced by the Bureau of Economic Analysis (BEA); the audit-based discrepancy measure of unreported taxable income produced by the Internal Revenue Service (IRS), and estimates of unreported income derived from various specifications of monetary models. These measures are reviewed and updated below.

Discrepancy measures

The US Government produces two discrepancy measures that are cited as indicators of underground activity. The first of these, compiled by the BEA, calculates the difference between adjusted gross income (AGI) as reported to the IRS and an independent estimate of AGI derived from National Income and Product Accounts (NIPA) estimates of personal income.

This "AGI gap" is not officially acknowledged as a measure of the underground economy: however, with a few qualifications (Carson, 1984; Feige, 1989), the AGI gap can be interpreted as a lower bound measure of non-compliance in the reporting of taxable income—i.e., a measure of unreported income.

Figure 1 sets the AGI gap estimates published by the BEA in 1985 beside the most recently revised estimates. The latest government figures showed that the earlier gap estimates had been much too low, and had to be expanded by $115 billion in 1983: by 1992, the AGI gap had risen to $500 billion. As a percentage of AGI,[5] the gap reached its peak of 16.1 in 1987 and then fell to an estimated 14 percent of AGI in 1992.

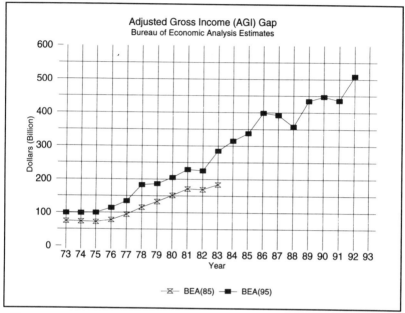

Figure 1

The IRS prepares an alternative discrepancy measure for unreported income using the data from its Taxpayer Compliance Measurement Program (TCMP). Responding to reports of a large underground economy that were based on monetary estimates, the IRS undertook a series of studies of the extent of non-compliance with US tax laws (IRS, 1979; 1981; 1983). The first study concluded that between $75 and $100

---

5 A common error in presenting estimates of unreported income is to display unreported income as a percentage of GNP. Since GNP includes non-taxable government and private expenditures, the appropriate scale measure for presenting estimates of unreported income is AGI, which forms the basis for assessing taxable income.

billion in legal source income had not been properly reported on individual 1976 tax returns. The agency estimated the resulting revenue loss to the government at between $12 and $17 billion. At the same time, illegal source unreported income was estimated at $25 to $35 billion, with a further revenue loss of $6 to $8 billion.

The 1983 IRS report increased the estimate for 1976 legal source unreported income by $30 billion: the associated estimate of lost tax revenue more than doubled. On the other hand, the 1983 report slashed the estimate of illegal source income to only $13 billion and cut the corresponding revenue loss from the illegal sector to roughly $4 billion.

Feige (1989) demonstrated the sensitivity of the results from the early IRS TCMP studies to small variations in the questionable set of assumptions used for estimating the magnitude of non-compliance. An IRS admission that 1981 total unreported income amounted to some $283 billion with a corresponding revenue loss of $90 billion led the BEA to undertake a major review of NIPA accounts. The BEA's 1985 "comprehensive revision" included changes in definitions and statistical methods, but its single most important element was an adjustment for income previously unrecorded due to understated tax source data. For 1984, the personal income adjustment for unrecorded wages, salaries, and non-farm proprietor income amounted to $101 billion, demonstrating the empirical connection between unreported and unrecorded income.

The latest IRS estimates of unreported income (IRS 1988) were based on the agency's TCMP audits of tax returns in the years 1973, 1976, 1979, and 1982 and include estimates of unreported income and corresponding losses in tax revenue projected out to 1992. These 1988 IRS estimates are presented in Figure 2 with the projections for the years 1983-1992.

For each audit year, a sample of roughly 55,000 tax filers was scrutinized by IRS auditors to pinpoint income that should have been reported and was not. Final estimates of unreported income for filers and non- filers from those years were obtained by combining information from audits, information returns, and special surveys. The IRS projections for the period 1985-1992 were based on Office of Management and Budget forecasts of personal income combined with an assumption of constant rates of non-compliance. The projections also assumed that taxpayer behaviour was unaffected by the tax reforms of

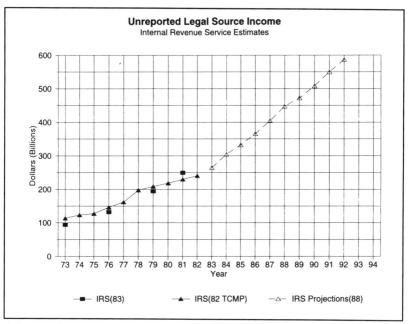

Figure 2

1986. By 1992, actual reported AGI fell more than $500 billion short of IRS projections. The overestimates of projected reportable income and the assumption that compliance rates were unaffected by tax cuts and tax reforms do suggest, however, that the IRS projections of unreported income were overstated.[6]

Whereas the earlier IRS studies had included estimates of both legal and illegal source unreported income, the 1988 study was limited to estimates of unreported legal source income. This study estimated illegal source income as $34.2 billion in 1981, roughly 15 percent of the

---

6   On page A-101 of the IRS 1988 report, the agency acknowleges the major limitations of its unreported income projections: "Because we essentially hold constant rates of noncompliance through 1992, these estimates do not reflect recent trends in noncompliance. Second we assume that tax reform has no impact on individuals' behaviour in terms of either their propensity for noncompliance or the types of incomes individuals will receive in future years. Third, these projections are sensitive to changes in macroeconomic model projections of incomes in future years."

revised legal source estimate for that year. If illegal income remained at roughly the same percentage of legal income, it would add an additional $88 billion in unreported illegal source income to the estimated $585 billion of unreported legal source income for 1992. [7]

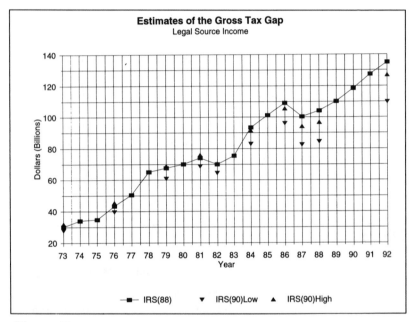

Figure 3

Figure 3 reports alternative IRS estimates of the "gross tax gap" on individual and corporate legal source incomes. The gross tax gap over-states revenue lost to the government through non-compliance to the extent that IRS enforcement activities collect some of the amounts due. The yield from these enforcement activities was estimated at $15.4 billion in 1981, $18.9 billion in 1984, and $21.9 billion in 1987.[8]

---

7   The IRS estimates reported above are based on the recommendations of the tax examiners. Since some of these recommendations are challenged by the taxpayer, the IRS also prepared an alternative set of estimates on an assessed basis (IRS, 1988).

8   IRS (1990), p. 10, Table 2.

On the other hand, the gross tax gap understates the loss of revenue to the government because it excludes revenue lost in illegal source income as well as losses from non-compliance with other federal taxes including employment, excise, gift, and estate taxes and customs duties. For the year 1987, income taxes represented only 56 percent of federal budget receipts: another 36 percent came from employment taxes and 5 percent from gift, estate, and excise taxes. Virtually no information is available on losses from non-compliance with these other important revenue sources and we have no estimates of amounts of public money wasted through benefit fraud.

Currency ratio models

The most common method of estimating the size of the unreported economy relies on some variant of the general currency ratio model described in Feige (1989). The most restrictive specification of the currency ratio model (Cagan, 1958; Gutmann, 1977) assumes that currency is the exclusive medium of exchange for unreported transactions; that the ratio of currency to checkable deposits is affected only by the growth of unreported transactions; that the income velocities of reported and unreported transactions are identical; and that in some base period, unreported income was zero, so that the observed base period currency deposit ratio serves as a proxy for the desired currency ratio in the official economy.[9]

Figure 4 shows estimated unreported income as a percentage of recorded AGI as obtained from the simple currency ratio model under the assumptions that in 1940 there was no unreported income and all currency outside the banking system was then held by the domestic public. As pointed out in earlier studies, the ratio of unreported income rose sharply during World War II and then declined to remain relatively stable until the early 1960s. Unreported income then spurted upwards from less than 5 percent of AGI in 1960 to 15 percent by 1980. The

---

9   As described in Feige (1989), the foregoing restrictions imply that the ratio of unreported (Yu) to reported income (Yo) can be estimated as follows: $Yu/Yo = (C-ko+D)/(ko+1)D$, where: C = Currency; D = Checkable Deposits; $ko = Co/Do$.

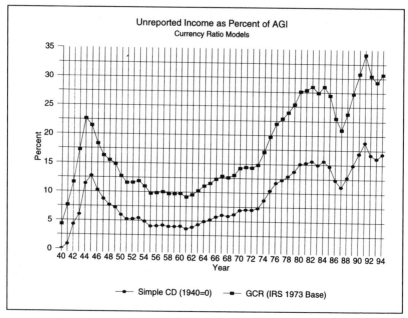

Figure 4

percentage of unreported income reached a plateau during the early '80s, and it actually declined around the time of the 1986 tax reform act before rising steeply between 1987 and 1991.

The figure also presents the results of a more general specification of the currency ratio model. The general currency ratio (GCR) model[10] takes the IRS estimate of unreported 1973 income as its benchmark and assumes that 75 percent of unreported income transactions are made in currency, with the remaining 25 percent made by checkable deposits. The resulting estimates display a time path similar to that of the more

---

10 The GCR model permits a relaxation of several of the assumptions employed in the simple currency ratio model. In particular, currency need no longer be the exclusive medium of exchange for unreported transactions, and any year can serve as a benchmark for which an independent estimate of unreported income is available. The GCR model can be solved to obtain the equation for the ratio of unreported income, which is: $Yu/Yo = (ku+1)(C-koD)/(ko+1)(kuD-C)$ where ku and ko respectively represent the currency deposit ratios in the unreported and reported economies.

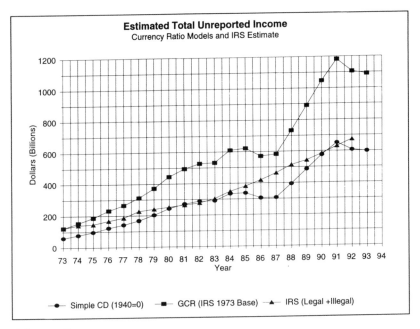

Estimated Total Unreported Income
Currency Ratio Models and IRS Estimate

Figure 5

restrictive estimates: however, the percentage of unreported activities is considerably higher in all periods.

Figure 5 shows three estimates of total unreported income from both legal and illegal sources for the period 1972-1993.[11] The IRS projections are remarkably similar to those obtained with the simple currency ratio model, suggesting that by 1991, total unreported income amounted to roughly $650 billion, or 17 percent of reported AGI. Assuming this unreported income had been subject to a marginal income tax rate of 20 percent, we find that $130 billion in tax revenues—roughly equal to 62 percent of the federal budget deficit—escaped government collection.

The GCR model results suggest that unreported income grew gradually during the first half of the 1980s to decline in mid-decade and then

---

11   The IRS estimate is the sum of the legal source unreported income estimate in Figure 2 plus a 15 percent imputation for illegal source income. The imputation for illegal source income is based on the estimates reported in the earlier study (IRS, 1983). The currency ratio models yield estimates of total unreported income from all sources.

resume growing until the early 1990s: in fact, unreported income appears to have risen to about $1 trillion in the latter years after doubling in the last half of the previous decade. Now all these currency ratio model estimates are predicated on the assumption that US currency exclusively is being used to fuel domestic transactions in both the official and underground economies. There is, however, a growing body of anecdotal evidence to suggest that US dollars also circulate as a medium of exchange in foreign countries. If a large and perhaps variable fraction of US currency is held abroad, conventional currency ratio models employing the total currency supply would be overstating the size of the domestic US underground economy.

Federal Reserve Surveys of Currency and Transaction Account Usage (SCTAU: Avery et al., 1986; 1987) reinforce the notion that a substantial portion of US currency holdings cannot be accounted for by the behaviour of US households. In both 1984 and 1986, SCTAU determined that US households admitted to holding at most 12 percent of the national currency supply. Since business firms are very concerned with efficient cash management to minimize interest losses associated with cash inventories, they are likely to hold considerably smaller cash inventories than households. The scant evidence on US currency holdings by business firms (Anderson, 1977; Sumner, 1990) suggests that domestic firms hold less than 3 percent of the currency in circulation.

A conservative estimate of the stock of currency required to sustain cash payments in the US unreported economy can be obtained with the IRS projection of 1992 unreported income as $675 billion. If we assume that roughly 75 percent of this unreported income is paid with cash, and take currency turnover[12] to be roughly 50 times per year, we get a stock of currency used for underground transactions that is less than 4 percent of currency in circulation with the public. In short, since US households

---

12   Also called the income velocity of currency. The methodology for estimating the velocity (turnover) of currency is described in Feige (1990b). The estimates are based on the Federal Reserve Survey of Currency and Transaction Usage, which finds that the income velocity of household cash holdings is roughly 50 turnovers per year. Share-weighted, denomination-specific velocities are obtained by estimating the average lifetime of each note denomination derived from Federal Reserve FR-160 data on currency issues (births) and redemptions (deaths).

admit to holding less than 12 percent of the nation's currency in circulation, firms hold roughly 3 percent, and underground transactions absorb another 4 percent, the ownership of more than 80 percent of circulating US currency is currently unexplained. This anomaly of missing currency gives rise to the stock component of the "currency enigma" (Feige, 1994a).

The flow component of this currency enigma denotes the volume of cash payments made with the outstanding currency stock. Admitted household holdings give rise to an estimated $1.7 trillion in cash payments for 1992, roughly 41 percent of recorded personal consumption expenditures. Business cash holdings generate some $400 billion, 70 percent of total intermediate payments, and the underground economy accounts for $675 billion in cash payments. If the stock of the remaining "missing" currency circulates at roughly the same rate as currency held by US households, it would generate an additional volume of unaccounted cash payments in excess of $10 trillion.

Several hypotheses have been advanced to explain these monetary anomalies. One holds that the US underground economy is substantially larger than currently estimated and domestic holdings of US currency are much larger than households tell currency surveys.[13] The "world dollarization" hypothesis suggests that a substantial fraction of US currency is held abroad by residents of other nations. The complementary "hoarding" hypothesis suggests that overseas hoards are being held as a store of value rather than as a medium of exchange. The dollarization hypothesis requires independent estimates of the fraction of US currency held abroad. The hoarding hypothesis requires evidence confirming that overseas holdings of US currency circulate at slower rates than domestic currency holdings.

Anecdotal reports of US currency circulating in parts of Latin America, the Middle East, Eastern Europe, and Russia are widespread, as are

---

13   The currency usage survey of US households is likely to understate actual domestic currency holdings for several reasons. The survey undersamples high-income households and may underestimate household hoards. Porter and Judson (1995) suggest that these two sources could add another 5 percent to domestic holdings. The survey may also understate actual domestic currency holdings as a result of self selection bias and underreporting bias, but the extent of these biases cannot be determined.

suggestions that foreign demand for US currency can fluctuate quite dramatically. Initial efforts to estimate the amount of US currency held abroad (Feige, 1994) range as high as 45 percent. Since the size, variability, and velocity of foreign US currency holdings have important implications for the measurement of the domestic underground economy and the conduct of domestic monetary policy, we now turn our attention to further efforts to locate this "missing" US currency.

Direct estimates of net outflows of US currency

At present, there is no information system collecting complete data on total amounts of US currency flowing in and out of the country. Large US currency shipments are typically handled by a small number of commercial banks that specialize in the business of wholesale bulk currency transport. These large currency shipments have been informally reported to the Federal Reserve Bank of New York cash office since 1988. Although the period spanned by the confidential estimates is short and the data are not comprehensive, being limited to major wholesale shippers operating largely in the New York Federal Reserve District, they provide useful information on a substantial segment of bulk cash shipments to and from the US.[14] We will denote the Federal Reserve bulk shipment outflow series as FSO and the bulk shipment inflow series as FSI. Net bulk outflows (FSN) equal FSO-FSI.

Interviews with Federal Reserve officials suggest that much of the currency for wholesale overseas currency shipments by the major transporting banks is supplied by the New York Federal Reserve Bank in the form of $100 bills. All Federal Reserve banks maintain monthly, denomination-specific records of the number of notes paid into circulation (PIC) and the number received from circulation (RFC). These records, main-

---

14 During the interwar period between 1923 and 1941, the Federal Reserve published data on net currency shipments to European countries (*Banking and Monetary Statistics: 1914-1941*, pp. 417-418). Over the entire period for which data are available, cumulative net inflows from Europe amounted to 4.8 percent of the average outstanding stock of currency during the period. The average annual net inflow of currency from Europe amounted to .25 percent of the average outstanding currency stock.

tained in the Federal Reserve system's FR-160 database, enable us to identify the net injections into circulation (PIC-RFC) of each denomination of currency by each Federal Reserve bank. Feige (1994a) observed a close relationship between the net value of $100 denomination notes injected into circulation by the New York Federal Reserve (NYN) and the net amount of currency shipped overseas as confidentially reported to the New York Federal Reserve Bank (FSN). Feige used NYN as a proxy for FSN, and this proxy was subsequently used by Porter and Judson (1995) as a measure of total currency flows overseas.

Although useful as a proxy for the confidential FSN series, net injections of $100 bills by the New York Federal Reserve (NYN) should not be viewed as an accurate measure of overall net currency flows abroad. The NYN proxy will overstate net outflows because some fraction of net injections of New York $100 notes are used to satisfy domestic demand. The proxy will understate true net outflows to the extent that it excludes the net export of smaller-denomination notes. Finally, the NYN proxy takes no account of net currency outflows from other Federal Reserve districts.

The most important direct measure of overseas currency inflows and outflows is collected as part of the regulatory responsibility of the US Customs Service. Enacted in October 1970, the *Currency and Foreign Transactions Reporting Act*, also known as the "Bank Secrecy Act," requires persons or institutions importing or exporting currency or other monetary instruments in amounts exceeding $5,000 to file a "Report of International Transportation of Currency or Monetary Instruments." Commonly known as "CMIRs," these reports have been collected by US Customs since 1977. In 1980, the reporting threshold was raised to $10,000.

Although the CMIR data system was established to record individual cross-border inflows and outflows of currency and monetary instruments, its micro-records can be usefully aggregated to study the size, origin, and destination of these cross-border movements. Since its inception, the CMIR system has collected 2.3 million inbound filings and more than 300,000 outbound filings. With the cooperation of US Customs and the US Treasury Department Financial Crimes Enforcement Network (FinCEN), the information contained in the millions of accumulated confidential CMIR forms was combined by a specially designed algorithm that aggregated CMIR currency inflows (CTI) and CMIR outflows (CTO) by mode of transportation, origin, and destination. Net CMIR outflows are represented by CTN=CTO-CTI.

The CMIR data system is the most comprehensive source of direct information on currency flows into and out of the US. It differs from the informal reports to the New York Federal Reserve in several important respects. CMIR records contain all reported currency inflows and outflows, including currency physically transported by currency retailers, non-financial businesses and individuals, and currency shipped by financial institutions specializing in wholesale currency transactions. The only transactions excluded are those that fall below the reporting requirements, direct shipments by Federal Reserve banks, and shipments that circumvent legal reporting requirements. [See 31 code of Federal Regulations 103.23(c)]. The CMIR data are thus more inclusive than the Federal Reserve (FED) informal series, which is limited to currency shipments to and from the New York Federal Reserve district by large wholesale bulk shippers.

Comparison of the estimated cumulative net outflows of US currency during the period spanned by each of the foregoing measures (1988-1994) reveals some important empirical differences. Informal FED reports (FSN) suggest that roughly $92.5 billion was added to foreign holdings, while the FR-160 proxy of net injections of $100 notes (NYN) suggests an $118.6 billion figure. The CMIR data as represented by CTN produce a much lower figure of $51.2 billion in cumulative net outflows. To track down the source of these important empirical discrepancies, we turn now to a detailed comparison of the conceptual differences in content and coverage among the three series.

Conceptual and empirical comparisons of direct measures of currency flows

Table 2 presents a conceptual comparison of coverage in the CMIR reporting system and the Federal Reserve informal system. The table reveals major differences in content and coverage between CMIR and FED currency flow data. To derive meaningful comparisons of information content in the two, we had to segregate total CMIR inflows (CTI)

Table 2: Content Comparison of CMIR and FED Currency Flow Reporting Systems

Characteristics	CMIR	Federal Reserve
Level of aggregation	Individual transactions	Aggregate transactions of wholesale bulk shippers
Number of records	2.3 million inflow records 300,000 outflow records	Approximately 62,000 records (7 years x 12 months x 8 banks x 93 countries)
Time periods	Monthly, 1977 - 1994	Monthly, 1988-1994
Private institutions	All reporting banks	Major New York banks
Federal Reserve banks	Not included	New York Federal Reserve
Retail currency dealers Non-financial firms Individuals	Reported cross-border currency transport ≥ $5,000 (pre-1980); ≥ $10,000 (1980-1994)	Not reported
Domestic coverage	Entire US (all Federal Reserve districts)	New York Federal Reserve Branch
Overseas coverage*	220 countries	93 countries

* The countries reported in the two data systems do not match exactly: differences reflect temporal name changes and different levels of country aggregation (e.g., United Kingdom vs England and Scotland). A separate comparison algorithm was written to resolve these difficulties and creates two country sets: those included in both the Federal Reserve and CMIR systems and those included in the CMIR system but not in the FED system.

and outflows (CTO) by mode of transportation.[15] An algorithm was therefore developed to aggregate the CMIR microdata into currency flows originated by wholesale bulk shippers and flows stemming from

---

15   To maintain the strict confidentiality of individual records in the CMIR data system, aggregations were performed at the offices of the US Treasury (FinCEN). Subsequent analysis was performed on the aggregated data. Since Federal Reserve banks are not required by law to file CMIR statements, the CMIR shipment series was augmented to include direct overseas currency shipments to and by the Federal Reserve Bank of New York. For a more refined breakdown of CMIR inflows and outflows by mode of transportation, origin, and destination, see Feige (1996).

Table 3: CMIR and Federal Reserve Currency Flow Notation

Mode of transportation	Wholesale bulk bank shipments	Physical transportation by individuals, currency retailers, and non-financial firms	Total
Gross Outflow Measures			
CMIR	CSO	CCO	CTO
FED	FSO	NA	NA
FED PROXY	NA	NA	NYO
Gross Inflow Measures			
CMIR	CSI	CCI	CTI
FED	FSI	NA	NA
FED PROXY	NA	NA	NYI
Net Outflow Measures			
CMIR	CSN	CCN	CTN
FED	FSN	NA	NA
FED PROXY	NA	NA	NYN

the physical transportation of currency by individuals, currency retailers, and non-financial firms.

Table 3 shows the notation used to describe alternative direct estimates of currency inflows and outflows. Total CMIR outflows (CTO) are divided into outflows originating from wholesale bulk bank shipments (CSO) and outflows physically transported by individuals, currency retailers, and non-financial firms (CCO).[16] Correspondingly, total CMIR inflows (CTI) are disaggregated into wholesale, bulk-shipped inflows (CSI) and physically transported inflows (CCI).

Since the Federal Reserve data are limited to wholesale bulk shipments, Federal Reserve recorded outflows (FSO) would be expected to be roughly comparable to CSO and, similarly, Federal Reserve recorded inflows (FSI) would be expected to be roughly comparable to the CSI

---

16 Non-financial firms include armoured carriers and travel transportation companies such as airlines and cruise ships.

derived from the independently collected CMIR data.[17] The FR-160 proxy flows (NYO, NYI, and NYN) cannot be disaggregated by mode of transportation; nor can we determine what fraction of net injections of $100 bills is used to satisfy overseas demand.

Table 4 shows the means of each of the quarterly flows in Table 3. Comparison of the mean Federal Reserve and CMIR inflow and outflow estimates reveals the CMIR data as considerably more inclusive than the FED. CMIR recorded average quarterly total currency outflows (CTO) exceed Federal Reserve recorded wholesale currency shipments (FSO) by some $1.39 billion per quarter. Similarly, CMIR recorded average total currency receipts (CTI) exceed Federal Reserve (FSI) wholesale currency receipts by $2.86 billion per quarter.

The finding that CMIR gross flows exceed Federal Reserve gross flows is to be expected because the CMIR data include the physical transportation of currency by individuals, currency retailers, and non-financial firms as well as currency flows with origins and destinations not included in the FED data. The asymmetry in the outflow and inflow discrepancies is due to the fact that individuals, currency retailers, and non-financial firms physically transport only 10 percent of reported total gross outflows but account for 31.8 percent of reported total gross inflows.[18] There is another reason for the discrepancy: though 82.9

17　The Federal Reserve database excludes currency shipments from or to the 11 non-New York Federal Reserve districts as well as shipments from or to countries other than those in the FED system. The FED data also exclude all inflows and outflows of currency physically transported by individuals or non-financial firms. Feige (1995, 1996) takes account of these finer distinctions.

18　The series on individual inflows and outflows appear to differ greatly from bulk shipments by financial institutions. There are two possible explanations for this significant disparity. The data for physical transportation by individuals include travel transportation companies such as airlines and cruise ships that generate US currency outside the US and regularly transport it back for deposit in their domestic banks. The discrepancy may also be due to differing levels of compliance with CMIR reporting requirements. Individuals transporting currency out of the country are not monitored as carefully by US Customs as individuals returning to the US. There may thus possibly be a lower rate of reporting compliance for physically transported outflows than for physically transported inflows.

Table 4: Direct measures of Quarterly Gross Currency Flows 1988-1994

Mean Quarterly Gross Outflow ($ millions)					
CCO	CSO	CSO*	CTO	FSO	NYO
724	6535	6015	7259	5869	6265

Mean Quarterly Gross Inflow ($ millions)					
CCI	CSI	CSI*	CTI	FSI	NYI
1729	3700	2765	5429	2567	2028

Mean Quarterly Net Outflow ($ millions)					
CCN	CSN	CSN*	CTN	FSN	NYN
-1005	2835	3250	1830	3303	4237

percent of wholesale bulk outflows originate in New York, only 50.9 percent of such shipments are returned there.

Given these differences in coverage, we find that the less inclusive Federal Reserve data understate gross outflows less than they understate gross inflows. This asymmetry in underreporting leads to an overstatement of net currency outflows in the FED data. This is even more strikingly true of the shipment proxy (NYN). Any conclusions derived exclusively from Federal Reserve data or from series closely correlated with FED data (such as NYN) are therefore likely to overstate net outflows and lead to the erroneous conclusion that foreign holdings of US currency have increased at a faster rate than is the case.

Table 4 also includes more refined measures of the CMIR flows that are conceptually comparable to the flows captured by the FED data system. CSO* represents CMIR gross reported bulk-shipped outflows originating exclusively from the New York Federal Reserve District and destined exclusively for countries included in the Federal Reserve's informal data collection system. Similarly, CSI* represents CMIR gross reported bulk-shipped inflows headed for the New York Federal Reserve District from countries included in the Federal Reserve data system. CSN* represents the corresponding net outflows (CSO*-CSI*). These adjusted flows are conceptually most comparable to the flows informally reported to the Federal Reserve.

When these refined CMIR measures (CSO* and CSI*) are compared with the conceptually comparable measures obtained from the FED data (FSO and FSI), they are, as expected, empirically compatible as well. The average discrepancy in estimated outflows of bulk shipments from the New York district (CSO* minus FSO) is $.15 billion per quarter and the corresponding discrepancy between comparable inflow measures (CSI* minus FSI) is $.20 billion per quarter. The comparable quarterly net outflow bulk shipment discrepancy (CSN* minus FSN) is only $.05 billion per quarter. CMIR and Federal Reserve data suggest that during the period 1988-1994, wholesale bulk currency shipments from New York resulted in a net cumulative outflow of between $92.1 (CMIR) and $92.5 billion (Federal Reserve). For the longer period covered by CMIR reports (1977-1994), cumulative net currency outflows in wholesale bulk shipments from New York amounted to $97.7 billion.

Table 5 presents the correlation matrix of quarterly inflows, out-flows, and net outflows for the period 1988-1994. Examining the relationship between alternate measures of net outflows, Table 5-C reveals that the Federal Reserve bulk shipment series (FSN) is very highly correlated with the proxy series of net injections of $100 notes in New York (NYN). As expected, both series have a much weaker relationship with the broader CMIR measure of all bulk shipments (CSN): however, the refined CMIR estimate of New York net bulk outflows (CSN*) is more closely related to the comparable FSN and NYN measures. This is confirmed when inflows and outflows are examined separately (Tables 5A and 5B).

We conclude that when comparable direct measures of inflows and outflows are examined, the CMIR data represent the most comprehensive and accurate estimate of bulk shipment activity to and from the New York district. Moreover, the CMIR data contain direct information on both bulk shipments and physical currency transportation that is not captured by either the Federal Reserve data or its New York $100 injections proxy. Table 5 reveals that the movements in the CMIR measures of physically transported currency (CCI, CCO) are virtually uncorrelated with the narrower New York bulk shipment measures. Indeed, as will be demonstrated below, the additional information contained in the more comprehensive CMIR measures tell a very differ-

Table 5A: Correlation Matrix of Quarterly Currency Inflows (1988:1-1994:4)

	CCI	CSI	CSI*	FSI	NYI
CCI	1.000	-0.109	-0.139	-0.158	-0.132
CSI	-0.109	1.000	0.987	0.924	0.904
CSI*	-0.139	0.987	1.000	0.954	0.935
FSI	-0.158	0.924	0.954	1.000	0.967
NYI	-0.132	0.904	0.935	0.967	1.000

Table 5B: Correlation matrix of Quarterly Outflows (1988:1-1994:4)

	CCO	CSO	CSO*	FSO	NYO
CCO	1.00	-0.001	-0.92	-0.171	-0.178
CSO	-0.001	1.000	0.983	0.925	0.916
CSO*	-0.093	0.983	1.000	0.945	0.946
FSO	-0.171	0.925	0.945	1.000	0.982
NYO	-0.178	0.916	0.946	0.982	1.000

Table 5C: Correlation Matrix Of Quarterly NET Currency Outflows (1988:1-1994:4)

	CCN	CSN	CSN*	FSN	NYN
CCN	1.000	0.384	0.197	0.190	0.137
CSN	0.384	1.000	0.904	0.654	0.579
CSN*	0.197	0.904	1.000	0.850	0.804
FSN	0.190	0.654	0.850	1.000	0.978
NYN	0.137	0.579	0.804	0.980	1.000

ent story from that suggested by the less comprehensive, New York-centred measures.

Direct CMIR estimates of total net currency outflows

Having demonstrated the close correspondence between the CMIR and Federal Reserve estimates of bulk-shipped inflows and outflows to and from the New York district, we now turn to direct CMIR estimates of other flows of US currency for which no other direct information source is available. These include:

- wholesale bulk shipments to and from Federal Reserve districts other than New York;
- reported currency physically carried into and out of the New York district; and
- reported currency physically carried into and out of other Federal Reserve districts.

Table 6 presents a breakdown of the key components of CMIR cumulative net outflows for different periods. The CMIR reports reveal that New York wholesale currency shipments resulted in a $92.1 billion cumulative net outflow of US currency during the period 1988-1994 as compared with a $5.7 billion net outflow for the decade 1977-1987. Wholesale shipments of currency to and from all other Federal Reserve districts produced a cumulative net currency inflow of $12.7 billion during 1988-1994 from $1.1 billion over the earlier decade.

Table 6: Direct Estimates of CMIR Cumulative Net Outflows ($ billions)

Period	Wholesale shipments New York	Wholesale shipments other	Carried New York	Carried other	All wholesale shipments	All carried	Net outflow
1977-1987	5.7	-1.1	-7.5	-33.9	4.6	-41.5	-36.9
1988-1994	92.1	-12.7	-2.7	-25.4	79.4	-28.2	51.2
1977-1994	97.7	-13.8	-10.2	-59.4	84.0	-69.6	14.4

CMIR reports are the only data source for currency transported by currency retailers, non-financial businesses, and individuals. These sources of physical currency transportation accounted for a cumulative net inflow of currency into the US of $28.2 billion in 1988-1994 and an even larger inflow of $41.5 billion in the previous decade. The combined estimates from all CMIR sources therefore suggest that cumulative net outflows of currency in the period 1988-1994 amounted to $51.2 billion and for the entire period 1977-1994, only $14.4 billion. It appears that failure to take account of physically transported currency and wholesale shipments from districts other than New York will lead to a serious overstatement of the amount of currency transferred abroad.

This conclusion is subject to several caveats. First, it is possible that the CMIR filing compliance rate is higher for currency physically transported by individuals entering the US than it is for currency physically transported by individuals leaving the US, since customs forms are routinely collected from incoming travellers only. The period 1988-1994 shows roughly nine inflow filings for every outflow filing. The average size of each inflow filing for physically carried currency was $39,000, whereas the average size of each outflow filing was $119,000.

The large average size of physically carried inflows and outflows suggests that most of these filings were probably made by currency retailers or non-financial businesses rather than individuals. Inflows mainly represent the physical transportation of currency consolidated from tourist centres and returned to the US by armoured carrier or courier: travel companies such as cruise ships, airlines, and hotel chains routinely collect small amounts of currency from outbound travellers and return these funds for deposit in the US. Businesses that regularly transport currency into and out of the US are aware of the legal filing requirements and liable to penalties if they fail to report. Individuals carrying large sums of currency into and out of the US, however, are more likely to file incoming rather than outgoing CMIR forms. A lower rate of outgoing individual filing compliance would impart a downward bias to physically transported net outflows. Without further analysis of the distribution of incoming and outgoing individual carriers, it is impossible to determine the magnitude of the bias.

Secondly, we must take account of currency flows that fall below the CMIR reporting requirement threshold. Unrecorded inflows include

US currency carried into the US by foreign travellers in amounts under $10,000. Similarly, unrecorded outflows include smaller amounts of US currency taken abroad by US travellers and net remittances of US funds sent abroad.

Unrecorded net outflows

Unrecorded net currency outflows from travel are estimated from data on total spending (net of air fares) in the US by foreign travellers and total overseas spending by US travellers going abroad. Net currency outflows from remittances are estimated as a percentage of net remittances sent abroad.[19]

We have estimated travellers' unrecorded net currency outflows falling below the filing threshold under two alternative scenarios. The first scenario (TR1) assumes that both foreign travellers to the US and US travellers to foreign countries make 20 percent of their purchases of goods and services with US currency and that 20 percent of net remittances are paid in US currency. The second scenario (TR2) assumes respective percentages of 20, 15, and 20. Since foreign travellers to the US will expect to make purchases with US dollars and typically have less access to credit cards than US travellers going abroad, the second scenario appears the more plausible.

Table 7 summarizes the assumptions underlying each of the scenarios and presents our estimates of cumulative net currency outflows below reporting requirements under each set of assumptions. The results suggest that for the period 1977-1994, cumulative unreported net currency outflows below the filing threshold ranged from $2.9 billion to $24.7 billion.

Estimating changes in the domestic stock of US notes

A change in domestic holdings of US banknotes outside the banking system (ΔN^d) can be estimated as the difference between the change in

---

19   The travel data were generously provided by the United States Travel and Tourism Administration, Washington, DC.

Table 7: Cumulative Unrecorded Net currency Outflows from Travel and Remittances ($ billions)		
Period	**Scenario 1**	**Scenario 2**
	Travel in, 20%; Travel out, 20%; Remittances, 20%	Travel in, 20%; Travel out, 15%; Remittances, 20%
1997 - 1987	18.9	10.2
1988 - 1994	5.8	-7.3
1977 - 1994	24.7	2.9

the total note stock in circulation with the public (ΔN) and the estimated change in overseas holdings (ΔN^o). Then,

$$(\Delta N^d) = (\Delta N) - (\Delta N^o) = (\Delta N) - (CSN + CCN + TR)$$

where CSN = net bulk shipments of currency abroad as reported on CMIR forms; CCN = net currency physically transported overseas by currency retailers, non- financial firms, and individuals as reported on CMIR forms; and TR = estimated unrecorded net currency outflows arising from travel and remittances falling below the filing threshold.

The stock of US notes in circulation with the public is calculated as the difference between the currency component of M1 minus coins in circulation. Net wholesale currency shipments (CSN) and net currency physically transported by currency retailers, non-financial businesses and individuals (CCN) are obtained from CMIR records. Unreported travel and remittance outflows (TR1 and TR2) are estimated from travel expenditure and remittance data as described in the previous section. All net outflows are assumed to be in the form of notes rather than coins.

Table 8 shows the allocation of net additions to the note supply for different periods under the assumption that a change in domestic holdings will equal a corresponding change in total holdings minus net outflows overseas. Using all available data, the results from direct measures of net currency outflows suggest that between 85.2 and 93.4 percent of the increase in the note stock between 1977-1994 was accounted for by increases in domestic holdings.

Table 8: Allocation of Net additions to Note Stock ($ billions)

Period	(ΔN)	CSN	CCN	TR1	TR2	(ΔN^{d}1)	(ΔN^{d}2)
1977-1987	110.6	4.6	-41.5	18.9	10.2	128.6	137.3
1988-1994	153.6	79.4	-28.2	5.8	-7.3	96.6	109.7
1977-1994	264.1	84.0	-69.6	24.7	2.9	225.0	246.8

Direct estimates of the share of US notes held abroad

Given direct estimates of net currency outflows and net additions to domestic stocks between 1977 and 1994, we can now simulate the current percentage of US notes held overseas, given alternative assumptions about the share of notes held abroad in 1977. Table 9 presents a range of estimates of the share of US notes presently held overseas for different starting values in 1977 and different combinations of measures of net outflows going abroad.

The results in Table 9 suggest that our estimates for US notes held abroad are sensitive both to CMIR estimates of physically transported

Table 9: Percentage of US Notes held Overseas, End 1994 (Alternative Estimates)

Estimated Outflows	1977=20%	1977=40%	1977=60%
CSN	25.5	29.8	34.1
CSN+CCN	4.8	9.1	13.4
CSN+TR(1)	32.9	37.2	41.5
CSN+TR(2)	26.4	30.7	35.0
CSN+CCN+TR(1)	12.6	16.4	20.7
CSN+CCN+TR(2)	5.7	9.9	14.2

currency and to various estimates of net travel and remittance outflows. On the basis of CMIR reports of wholesale shipments alone, the percentage of currency now held abroad ranges between 25.5 and 34.1 percent. However, the inclusion of reported net flows physically transported by currency retailers, non-financial firms, and individuals reduces the estimated range of overseas holdings to between 4.8 and 13.4 percent. The further addition of estimated unreported net currency travel and remittance flows that fall below the filing threshold produces a range of 5.7 to 20.7 percent.

If we entirely ignore the CMIR evidence on reported physical currency transportation but include estimates of unreported travel expenditures and remittances, we obtain an upper-bound estimate suggesting that between 26.4 and 41.5 percent of US currency is held abroad. The hypothesis that from 60 to 95 percent of US currency is held domestically contrasts starkly with evidence from surveys of US currency use that only 20 percent of US currency is so held.

In the light of the substantial range of estimated overseas holdings reflecting combinations of different components of overseas flow estimates, we now turn to the empirical relationship between the known change in the total stock of notes and empirical proxies for domestic and overseas changes. Let change in demand for domestic notes depend on change in domestic personal income (ΔPI) and the Federal Funds Rate (R). Change in overseas stock is measured by the various components of estimated currency outflows. Change in total note stock (ΔN) is represented as:

$$(\Delta N) = f(\Delta PI, R) + g(CSO, CSI, CCO, CCI, TR)$$

Table 10 reports the results of regressing the change in total stock of notes on determinants of the change in domestic note demand and CMIR measures of inflows and outflows. Change in personal income does not significantly affect change in note demand, but the Federal Funds Rate is significant and has the expected sign. All CMIR flow variables have the expected signs, although the coefficient for physically transported outflows is not significant, reinforcing the view that there may be a downward compliance bias in this component.

It is also noteworthy that the coefficient estimates of the flow variables suggest that only some fraction of each dollar of inflow or outflow effects the change in the total stock of notes held outside the

Table 10: Regression Estimates*

Dependent variable is change in total note stock, 1977:1 - 1994:4			
Variable	Coefficient	Std. Error	T-Statistic
ΔPI	0.0007	0.0015	0.493
FFR	-120.196	44.886	-2.739
CSO	0.778	0.067	11.572
CSI	-0.326	0.139	-2.350
CCI(-1)	-0.249	0.130	-1.913
CCO(-1)	0.208	0.254	0.819
TR2	1.398	0.855	1.634
C	3741.381	1893.149	1.976
AR(4)	0.873	0.078	11.217
MA(1)	0.561	0.118	4.756
MA(2)	00.629	0.120	5.249
Regression statistics	**R - squared**	**Durbin-Watson Statistic**	
	0.917	1.810	
*Heteroskedasticity Consistent Standard Errors and Covariances.			

banking system. This observation is consistent with the hypothesis that some recorded cross-border flows simply represent a transfer between domestic and overseas currency hoards that are held outside the international banking system. Such transfers would leave the total note stock unaffected. Our results suggest that this is more likely to be the case for physically transported currency than for bulk currency shipments.

Indirect methods of estimating foreign holdings of US currency

As will be demonstrated below, we are able to estimate the share of currency held overseas by a variety of indirect methods. Unlike the direct observations of reported currency flows discussed in the preceding sections, indirect methods require behavioral assumptions about domestic and overseas demand for US currency. Since the US government satisfies all domestic and overseas demand for its dollars, the total amount of currency outstanding is completely demand-determined.

Monetary demography model (MDM)

Consider the general demographic problem of estimating the proportions β_1 and β_2 of members in two sub-populations C_1 and C_2, which comprise the total population C, and X_1 and X_2 the corresponding measured characteristic in sub-populations C_1 and C_2. The average population characteristic X can be represented as a weighted average of the sub-population characteristics with the weights being the unknown proportions β_1 and β_2.

$$(1) \quad X = \beta_1 X_1 + \beta_2 X_2$$

Since $\beta_1 + \beta_2 = 1$, it follows that the proportions can be estimated from the measured characteristics:

$$(2) \quad \beta_1 = (X - X_2)/(X_1 - X_2)$$

$$\beta_2 = (X_1 - X)/(X_1 - X_2)$$

A meaningful solution for parameters β_1 and β_2 exists so long as the characteristics of the sub-populations are different ($X_1 \neq X_2$) and the calculated proportions lie between 0 and 1.

This demographic framework suggests a monetary demography model (MDM) capable of estimating the proportion of US currency held domestically (β^d) and the proportion held overseas (β^o). To estimate these unknown proportions, we require measures of characteristics of the overall US currency population and of its domestic and overseas components. Examples of measurable characteristics which might be employed to estimate the MDM are the age, quality, velocity, denomination, series or seasonal characteristics of the US currency population and its domestic and overseas sub-populations.

Given estimates of any currency population characteristic X and the corresponding domestic (X^d) and overseas (X^o) currency characteristics, the proportion of notes circulating domestically (β^d) can be estimated as:

$$(3) \quad (\beta^d) = (X - X^o)/(X^d - X^o)$$

MDM using age and quality characteristics

Applying general demographic concepts to currency populations leads naturally to a consideration of possible differences in the age and quality of denomination-specific notes circulating domestically and overseas. Estimates of the age, quality, and quality by age distributions of the corresponding domestic and overseas sub-populations were obtained from a special study conducted by the Federal Reserve.[20] Based on a sample of some 4 million individual notes, note quality was ascertained by recording light reflectivity measures from an optical densitometer that scanned individual notes during routine processing by high-speed sorting machines at the Federal Reserve banks in all 12 Federal Reserve districts.

Individual serial numbers were recorded for a subsample of approximately 150,000 domestic and returning overseas notes to determine the date when the Bureau of Engraving and Printing had sent each note to a Federal Reserve bank. An inventory model was then used to estimate the date when the note had actually been put into circulation, thereby establishing its date of birth. Each note's age was then determined as the difference between this date of birth and the date of sampling. For each denomination—$1, $5, $10, $20, $50, and $100—it was thus possible to construct univariate age and quality distributions for notes sampled domestically and notes returning from abroad.

Casual observation suggests that domestic notes are likely to be used predominantly as a medium of exchange, whereas overseas notes are more likely to be held as a store of value. Accordingly, it was anticipated that the univariate age and quality distributions of domestic and overseas notes and the corresponding bivariate quality by age distributions would differ greatly. Domestic notes sampled on their return to the Federal Reserve were expected to be relatively younger than notes coming back from abroad and generally of poorer quality for a given age. Considering these expected differences in domestic and

---

20   See the Federal Reserve Soil Level Impact Task Force (SLITF) study entitled "Comprehensive Assessment of US Currency Quality, Age & Cost Relationships" (1990).

overseas characteristics, age, quality, and quality by age distributions were thought to be promising characteristics for estimating the percentage of notes held overseas.

Surprisingly, analysis of the quality and quality by age distributions of the domestic and overseas samples revealed that they were not sufficiently different to yield robust estimates of percentages of notes held domestically and overseas. Initial efforts to estimate the MDM were therefore based on differences in univariate age distributions between overseas and domestic notes for each specific note-denomination population. Denomination-specific age distributions for the entire population were derived from FR-160 data on note births and deaths (redemptions) combined with estimates of average note lifetimes.

Given the age characteristics of the relevant populations, the problem is then to estimate the proportions of US currency circulating domestically (β^d) and overseas ($\beta^o = 1-\beta^d$) from the MDM(A) specified for each denomination as follows:

$$(4) \quad A = \beta^d A^d + (1-\beta^d) A^o,$$

$$\text{and } \beta^d = (A - A^o)/(A^d - A^o)$$

where A, A^d, and A^o respectively represent the denomination-specific age distributions for the total, domestic, and overseas note populations. Estimated percentages of notes of different denominations circulating abroad in mid-1989 were then obtained from estimates of the notes' overall, domestic, and overseas age distribution.[21]

Table 11 presents the resulting denomination-specific estimates of percentages of banknotes held overseas. The MDM(A) estimates for age distribution characteristics suggests that between 45.8 and 53.0 percent of the US currency stock was held overseas in 1989: 68.3 percent in large-denominations—$100s and $50s; approximately 28 percent in

---

21   The estimates for the $1, $5, $50, and $100 denominations are averages from Baselines 1 and 2 of the SLITF study (n. 20). The Baseline 1 model for the $10 denomination and the Baseline 2 estimates for the $20 denomination failed to converge, requiring significant outliers to be deleted from the samples. We therefore report a range of estimates for these two denominations. The similarity of the age distributions for overseas and domestic notes suggests that the reported results are likely to be imprecise.

Table 11: Estimates of the Demographic Model: MDM(A) age distribution characteristics

Denomination	Overseas share in 1989 (%)	Notes in circulation ($ billions)	Value of notes overseas, 1989 ($ billions)	Denomination composition of overseas notes (%)
	(1)	(2)	(4)	(5)
$1	35.7	4.0	1.4	1.6
$5	37.6	5.0	1.8	2.1
$10	19.3 - 35.0	10.3	2.0 - 3.6	4.0
$20	49.0 - 69.3	54.7	21.9 - 37.9	24.1
$50	45.3	26.3	11.9	13.1
$100	51.1	98.2	50.1	55.2
Total	45.8 - 53.0	198.3	89.2 - 106.8	100.0

mid-sized denominations—$20s and $10s, and 3.6 percent in small denominations—$5s and $1s.

MDM using seasonality, series and coin/note ratio characteristics

Porter and Judson (1995) employ several variants of the MDM to estimate the proportion of US currency held overseas by exploiting assumed differences in seasonality, series, and coin/note ratio characteristics of domestic and overseas US currency holdings.

Since the seasonal characteristic of the total US currency population (S) is directly measurable while the seasonal characteristics of the domestic (S^d) and foreign (S^o) stocks are unobservable, Porter and Judson assume that for the period 1947-1994, seasonal variations in domestic US currency holdings are identical to the observed seasonal pattern for the Canadian currency supply.[22] They further assume no significant seasonal component in foreign demand for US currency, so that the seasonal characteristic of overseas US currency holdings (S^o) can be

---

22 The assumption is justified by the argument that the US and Canada have similar currency denomination structures and that the Canadian dollar is rarely used overseas.

Table 12: Estimates of the Demographic Model: MDM(S) annual seasonal characteristics

Denomination	Overseas share in 1989 (%)	Notes in circulation, 1989 ($ billions)	Value of notes over seas, 1989 ($ billions)	Denomination composition of overseas notes (%)
	(1)	(2)	(3)	(4)
$1	10.0	4.0	0.4	0.3
$5	54.2	5.0	2.7	2.2
$10	44.2	10.3	4.5	3.7
$20	59.1	54.7	32.3	26.1
$50	50.7	26.3	13.3	10.7
$100	72.0	98.2	70.6	57.0
Total	62.4	198.3	123.9	100.0

assumed to be equal to unity. The seasonal variant of the MDM(S) can then be estimated with the equation:

$$(5) \quad S = \beta^d S^d + (1 - \beta^d) S^o$$

where the seasonal characteristics are time-dependent and $S = S^{US}$, $S^d \approx S^{CAN}$, and $S^o \approx 1$. From (3), it follows that the domestic share of currency holdings (β^d) is estimated as:

$$(6) \quad \beta^d = (S - 1)/(S^d - 1)$$

Table 12 presents Porter and Judson's reported estimates of the denomination-specific share of US currency held overseas in 1989. The denomination-specific MDM(S) yields an overall estimate of 62.4 percent as compared with the 45.8 to 53.0 percent range obtained with the age characteristic model. The MDM(S) results suggest that 67.8 percent of foreign holdings are in large denominations, with 29.7 and 2.5 percent in mid-sized and small denominations respectively.

A second variant of the MDM exploits differences in the series composition characteristics (SR) of domestic and overseas notes to estimate percentages of $100s and $50s circulating abroad. In 1991, the Federal Reserve introduced a 1990 series note which was distinguished from the pre-1990 notes in circulation by a polyester strip and micro printing to frustrate counterfeiters. Let the series characteristic (SR) be the proportion of the circulating note population (N) made up of new 1990 series notes (N^{90}) so that:

$$(7) \quad (SR) = N^{90}/N.$$

The series composition of the total currency population is known, but the domestic and overseas components are not. Porter and Judson assume that the series composition of overseas notes is adequately proxied by an estimate of the series composition of notes processed by the New York Federal Reserve, and that an estimate of the series composition of the notes processed by all other Federal Reserve banks adequately reflects domestic composition.[23] The MDM(SR) can then be represented as:

$$(8) \quad SR = \beta^d SR^d + (1-\beta^d)SR^o$$

where $(SR) = N^{90}/N$ is known and, by assumption, $SR^d \approx SR^{\text{Non NY}}$ and $SR^o \approx SR^{NY}$.

The proportion of notes held domestically can then be estimated as:

$$(9) \quad \beta^d = (SR - SR^o)/(SR^d - SR^o)/$$

$$\approx (SR - SR^{NY})/(SR^{\text{Non NY}} - SR^{NY})$$

Porter and Judson use two different procedures for estimating domestic and overseas series characteristics. Table 13 presents their upper- and lower-bound estimates for the $50 and $100 denominations.

A third MDM variant uses the ratio of coins to notes as the characteristic distinguishing domestic from overseas currency holdings. The coin/note ratio of the total US currency population is directly observable: it remains to identify the coin/note ratio of domestic and overseas holdings. The domestic coin ratio is proxied by Canada's coin/note ratio, and the overseas ratio is zero with virtually no US coin held overseas.

---

23 Porter and Judson claim that almost all currency sent to and received from abroad is processed by the New York Federal Reserve Bank. The veracity of this assumption can be tested by an examination of CMIR data disaggregated by Federal Reserve district of origin and destination. The CMIR data reveal that only 52 percent of all reported currency inflows for the period 1977-1994 had the New York Federal Reserve District as their point of destination. The New York district was reported as the point of origin for 85 percent of total outflows during the period.

Table 13: Estimates of the Demographic Models MDM(SR) and MDM(C/N)
series and coin ratio characteristics

Denomination	Series model (% overseas, 1994) lower bound	Series model (% overseas, 1994) Upper bound	Series model (% overseas, 1994) average	Coin Ratio (% overseas, 1989)
	(1)	(2)	(4)	(5)
$1-20	NA	NA	NA	NA
$50	28.0	48.0	38.0	NA
$100	55.6	70.7	63.2	NA
Total	NA	NA	NA	20.9

Let C/N represent the population ratio of coins to notes, $(C/N)^d$ the domestic coin ratio, and $(C/N)^o$ the overseas coin ratio. If β^d represents the fraction of US currency held domestically, then it follows from equation (1) that the MDM(C/N) can be represented as:

$$(10)\ (C/N) = \beta^d (C/N)^d + (1-\beta^d)\ (C/N)^o$$

By assumption, $(C/N)^d \approx (C/N)^{CAN}$ and $(C/N)^o \approx 0$. Therefore, (10) reduces to:

$$(11)\ \beta^d = (C/N)/(C/N)^{CAN}$$

As shown in Table 13, the MDM(C/N) estimates 20.9 percent of US currency held abroad in 1989. This estimate falls within the range of estimates obtained from the CMIR data.[24]

To test the robustness of the Porter and Judson MDM(S) results, we reestimated the model with the X11 ARIMA method for calculating the multiplicative seasonal component of notes in circulation for the US and

---

24   The reported results included an adjustment of the coin/note ratio to take account of the introduction of a $1 coin in Canada in July, 1987. The Bank of Canada continued to issue $1 banknotes until June 30, 1989, at which time there were 246 million $1 coins in circulation. By the end of 1989, the number of $1 coins in circulation had risen to 464 million. The reported results are based on a time series forecast of what the coin/note ratio would have been in the absence of the introduction of the $1 coin.

Canada.[25] Our reestimate of the MDM(S) confirms the Porter and Judson finding that the model is incapable of producing sensible monthly or quarterly estimates. Indeed, monthly and quarterly estimates of the overseas share of US currency reveal a strong seasonal component, suggesting that the assumption that ($S^{o} \approx 1$) may be unsustainable. Even annual time series estimates of overseas share obtained from the annual average of monthly seasonal components are quite different from Porter and Judson's result with their seasonal amplitude metric of the difference between the December and February seasonals.

Figure 6 presents the Porter/Judson time series of estimated overseas share, MDM(S):DEC-FEB, and the corresponding estimate based on average monthly seasonal components: MDM(S):Monthly Average. The figure also includes the range of 1989 point estimates from the age characteristic model, MDM(A1) and MDM(A2), the overseas shares derived from the coin ratio model, MDM(C/N), and the average share of $100 notes obtained with series characteristic model MDM(SR).

As shown in Figure 6, the monetary demographic models produce a wide range of estimates of the overseas share of US currency and different temporal patterns for change in overseas holdings. Given the diversity of these results and the strong assumptions required to pro-

---

25 Porter and Judson obtained their seasonal components by applying the STL seasonal adjustment procedure to the currency component (coin plus notes) of the Canadian and US M1 series. In our replication, we used the X11 ARIMA procedure on the Canadian and US notes in circulation series, since neither Canadian nor US coins are assumed to circulate overseas.The results reported by Porter and Judson are based on the ratio of seasonal amplitudes of the US and Canadian series, derived by taking the difference between the December and February seasonals (Porter and Judson, 1995, pp. 16-17). Our replication suggests that the results are relatively insensitive to the use of different seasonal adjustment procedures and the substitution of the note series for the currency component series. However, the time series estimates of the share abroad is quite sensitive to the use of the seasonal amplitude metric employed by Porter and Judson. In particular, when the MDM(S) is estimated on a monthly or quarterly basis and the estimated monthly or quarterly overseas share are estimated as the ratio of each of the seasonal components minus one as suggested by equation (6), the estimated monthly and quarterly shares abroad fluctuate wildly within a year, often yielding estimates of the share abroad that exceed 100 percent.

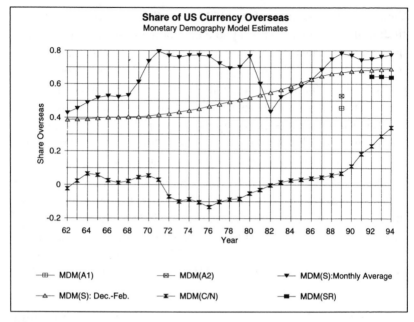

Figure 6

duce them, it is difficult to view them with much confidence. The age characteristic model required the elimination of sample outliers before convergence could be obtained. The coin ratio model produces negative overseas shares for the period 1972-1982, and the seasonal characteristic estimates yield implausible results at monthly and quarterly frequencies. Both the seasonal and serial characteristic models require strong assumptions concerning unobserved domestic and overseas characteristic specifications. Given these difficulties, we turn to some alternative approaches for estimating the share of US currency held abroad.

Note ratio models

The Note Ratio Model (NRM) provides an alternative means of indirectly estimating the currency percentage held abroad. The known amount of US notes in circulation (N) can be broken down into unknown quantities of notes in domestic and overseas circulation (N^d and N^o). Let Z denote any scale variable assumed to affect the demand for notes. Then:

$$(12)\, N/Z = N^d/Z + N^o/Z$$

As with the MDMs, we assume that the domestic US ratio (N^d/Z) can be proxied by the same ratio in Canada, so that:

$$N^d/Z \approx (N/Z)^{Can}$$

Substituting the Canadian ratio $(N/Z)^{Can}$ into equation (12), multiplying through by Z and dividing both sides by N yields a solution for the unknown fraction of notes overseas (β^o):

$$(13)\, (\beta^o) = N^o/N = [N - (N/Z)^{Can}.Z)]/N$$

The simple note ratio model (NRM) is estimated for several variants where Z alternatively represents:

- personal consumption expenditures (PCEs),
- personal disposable income (PDI), or
- population (POP) x the Consumer Price Index (CPI).

Figure 7 presents the estimated share of US currency held overseas obtained from each variant of the note ratio model: NRM(PCE), NRM(PDI), and NRM(POP). The results suggest that the overseas share

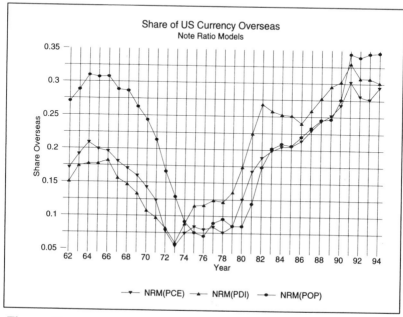

Figure 7

Table 14: Correlation Matrix of Indirect Annual Estimates of Overseas Currency Shares, 1962-1994

	MDM (C/N)	MDM (S)	MDM (S-PJ)	NRM (PCE)	NRM (PDI)	NRM (POP)
MDM (C/N)	1.000	0.079	0.601	0.879	0.744	0.835
MDM (S)	0.079	1.000	0.393	-0.136	-0.026	-0.301
MDM (S-PJ)	0.601	0.393	1.000	0.678	0.864	0.231
NRM (PCE)	0.879	-0.136	0.678	1.000	0.916	0.828
NRM (PDI)	0.744	-0.026	0.864	0.916	1.000	0.552
NRM (POP)	0.835	-0.301	0.231	0.828	0.552	1.000

declined for almost a decade between the early 1960s and early '70s, then rose significantly over the following two decades. The peak in overseas holdings appears to have come in 1990, when roughly 30 to 35 percent of US notes in circulation are estimated to have been held abroad. The time series of estimated shares of overseas currency derived from the NRMs are markedly lower than the results from the seasonal MDM and higher than the MDM(C/N) results.

Table 14 presents the correlation matrix of overseas currency share estimates obtained by each of our indirect methods. This matrix shows relatively close correlations among all the NRM estimates and the MDM(C/N) estimate. Comparison of the MDM(S) estimate with the MDM(S-PJ) estimate reveals that the two alternative methods of computing the seasonal estimates yield very different results. The correlation between the two seasonal estimates is only .393, suggesting that the model is quite sensitive to the arbitrary choice of a metric. The MDM(S) shows low and negative correlations with the other estimates, whereas the smoothed MDM(S-PJ) series displays positive correlations with the others.

Indirect estimates of net outflows of US currency

Given the wide range of overseas share estimates produced by our various models, we now turn to estimate the net currency outflows implied by each of the MDM and NRM variants. Given the known total stock of notes in circulation and indirect estimates of the share of

Table 15: Correlation Matrix of Annual Indirect Estimates of Net Outflows of Currency Overseas: 1962-94

	MDM (C/N)	MDM (S)	MDM (S-PJ)	NRM (PCE)	NRM (PDI)	NRM (POP)
MDM (C/N)	1.000	0.884	0.859	0.770	0.660	0.872
MDM (S)	0.884	1.000	0.990	0.793	0.732	0.853
MDM (S-PJ)	0.859	0.990	1.000	0.791	0.758	0.847
NRM (PCE)	0.770	0.793	0.791	1.000	0.726	0.763
NRM (PDI)	0.660	0.732	0.758	0.726	1.000	0.769
NRM (POP)	0.872	0.853	0.847	0.763	0.769	1.000

currency abroad, we can develop year-end estimates of the total stock of currency held abroad.[26] The difference in these estimated year-end overseas stocks yields estimates of annual net outflows of currency from the US.

Table 15 shows the correlation matrix for estimated net outflows derived from each of the indirect methods. The net outflow estimates from the different models appear to be more highly correlated than the share estimates, suggesting that the indirect methods may produce more accurate estimates of outflows than shares abroad.

Comparing direct and indirect estimates

Table 16 summarizes the cumulative net outflows for different periods as estimated by direct and indirect methods. For the period 1977-1994, cumulative outflows obtained with NRMs fall within the range produced by summing CMIR bulk shipments and unreported travel and remittance outflows. The two significant outliers are the CMIR estimates of the sum of reported bulk shipments and reported physically transported currency (CTN) and the MDM(S-PJ) estimate. The CTN estimate puts cumulative net outflow for the period at only $14.4 billion, while the MDM(S-PJ) estimates a cumulative outflow of $209.0 billion.

---

26   Throughout the analysis, we assume that all US coin is held domestically.

Table 16: Cumulative Net Outflows of US Currency ($ billions)

	CSN	CTN	CSN + TR1	CSN + TR2	C/N	PCE	PDI	POP	MDM (S-PJ)
1977-1987	4.6	-36.9	23.5	14.8	16.8	35.5	37.2	36.7	90.9
1988-1994	79.4	51.2	85.2	72.0	113.1	67.0	51.5	74.5	118.1
1977-1994	84.0	14.4	108.7	86.8	129.9	102.4	88.7	111.2	209.0
1962-1994	NA	NA	NA	NA	122.2	103.9	93.5	108.8	235.0

Two hypotheses may explain the divergence between the indirect methods and the direct methods that include physically transported currency flows. The first stems from the possibility already mentioned of a downward compliance bias in reported CMIR outflows of physically transported currency. In such a case, physically transported outflows will be underestimated and so will the share of US currency held abroad. An alternative hypothesis is that physically transported net currency flows represent offsetting changes between domestic and overseas currency hoards that do not affect the total currency supply. Since each of the indirect methods is based on changes in the total currency supply, these methods would be incapable of reflecting currency hoard shifts from overseas to the US. While such hoard shifts do affect the

Table 17: Estimated Percentages of Currency Abroad: 1976 = 30%

Dec. 31	CMIR1*	CMIR2*	CSN	CTN	C/N	PCE	PDI	POP	MDM (S-PJ)
1976	30	30	30	30	30	30	30	30	30
1980	22	20	25	20	24	29	31	24	42
1985	6	2	18	-2	22	30	32	30	56
1990	14	8	26	3	27	35	37	37	66
1994	18	11	31	11	45	37	33	40	69
*CMIR1 = CCN+CSN+TR1 and CMIR2 = CCN+CSN+TR2									

Table 18: Estimated Percentages of Currency Abroad: 1994 = 30%

Dec. 31	CMIR1*	CMIR2*	CSN	CTN	C/N	PCE	PDI	POP	MDM (S-PJ)
1976	79	106	21	110	-36	-3	17	-11	-133
1980	60	80	20	83	-25	6	22	-7	-83
1985	32	43	15	40	-11	15	26	9	-29
1990	32	35	24	31	6	25	33	23	10
1994	30	30	30	30	30	30	30	30	30

*CMIR1 = CCN+CSN+TR1 and CMIR2 = CCN+CSN+TR2

proportion of currency held abroad, they will not affect the total stock. If we accept this interpretation, indirect measures will overestimate the share of currency held abroad.

To test the sensitivity of the estimated percentage of US currency held overseas, we turn now to the implications of the alternative estimates of net outflows to different beginning and terminal assumptions about this percentage. Table 17 presents percentage estimates based on different net currency outflows and assuming that 30 percent of US currency was held abroad at the end of 1976. Table 18 presents percentage estimates that reflect the assumption that the terminal share of currency at the end of 1994 was 30 percent.

The starting assumption that 30 percent of US currency was abroad in 1976 leaves us with a range of estimates of 11 to 69 percent for the current situation. All estimated percentages except the CTN result are within the permissible 0-100 range. However, when a terminal share of 30 percent abroad is assumed, only CMIR1, CSN, and PDI yield estimates within the permissible range. What these simulations reveal is that the alternative estimates have a "knife edge" characteristic in the sense that plausible temporal estimates exist only for narrow ranges of terminal conditions. The full CMIR direct estimates give plausible results only for terminal conditions in the 20 to 25 percent range, whereas the NRMs give plausible estimates for terminal conditions between 35 and 50 percent. The MDM(S-PJ) yields plausible results only for terminal conditions in the range of 60 to 80 percent.

Composite estimates

Given the diversity of indicators of unknown net flows of currency overseas, we will now combine these measures to obtain a single estimate based on all available information. One approach here is to use a factor analysis model to estimate the common signal or latent variable (L_t) associated with different indicators of net overseas currency flow (M_{it}). In the factor model

$$(14) \quad M_{it} = \delta_i L_t + \varepsilon_{it}, \, (i = 1, 2, \dots N)$$

each of the M_i indicators of net outflow[27] is linearly related to the latent common factor (L_t). The δ_is represent the factor loadings and the ε_{it} are the temporal measurement errors in each of the N measures of net currency outflow. The latent factor L_t is computed as a weighted average of the observed indicators with the weights constrained to sum to unity.

Since different estimates of net outflows are available for different time periods and different frequencies, we estimated several factor models for both annual and quarterly frequencies to test the stability of our results. The variables used and periods covered by these estimates are described in Table 19.

Figure 8 shows maximum likelihood estimates of annualized net outflows as derived from each of the foregoing factor models. The

Table 19: Factor Model Specifications

Factor Model	Period	Variables
Annual Model AF(1)	1962-1994	NRM(PCE); NRM(PDI); NRM(POP); MDM(C/N); MDM(S); TR2
Quarterly Model QF(1)	1961:1-1994:4	NRM(PCE); NRM(PDI); NRM(POP); MDM(C/N)
Quarterly Model QF(2)	1977:1 -1994:1	CCN; CSN; NYN; NRM(PCE); NRM(PDI); NRM(POP); MDM(C/N)

---

27 A general discussion of factor analysis models can be found in Mulaik (1972). Bollen (1989) contains a review of factor analysis in the context of latent variables.

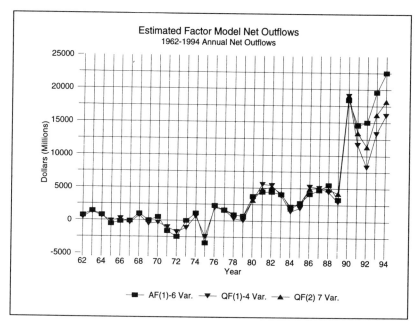

Figure 8

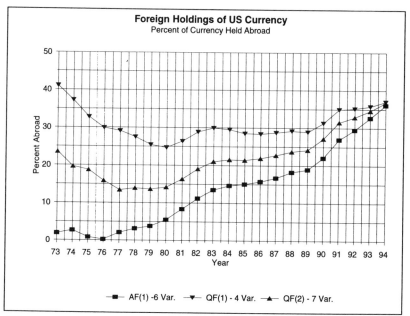

Figure 9

temporal patterns are broadly similar in all estimates, which suggests a rising level of net outflows during the decade of the 1980s and a significant upward shift in net outflows during the early '90s associated with increased use of US currency as a co-circulating medium of exchange in Eastern Europe and the newly independent republics of the former Soviet Union. The seven-variable annual factor model AF(1) produces the highest estimated net outflows for recent years, while the four-variable quarterly model QF(1) produces the lower-bound net outflow estimates.

Simulations employing the factor model outflows for different beginning and terminal values reveal that the most plausible estimate of the share of US notes presently held abroad is roughly 40 percent, which implies that something like 36 percent of all US currency (notes plus coin) is held abroad. Using this current value, Figure 9 displays the implied time series of the share of currency held overseas between 1973 and 1994 for each of the factor model net outflow estimates.

Implications for the domestic unreported economy

These provisional estimates of overseas dollar holdings suggest that earlier currency ratio model estimates of the unreported economy were erroneous in assuming that the entire stock of US currency was held domestically. We are now able to reestimate the currency ratio models with our new alternative estimates of the domestic US currency stock.

Figure 10 displays estimates of total unreported income obtained from a GCR model using alternative factor model estimates of the domestic US currency stock. Figure 11 shows GCR estimates of unreported income as a percentage of AGI.

Total unreported income appears to have grown secularly until 1985, declined briefly around the time of the 1986 tax reform, and then peaked in 1991. The temporal pattern of the alternative GCR estimates of unreported income as a percentage of AGI tell essentially the same story. Unreported income appears to have grown rapidly from 1966 and peaked as a percentage of AGI in 1980. The percentage of unreported income then declined until 1987, rose again until 1991, and fell again to a level approximating levels last observed in the early 1970s.

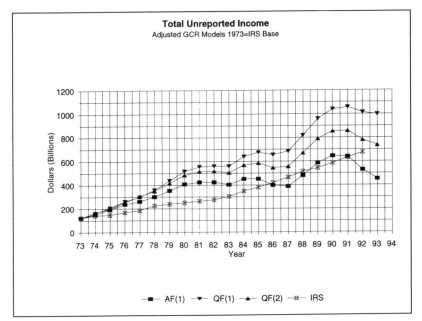

Figure 10

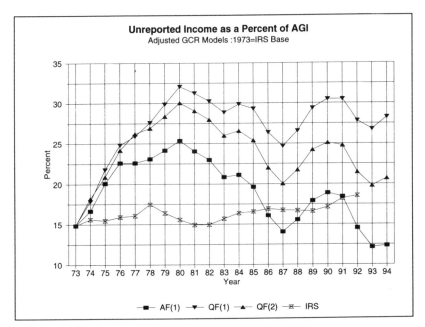

Figure 11

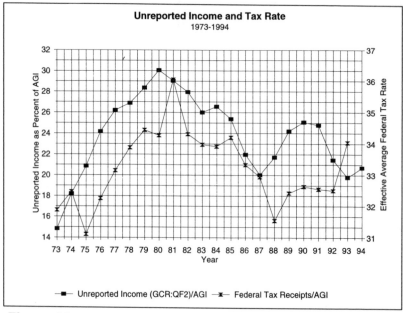

Figure 12

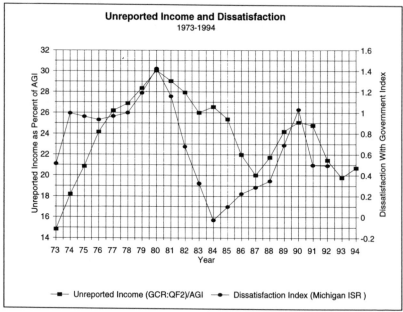

Figure 13

Of the three factor model estimates of the domestic currency supply, the QF(2) may be the most reliable, being based on quarterly frequencies and the largest amount of direct and indirect information concerning net currency outflows. Employing the QF(2) estimates in the GCR model suggests that total unreported income in 1994 was roughly $700 billion, or approximately 20 percent of AGI.

The main conclusion to be drawn from these revised estimates of unreported activity is that once account is taken of foreign US currency holdings, the range of uncertainty about the magnitude of unreported income is substantially reduced. The difference between the unadjusted GCR estimates of unreported income and the IRS estimates for 1992 amounted to more than $400 billion. The revised estimates in Figure 10 reveal that the difference between the IRS and the QF(2) estimates is now reduced to roughly $100 billion.

Figure 11 reveals that unreported income as a percentage of AGI varies considerably over time. The two most plausible explanations for these fluctuations are changes in average tax rates and variations in levels of dissatisfaction with government.

Figure 12 shows the relationship between the QF(2) revised estimates of unreported income as a percentage of AGI and the average effective federal tax rate, and Figure 13 displays the relationship between unreported income and an index of dissatisfaction with government.[28] As we can see in the first of these figures, tax evasion does appear to rise in response to higher average taxes and fall when incentives to cheat are reduced by lower rates. Similarly, Figure 13 confirms the expected relationship between tax evasion and level of dissatisfaction with government. The dramatic fall in the level of dissatisfaction with government between 1980 and 1984 coincided with a drop in the relative level of tax evasion. Conversely, increases in the level of dissatisfaction

---

28   The average effective federal tax rate is simply the sum of federal government tax receipts divided by AGI. The dissatisfaction with government index is constructed as an equally weighted average of three normalized indices representing answers to the University of Michigan's Institute for Social Research (ISR) surveys on whether government officials can be trusted, whether they are crooked, and whether the government is wasting taxpayers' money. I am indebted to the ISR for providing the underlying data.

with government observed in the later 1980s are associated with a relative surge in evasion. It seems that when taxpayers perceive their public representatives as dishonest and see benefits from their tax dollars decline, they are more likely to engage in tax evasion.

The finding that a substantial portion of US currency is held overseas provides a partial resolution of the currency enigma. It will be recalled that Federal Reserve surveys showed that US households admit to holding only 12 percent of the nation's currency, firms account for roughly 3 percent, and the unreported economy employs about 4 percent. We now find that another 35 to 40 percent is held abroad and believe that the percentage held domestically is larger than admitted.

Porter and Judson (1995), who place considerable emphasis on the MDM(S-PJ) and MDM(SR) results, have suggested that as much as 50 to 70 percent of US currency is held abroad. We are more inclined to believe that surveys of currency usage are subject to self-selection and underreporting biases which result in a substantial understatement of the actual amount of currency held at home. Whether these domestic cash hoards are derived from underground activities that we continue to underestimate or from legitimate activities that are simply underrecorded in our NIPA accounts remains to be resolved.

Our overseas finding raises another monetary puzzle. Are foreign holdings of US currency being used solely as a store of value or do they function as a co-circulating medium of exchange? An investigation of the age and quality of a large sample of individual banknotes (Feige, 1994b) suggests that the age/quality distributions of domestically circulating notes and notes returning to the US from abroad are quite similar. This suggests that the average velocity of domestically held currency is not that different from the velocity of currency held abroad. If foreign US currency holdings circulated at the same rate as US household holdings, they would generate a flow of annual cash payments approaching the size of the United States GDP.

Thus, the partial resolution of the currency enigma for the US merely creates another monetary anomaly for the rest of the world. The world economy appears to subsume a US-sized unrecorded economy which employs US currency as its medium of exchange. This global currency enigma deepens when we consider that our revised estimates of US per-capita currency holdings are still modest compared with the per-capita currency holdings of other developed European and Asian nations. The missing currency problem is not limited to the US dollar: it extends to other major currencies, most importantly the German mark and the Japanese yen.

Conclusion

In an effort to mitigate uncertainty about the size of the domestic underground economy, we have examined a variety of measures of net US currency outflows to determine what percentage of US currency is held abroad and thus the amount of US currency circulating in the domestic economy. While alternative methods of estimating overseas US currency holdings still yield a wide range, we conclude that the most plausible estimates are in the range of 25 to 45 percent. Given the importance of forming a more accurate estimate of the domestic US money supply, both for the purpose of gauging the size of the domestic underground economy and for more refined monetary policy analysis, it seems necessary to continue research into the matter of the precise amount of US currency held domestically and overseas.

The introduction in 1996 of a newly designed US currency series with modern counterfeit protection provides a unique opportunity to establish a currency census system which, like the population census, would aim at precision concerning amounts of US currency circulating domestically and overseas. A currency census system would not require the burden of human reporting: all necessary information on banknote life cycles could be electronically captured as notes are routinely and anonymously processed by high-speed sorting machines at the times of their issue and return to the Federal Reserve banks. A currency census system would fully preserve the anonymity of currency use by individuals and firms while maintaining automated records of a note's age, quality, birthplace, location, and final redemption. Such a system would provide the data required to construct currency migration matrices and all other demographic characteristics of the note population.[29] In short, the establishment of a currency census system would provide us with reliable estimates of the domestic money supply and so enhance our ability to conduct domestic monetary policy.

References

Abt Associates (1984), "Unreported Taxable Income From Selected Illegal Activities": US Government Printing Office, September 1984, p. 62;112.

Anderson, P. (1977), "Currency in Use and in Hoards," in *New England Economic Review*, Federal Reserve Bank of Boston, March/April, pp. 21-30.

Avery, R.B., G.E. Elliehausen, A.B.Kennickell, and P.A. Spindt (1986), "The Use of Cash and Transaction Accounts by American Families," in *Federal Reserve Bulletin*, vol. 72 (February 1986) pp. 87-108.

——————— (1987), "Changes in the Use of Transaction Accounts and Cash from 1984 to 1986," in *Federal Reserve Bulletin*, vol. 73 (March 1987), pp. 179-196.

Bollen, K.A. (1989), *Structural Equations with Latent Variables*: New York, John Wiley and Sons.

Cagan, P. (1958), "The Demand for Currency Relative to Total Money Supply," in *Journal of Political Economy*, vol. 66 (August), pp. 303-28.

Carson, C. (1984), "The Underground Economy: An Introduction," in *Survey of Currency Business*, US Department of Commerce–Bureau of Economic Analysis, vol. 64, no. 5, (May and July).

Federal Reserve System (1990), *A Comprehensive Assessment of the U.S. Currency System, Quality, Age and Cost Relationships*: Federal Reserve System, 1991.

Feige E. L., ed. (1989), *The Underground Economies: Tax Evasion and Information Distortion*: Cambridge, Cambridge University Press.

---

29 The application of demographic theory and methods to currency populations is developed in Feige (1990b), which includes estimates of age-specific currency mortality and survival rates. Feige (1994b) presents a full demographic model describing the life cycle of the individual note and the dynamics of note populations and cohorts.

——— (1990a), "Defining and Estimating Underground and Informal Economies: The New Institutional Economics Approach," in *World Development*, vol. 18, no. 7 (July), pp. 989-1002.

——— (1990b), "Currency Velocity and Cash Payments in the US Economy: The Currency Enigma," Department of Economics, University of Wisconsin-Madison, unpublished.

——— (1994a), "The Underground Economy and the Currency Enigma," in *Public Finance and Irregular Activity*, Werner W. Pommerene, ed., supplement to *Public Finance/Finances Publiques*, vol. 49 (1994), pp. 119-136.

——— (1994b), "The Cash Payment System: Monetary Demography," report prepared for the Board of Governors of the Federal Reserve System and the Financial Crimes Enforcement Network.

——— (1995) "The Cash Payment System: The International Migration and Location of US Currency," Report prepared for the Board of Governors of the Federal Reserve System and the Financial Crimes Enforcement Network.

——— (1996), "Overseas Holdings of US Currency and the Underground Economy," in Susan Pozo, ed., *Exploring the Underground Economy*: W.E. Upjohn Institute for Employment Research, Kalamazoo, Michigan.

Gutmann, P. (1977), "The Subterranean Economy," in *Financial Analysts Journal*, vol. 33 (November/December 1977), pp.24-27.

Internal Revenue Service (1977), "Estimates of Income Unreported on Individual Tax Returns," Department of the Treasury Publication 1104 (9-79), Washington, DC.

——— (1981), "Study of the Information Returns Program": Department of the Treasury, Internal Revenue Service, Research and Operations Analysis Division, Washington, DC (July).

——— (1983), "Income Tax Compliance Research": Department of the Treasury, Washington, DC (July).

——— (1988), "Income Tax Compliance Research": supporting appendices to Publication 7285, Department of the Treasury, Internal Revenue Service, Research Division Publication 1414 (7-88).

——— (1990), "Income Tax Compliance Research–Net Tax Gap and Remittance Gap Estimates": Department of the Treasury,

Internal Revenue Service, Research Division Publication (1415 (4-90).

Krueger, Russell and Ha, Jiming (1995) "Measurement of Co-Circulation of Currencies," working paper 95/34, International Monetary Fund.

Laurent, Robert (1974), "Currency in Circulation and the Real Value of Notes," in *Journal of Money, Credit and Banking*.

Muliak, S.A. (1972), *The Foundations of Factor Analysis*: New York, McGraw-Hill.

Porter, R. (1993), appendix to "Nominal Income targeting with the Monetary Base as Instrument: An Evaluation of McCallum's Rule": Federal Reserve Board, Finance and Economics Discussion Series, Working Study No. 1.

Porter and Judson (1995), "The Location of U.S. Currency: How Much is Abroad?": Board of Governors of the Federal Reserve System, unpublished.

Reuter, Peter (1996) "The Mismeasurement of Illegal Drug Markets," in Susan Pozo, ed., *Exploring the Underground Economy*: W.E. Upjohn Institute for Employment research, Kalamazoo, Michigan.

Summer, S. (1990), "The Transactions and Hoarding Demand for Currency," in *Quarterly Review of Economics and Business*, vol. 30, no. 1 (Spring 1990), pp. 75-89.

Sprenkel, C. (1993), "The Case of the Missing Currency," in *Journal of Economic Perspectives*, vol. 7, no. 4 (Fall 1993), pp. 175-184.

The Underground Economy in Britain

John Burton

Public disquiet versus academic quietude

There is a yawning gulf in Britain between the public perception of the underground economy on the one hand and the academic and official evaluations of this phenomenon on the other.

It is impossible to open either a tabloid or a serious newspaper in the UK without reading about various aspects of the underground economy that range from the nefarious, often murderous activities of crack cocaine dealers through benefit fraud and moonlighting to the ongoing growth of the theft industry.

UK newspapers, like media everywhere, report these matters because they are of consuming public interest. We now have an immense volume of personal and anecdotal evidence on the underground economy. Everyone in the UK knows of—and commonly deals with—"cash only" entrepreneurs, be they window cleaners, builders and painters, or small business people. With disgruntlement, everyone in Britain will talk about their experience of burglary over recent years, and more and more commonly, the car theft they have suffered.

Given this widespread public interest and concern about the underground economy in contemporary Britain, it might be assumed that there are plenty of up-to-date estimates of its size. Such, however, is not the case. There was a flurry of research in the first half of the 1980s attempting to quantify the British underground economy, and which harked back to earlier decades, particularly the 1960s and 1970s.[1] Since that time, however, academic economic interest in the topic seems to have disappeared entirely.

This is probably not due to genuine lack of interest: economists are reputed to be human beings and must at least occasionally be aware that the rest of the British population are very much concerned about these matters. In fact, the decline or disappearance of up-to-date research on the UK underground economy is more probably due to the difficulties and frustrations of this particular field. The studies published in the first half of the 1980s used a wide variety of techniques to quantify the phenomenon and came up with a wide variety of estimates, ranging from a low of 3 percent of UK national income (Dilnot and Morris, 1981) to a high of 22 percent (Feige, 1981). Others, using yet other techniques, came up with figures that fell somewhere in between, such as 14 percent (Matthews and Rastogi, 1985).

It does seem that no particular strategy for estimating the size of the underground economy was able, in the studies of early 1980s vintage, to demonstrate a convincing "win" over other approaches. Apparently this is still the case even today. There also appears to be a quietly deployed rule of thumb in the contemporary economics profession that "if you can't (convincingly) estimate something, it is best to ignore it." More charitably, it may be that British economists recognize that the task of estimating the significance of the underground economy is, like the quest for the Holy Grail, likely to be without conclusion.

---

1   For surveys, see Heertje, Allen, and Cohen (1982); S. Smith and S. Wied-Nebbeling (1986); and Pyle (1989)

The 7.5 percent solution

In this contemporary academic vacuum concerning the extent of the UK underground economy, a sort of conventional wisdom has emerged that it is in the order of around 7.5 percent of UK national income.

The history of this magical figure bears some recounting. In 1979, Sir William Pile, a former chairman of the Board of Inland Revenue giving evidence to the British House of Commons Expenditure Committee, estimated the possible extent of tax evasion at something like 7.5 percent of UK national income. Neither Sir William nor the Inland Revenue, at that time or any subsequent time, has ever presented any methodology or basis for this particular figure. As Matthews and Rastogi would comment (1985, p. 21):

> A cynic might be forgiven for thinking that the figure of 7.5 percent is a particularly comfortable one. It is large enough to cause official concern and warrant further manpower resources to the Inland Revenue. However, it is not so large that it would give the impression that the Board of Inland Revenue is not effective in this area.

The Conservative Party *Election Manifesto* of 1979 pledged that an incoming Conservative government would review the powers of both the Customs and Excise and Inland Revenue departments. This had been a matter of considerable public disquiet during the 1970s—especially among Britain's small traders—following the passage of the Finance Acts of 1972 and 1976 that gave the taxing agencies extensive powers of search.

In July 1980, having gained office in late 1979, the new Conservative government of Mrs. Thatcher announced the establishment of a Committee on Enforcement Powers of the Revenue Departments under the chairmanship of Lord Keith of Kenkel, subsequently known as the Keith Committee. This inquiry began publishing its conclusions in 1983, eventually issuing four volumes with a total of some 1,378 pages.

The Association of Her Majesty's Inspectors of Taxes gave evidence to the Keith Committee in April 1981 (*Keith Report*, 1983, n. 41). The tax inspectors accepted that the size of the black economy (tax evasion component) was "debatable," but once again plumped for the 7.5 percent figure as probably correct. In all its deliberations, the Keith Committee failed to consult or discuss any other estimate of the UK underground economy apart from one by a Central Statistical Office employee (Macafee, 1980). It grandly ignored the application of Feige's transactions approach to the UK situation as it did all other work by academic economists on this issue. The only "evidence" referred to in the Keith Committee's published report is the Sir William Pile "guesstimate" noted above.

The outcome of all this was that "the [Keith] Committee eventually announced that it felt 7.5 percent was probably the level of unofficial activity in the country" (Heertje et al., 1982, p. 63). Thus, by a process of bureaucratic reiteration combined with selective avoidance of alternative views, the idea that the tax evasion component of the UK underground economy stands at or around 7.5 percent of British national income was to become entrenched as the semi-official view (Matthews and Rastogi, 1985, p. 21).

This figure—which seems to have been plucked out of thin air—has taken tenacious hold and survives to this day as the most commonly quoted statistic of the "probable" size of the UK black economy. In early 1994, for example, the *Economist*, a journal not normally given to much truck with official figures when it is discussing the size/growth of the UK formal economy, quoted a 7.5 percent figure to represent the UK black economy as a percentage of GDP. We can only presume that on this occasion the *Economist*—possibly lacking, like the rest of us, any better ideas—decided to plump for the convenient, conventional "wisdom."

Reflections

If—and that is a very big "if"—we were to accept the "semi-official" figure of 7.5 percent of UK GDP as representing the extent of tax evasion in the late 1970s and early '80s, two observations follow.

In the first place, the total size of the UK underground economy would have been very considerably larger than this, as the Pile guesstimate referred only to what Feige (1993) calls the "unreported economy." The full underground economy—or what Smith and Wied-Nebbeling (1986) call the "shadow economy"—also includes the "illegal economy" (drug trafficking, alien smuggling, theft, fraud, arson, prostitution) and the "self-service economy" involving housework, DIY home repairs, gardening, child care, volunteer work for charities and clubs, informal aid to friends and neighbours, etc.

This full underground economy may also be taken to include what I have elsewhere called the "grey economy" (Burton, 1993) composed of economic activities that may be largely captured in the national income figures but which are either technically illicit or else stand in a grey area legally. An example of the latter in the Britain of the early 1980s was the substantial volume of Sunday trading conducted in England and Wales in contravention of the 1950 *Shops Act*.

Finally, there is a "very good question"—in the absence of up-to-date quantitative studies—as to how the underground economy has waxed (or waned) in the UK since those times. The writer's somewhat subjective impression as a Briton is that the UK underground economy is even more extensive now than it was in the 1970s and '80s.

Frey and Weck-Hanneman (1984), in their "soft-modelling" approach to the black economy, suggest four major determinants of underground activity:

- the burden placed on individuals by both taxation and regulation,
- the extent of tax morality,
- the incentives to black economy activity created by unemployment, and
- the level of economic development.

On the first three of these counts, incentives to participation in black economy activity have probably multiplied in the UK over the past two decades.

Taxation and regulation: while some significant cuts in the marginal rate of income taxation were made in 1988, the overall burden of British taxation went up under Mrs. Thatcher in that decade from approximately 41 percent of GDP at factor cost to 43 percent. This trend continued as sharp tax increases were introduced in 1994.

There was much talk of deregulation during the Thatcher years, but the practical realities were very modest, one example being the deregulation of bus transportation. There has also been an enormous pile-up of regulation coming into Britain at the behest of the Brussels Eurocracy. It is impossible to quantify this tidal wave—suffice it to say that the "curvature" of British cucumbers is now under EC regulation (Boyfield, 1993).

Tax morality: there is no time-series UK evidence on this. The writer's impression is that there has not been any remarkable surge in British tax morality over the past 15 years: if anything, we have seen the reverse.

Unemployment: the measured British unemployment rate at the time of the conference was a sliver under 10 percent of the workforce. This may be a low figure compared with some other European countries— Spain has averaged 18 percent over the last decade—but it is high by UK standards from the 1960s or '70s. Many more people may be being pushed into the black economy than, say, in the seemingly halcyon '60s. Unlike previous postwar recessions, this one includes a large contingent of redundant managerial/professional workers, many of whom have turned to "self-employed consulting," an activity notorious for under-reporting income to the tax authorities.

The illegal economy: there can be little doubt that the illegal economy component of the underground economy has grown significantly in Britain over the past two decades, notably in such areas as car theft, burglary, and drug trafficking. The last pursuit got a boost with the completion of the Internal Market on January 1, 1993. The Internal Market features a new British Customs "blue channel" through which most travellers from the EC pass without a check. It is estimated that 65 percent of illegal drugs enter Britain from other EC countries.[2]

All in all, it would seem that the Frey/Weck-Hanneman determinants of black economy activity have been on the increase in the UK over the past decade. It will not be surprising to find, when up-to-date economic studies are eventually undertaken, that the UK's underground economy proves to be significantly larger than it was at the end of the 1970s.

---

2   "One expert estimates that the [UK] street price of cocaine, having stayed at about £70 a gramme for several years, has fallen to £65 over the past six to nine months, a sign that there is more of the stuff about." *The Economist*, "Crime Without Punishment," June 26, 1993, p.27.

References

Boyfield, K. (1993), *The Regulated Society*: London, Aims of Industry.

Burton, J. (1993), *Whither Sunday Trading?*: London, Institute of Economic Affairs.

Burton, J. and Parker, D. (1991), "Rolling Back the State?: UK Tax and Government Spending Changes in the 1980s," in *British Review of Economic Issues*, vol. 13, no. 31 (October), pp. 31-66.

Dilnot, A. and C.N. Morris (1981), "What Do We Know About the Black Economy?" in *Fiscal Studies*, vol. 2, pp. 58-73.

Economist (1994), "Working in the Shadows," February 12, p. 81.

Feige, E. (1981), "The UK's Unobserved Economy," in *Journal of Economic Affairs* (July), pp. 205-213.

Frey, B.S. and H. Weck-Hanneman (1984), "The Hidden Economy as an 'Unobserved' Variable," in *European Economic Review*, vol. 26, pp. 33-53.

Heertje, A., M. Allen, and H. Cohen (1982), *The Black Economy*: London, Pan Books.

Keith Report (1983), The Committee on Enforcement Powers of the Revenue Departments: London, HMSO, Cmnd 8822, 9120, and 9440.

Macafee, K. (1980), "A Glimpse of the Hidden Economy in the National Accounts," in *Economic Trends* (February), pp. 81-87.

Matthews, K. and A. Rastogi (1985), "Little Mo and the Moonlighters: Another Look at the Black Economy," Liverpool Research Group in Macroeconomics *Quarterly Economy Bulletin*, vol. 6, no. 2, pp. 21-24.

Pyle, D.J. (1989), *Tax Evasion and the Black Economy*: London, Macmillan.

Smith, S. and S. Wied-Nebbeling (1986), *The Shadow Economy in Britain and Germany*: London, Anglo-German Foundation for the Studies of Industrial Society.

The Size and Some Effects of the Underground Economy in Mexico

Raymundo Winkler

Mexico's Underground Economy

The Mexican informal economy is very extensive. According to estimates by the Centre for Economic Studies of the Private Sector, the informal economy in Mexico represents, depending on the method employed, between 25 percent and 35 percent of the formal gross domestic product. The first Mexican study on this subject was conducted by the Centre in 1988, and since then many other studies have been done by both independent researchers— that is, people who do not work for the government—and universities. These studies produced similar results to those of the Centre even though different and finer approaches were used. In general, the methods employed were the monetary approach and the input of generalized use—namely, electricity consumption. More recent studies have focussed on surveys of various kinds with similar results.

The most recent estimates, including our reestimate, show that the global size of the informal economy as a proportion of GDP has never surpassed 35 percent, even though there has been a clear increase in these activities in the main cities. This contrasts with the trend observed over the past two decades, when the informal economy rose very fast—from 10 percent in 1970 to 30 percent in 1988. This could be explained by the recovery of the Mexican economy that began in 1989: it might also be due to the fact that the informal economy has a natural limit to its expansion because of the limited size of the total consumer market and, above all, because many informal companies find that in certain circumstances of size or scale it is necessary to enter the formal economy looking for, say, credit, a better-educated labour force, and other vital services.

As expected, the main causes of the informal economy found in most of the studies were the typical ones: higher taxes, excessive government regulation of economic activities, corruption, and bureaucracy. In Mexico's case, the job shortage during the last decade also markedly influenced the creation of a highly informal economy.

The initial reaction of the Mexican government to these studies was very skeptical, and there was a refusal to see them as worthy of attention. However, during the last few years the government has begun to conduct surveys among the population engaged or employed in informal activities and has also put some measures into effect to attack the underlying causes of the informal economy, especially tax evasion.

According to the national statistical agency, the population engaged or employed in the informal sector numbers 4.5 million people or 22 percent of the labour force. Based on estimates of productivity in that labour force as well as perceived income and sales, the Mexican statistical agency guesses that the underground economy amounts to only 10 percent of recorded gross domestic product. Most of the independent studies show that this figure clearly understates the real size of the informal economy. Nevertheless, this acknowledgement represents a sea change in the attitude of the Mexican government compared to its previous denial of the existence of this phenomenon, and in any case, 10 percent of GDP should be considered a significant proportion.

At the same time, the official figures contradict, or are incompatible with, the numbers the government collects on underemployed people in Mexico. Although the open unemployment rate in Mexico is just about 3.5 percent, the official underemployment rate is 25 percent of the labour force—more than 5 million people. It is felt that practically all that population is engaged in informal activities that do not pay taxes.

Some effects

Some of the main impacts of the informal economy are the following:

- A high level of tax evasion, which means a big loss of fiscal revenues: this dictates a need to get higher taxes from a reduced number of contributors or taxpayers. The top marginal tax rate for individuals, 35 percent, is reached by people earning no more than US $8,000 a year. This situation tends to feed back into informal activities and/or tax evasion, creating a vicious circle.
- Statistical distortions: for economists, analysts, and for the government itself, it is difficult to know what is really going on with such matters as the actual size of the economy, its growth rate, inflation performance, employment, unemployment, income and expense levels, income distribution, international trade (mainly imports), and so on. The actual effects of some macroeconomic policies are anybody's guess.
- Contraband: this activity has been estimated at US $15 billion for 1993, equivalent to 30 percent of the total amount of Mexico's imports in that year.
- The informal participants are both strong and unfair competitors for formal market participants. According to some surveys carried out by CEESP among almost 500 companies located in several Mexican cities, between 30 and 40 percent of producers and retailers consider that the informal economy has a big presence in their markets and that they have been partially or totally wiped out of markets by informal business. The formal companies say that this problem is as acute as the phasing-out problem produced by legal imports that is associated with

opening up the economy to international trade. According to them, trade liberalization and the informal economy are the main problems they are facing as they attempt to generate higher growth rates in production and sales.

- Another important impact is that, due to the fact that the informal economy is a refuge for many unemployed workers, this sector exerts upward pressure on wage levels.

Strategies to combat the informal economy

The Mexican government has undertaken a series of measures to diminish the informal economy that include reducing administrative procedures and general taxes for both individuals and companies and a remarkable effort to punish tax evaders. Law enforcement in this area has recently been very strong—some would say Draconian. However, it has not been enough: participants in the informal economy still continue to think that the perceived risk is not high enough to offset the benefits they can obtain from their informal activities. For millions of people in Mexico, the informal economy does still pay.

The enforcement drive of the Mexican tax authorities has had some dramatic results. The number of active federal taxpayers—as distinct from those considered captive because they work for a formal company which collects their taxes and remits them to the tax authorities—grew from 1.5 million people in 1988 to almost 5 million in 1993. Tax collection has shown an average annual growth rate of more than 8 percent since 1988. This has reduced tax evasion and improved the public finances but, as already mentioned, it has not necessarily reduced the size of the underground economy. At best, the government measures may have contributed to somewhat arrest the expansion of the informal economy.

Conclusion

The underground economy in Mexico is very big compared with what is reported for industrialized nations but fairly "normal" in terms of standards for developing countries. Its causes are similar to those found in most of the industrialized world, but in Mexico the high unemployment rate, and specifically the underemployment rate, play a very important role in determining its size.

The Mexican government has at least begun to acknowledge the existence of this economy and its impacts, and as a result is attacking some of its main causes. For Mexico, this represents an encouraging change of attitude on the part of the government.

The informal economy is a big challenge for formal economic participants, a strong competitor with such cost advantages as less taxes and non-compliance with regulations.

Even though opening up the Mexican economy to legal imports could mean reduced cost-attractiveness for contraband, many products still offer advantages. One important aspect is that the informal economy is becoming the most effective way of distributing products that get into the country through dumping practices. These include clothing, footwear, old machinery, and a host of other products.

What are the prospects for the Mexican informal economy? Well, this sector is one of the very few in Mexico that can look forward to a marvellous future. It will continue to provide a refuge for millions of people who cannot finds jobs in the modern sectors of the formal economy.

The Mexican economy in the context of NAFTA will be looking mainly for a skilled workforce. For unskilled workers, their destiny will be the informal economy and/or emigration to other countries. Certainly the NAFTA will create jobs, but not immediately in the numbers needed to absorb the more than 1 million people annually entering the Mexican labour market.

The Growing Importance of Informality and Possibilities for Integration

Enrique Ghersi

Introduction

Despite the fact it represents a historical problem, its deep causes lie in the countries legal structure and some of its most outstanding aspects have made it very visible during the last few years, only recently has informal economy has become a topic for debate. Nevertheless, in a very short time a new intellectual discipline has developed, so called "informology."

What is informality?

Before analyzing the informal economy, we should define its concept, thus there isn't unanimity regarding it's definition.

The International Labour Organization (ILO) and the Regional Employment Program for Latin America and the Caribbean (REPLAC) understand informality as related to economic activity scale: for them, informality is synonymous to small business.

We find this concept essentially inaccurate. Any definition on economic activities quantitative aspects is bound to be altogether arbitrary, as no objective measure exists to tell the difference between big and small. Economic activity scale is an effect and not a cause: therefore we cannot consider that it defines informality—rather, it is one of its multiple consequences. The small business definition is also inadequate to explain existing qualitative differences. For example, there are more economic differences between a small business that is duly registered, pays its taxes, and is protected by the law, and a small one that is not, than between a midsize company and a small business.

On the other hand, the classic anthropological literature which specializes in this subject identifies "informal" with "marginal." This seems to imply that informal activities are performed as a means of survival or a last resort, which seems to be a criterion of verification more than a definition. Now since, according to research carried out by the ILO itself, informality in our country involves at least 48 percent of the economically active population and 61.2 percent of man/hours worked, it cannot be said that informal workers are marginal. On the contrary, the real marginal individuals are more likely to be the ones commonly considered "formal."

Taking all these difficulties into account, the ILO has tried to develop a concept of informality that conforms more closely to what actually exists in our country. Briefly, this concept considers as informal those economic activities which use illegal means to achieve legal objectives. It is very probable that the people directly involved in such activities, as well as the society in general, are better off if the law nominally applicable is infringed rather than complied with.

It is not the individuals who are informal, but their activities. Informality is not a specific, static sector, but an indefinite borderline with a considerable frontier of contact with legality where individuals take refuge when the costs of complying with the laws exceed the benefits. Thus understood, informality is nothing but an analytical concept that refers us to concrete cases where economic agents cannot abide by government regulations even if they do adapt to socially accepted behaviour.

This criterion applies both to activities that we could call classically informal—street trading, for example—and to the duly recorded production of the formal factories and even the process of informal urbanization, which is typical to emerging small towns or housing associations and cooperative organizations.

Quantifying informality

It was estimated in 1984 that informality in Peru covered 48 percent of the economically active population engaged full-time. However, should part time informals be considered—that is, people who, like "pirate" cab drivers or occasional street vendors, devote only part of the working day to these occupations? With them included, informality would account for an estimated 61.2 percent of total man/hours worked in the country.

Informality also contributes with a highly significant volume both of goods produced and of services rendered in the Peruvian economy. In 1984, informal activity produced the equivalent of 31.7 percent of total GNP. Since a substantial part of it is not considered by official statistics, we estimate that GNP was undervalued by 18.4 percent, This means that in 1984 we were 18 percent wealthier thanks to the informal workers, nevertheless we didn't know it.

Informal housing

This category covers all provisional settlements either acquired, urbanised, or built without abiding by or even against legal provisions, which may eventually benefit from a system of administrative exception to allow them some form of official acceptance. We include here the so called shanty towns, marginal neighbourhoods, emerging small towns, shelters, "popular urbanizations of social interest" (UPIS), urban expansion areas, marginal provisional settlements, municipal provisional settlements, housing associations, and cooperative organizations.

Among all existing houses in the capital city in 1982, 42.6 percent belonged to informal marginal settlements, 49.2 percent to the formal sector, and the remaining 8.2 percent to the poorest sections located in former "formal" areas. Measured in terms of people, these informal settlements have provided lodging to 47 percent of Lima's population. It is estimated that an additional 20 percent lived in the poorest sections, that is in areas of much misery within traditional urban sites, and that only the remaining 33 percent lived in what could be considered formally fit urbanizations. Even so, these indicators cannot reflect the immense proportion of cases in these urbanizations where applicable rules and regulations for accommodations or construction had not been complied with.

Beyond their unquestionable social importance, the informal settlements also have significant economic importance. In 1984 again, to calculate the value of the real property located in such settlements, each house was appraised separately. According to this appraisal, the total value of the informal settlements amounted to $8,319.8 million, equivalent to 69 percent of Peru's external longterm debt.

What is also remarkable about all this is that the value was generated by the informal occupants themselves with no aid or investment provided by the state. As evidence of its significance we only need to say that during the same period when these informal settlements developed—between 1960 and 1984—the state spent only $173.6 million in housing projects: that is only 2.1 percent of what the informals had invested with their own efforts.

Informal trade

Informal trade includes all commercial activities that take place without abiding by or in defiance of the official provisions nominally regulating it. Such activities comprise the ones conducted out in the public road—street trading—and the ones occurring in markets built especially to keep business off the street.

Despite the fact that it is considered to be the informal activity par excellence, official figures on street trading in Lima are unsatisfactory. The only count ever done by the government dates back to 1976 and was based on a limited sample which, given the features of the current crisis, could be used as valid. This made it necessary to take new counts in 1985 and 1986, when the population engaged in street trade and their main specializations were recorded.

As of January 1986, then, 91,455 street vendors were counted throughout the city, distributed in 79,020 stands at a rate of 1.16 per stand. Of the total number of stands, 59.5 percent were selling foodstuffs; 17.5 percent were selling articles for personal use, 13.7 percent, services and 9.3 percent, home and office supplies.

Apart from their social importance, their economic significance was also determined. According to an income survey carried out in 1985, the street traders gross sales totalled $322.2 million a year, which made the per-capita income derived from this activity 38 percent higher than the minimum legal remuneration. Obviously, an unqualified individual would have found it economically much more attractive to work in street trade than to try for a job at the minimum wage.

As for the second type of informal trade, the trade that takes place in informally built markets, it was found that Peru's capital city counted with 274 of these markets as compared with only 57 erected by the state, and that these markets were occupied by some 38,897 individuals who used to be street vendors, distributed in 29,693 stands at an average of 1.31 per stand. These informal markets had an appraised value of $40.9 million.

Informal transportation

Probably the economic activity with the highest index of informality in Lima is urban transportation. This has been the case since at least 1930, when a big strike of group passenger transport drivers paralyzed the city. Since 1965, when the old private bus companies went bankrupt, the growth of informality in this area has been constant. This particular universe has two clearly defined levels. The first, of higher relative legality, is composed of minibus and cab drivers who have government permits in the form of concessions; the second, of lower relative legality, is formed by minibus drivers and "pirates" or provisional cab drivers who conduct their activities without permits.

As to numbers, if we consider minibuses and buses, informality accounts for 91.4 percent of the service: if the universe is expanded to include small group transportation by automobiles and taxis, the informality percentage reaches no less than 94.8 percent. We should consider, however, that these figures will have varied more recently to reflect the government's decision to accept "rural station wagons"—a regulatory euphemism for "pirate" minibuses. The replacement value of this fleet amounts to $620 million, to which $400 million should be added for infrastructure—gas stations, mechanics' garages, and other facilities.

Informal industry

Informality continues to predominate, at least in the same activities where it was already significant according to a study conducted by the UN. Leading categories are shoemaking, apparel manufacture, and furniture. Lima is estimated to have about 8,000 companies engaged in the manufacture of clothing and 2,000 shoe workshops, 90 percent of which have not been registered. At least 85 percent of wooden and metallic furniture originates in informal industries that sell both to the public and to legally approved companies that affix their own trade-marks to it.

Possible causes of informality

The underlying cause of informality in Lima can be identified as the formal systems inadequacy to meet the needs of the emerging popula-tion. This can be clearly seen in at least two specific instances.

The migrant who leaves the countryside to come to the city is not a neutral economic agent. He needs access to economic opportunities, not only a job but also housing, transportation, commerce, and in general anything he may need. Given the national ruling tradition, however, there is no easy access. The fact that someone wants to sell in a market, build a house, make fit a piece of land, or start a business or industry does not mean that he can just go ahead and do it. First he should obtain licences: he should pass through the screen of the law—and this repre-sents the first step of confrontation between the individual and the institutional system. In our attempt to identify the causes of informality, we shall refer to this first step as the cost of access to formality.

Our second specific instance is once access has been obtained. Our individual wants to do something—build a house, provide a service, work in an industry or in commerce— but he cannot go outside the law to operate officially. His conduct is supposed to be conditioned by the institutional system. Taxes should be paid, the law complied with, job stability respected, concessions obtained, and buildings must be subject to the very particular requirements of the National Rules and Regulations for Construction. Thus, it does not suffice to obtain legal access: legality should be maintained. We will call this second phase, "costs of permanence" within formality.

To quantify these costs, a simulation was conducted in 1984 to cover all the steps required to legally constitute a small clothing workshop on the central highway. The goal was to go through the whole process like any citizen, without either technical information or professional advice and with an eminently honest purpose. Consequently, it was decided not to pay any graft to expedite the procedure.

The final result was that 289 days were required to get the 11 permits required at a total cost of $1,231 between expenses actually disbursed and loss of profits. Graft was demanded about ten times and had to be paid on two occasions: thus, in spite of compliance with regulations, bribery to some officials could not be avoided.

To verify whether the problem might be universal, the experiment was repeated in Tampa, Florida, USA, where it was discovered that processing the legal founding of a small clothing workshop took only three hours. The astounding difference between these results requires no further comment, except that they apparently reflect the two countries' levels of development.

For obvious reasons, no simulation could be undertaken for housing, and we decided to study actual legal files. As a result, it was found that the formalities for adjudicating, making ready, and obtaining construction licences—all of which were required for the use of an uncultivated lot owned by the state—take an average of 80 months and involved no fewer than 207 different administrative steps even with the intervention of the President of the Republic. The sole cost of awarding the land to an average residents' association amounted to about $2,156 dollars per member, 52 times the minimum legal remuneration in force at the time of the estimate.

The case of retail trade turned out to be equally pathetic. Costs of access to a formal store and a supply market were examined, since these represent the two most common options for this activity. In the first case, a simulation indicated that the formalities for opening a small grocery store take about 43 days at a cost of $600. As for the second possibility, study of five actual cases revealed that the formalities for legally building a market last an average of 18 years.

In the case of transportation, the matter is much simpler but at the same time dramatic, as there is no access at all. To work in this service, a person has to invade and then either demand or negotiate politically for legal admittance. Only when the transporters have been formally admitted they are allowed to participate in the bidding that is so ostentatiously called for by the municipality.

As to the costs of permanence within formality, these have been found, based on a sample of 50 small industrial businesses, to represent 347.7 percent of their profit after taxes and 11.3 percent of their production costs. Some 21.7 percent of the costs of permanence go in taxes, 72.7 percent are related to labour and bureaucratic expenses, and the remaining 5.6 percent represent costs for the use of utilities. All of this suggests that taxation is a much less important factor than it is commonly considered to be in defining the formality or informality of businesses. Instead, the state-imposed labour and bureaucratic costs for maintaining businesses under protection account for the bulk of our costs of permanence.

Thus, the causes of informality can be determined by examining the costs of access and permanence in various economic areas. The mechanism is simple: given that people are inclined by nature to do what is cheapest and avoid that which is most expensive, compliance with the law—materially speaking—depends on whether its costs are lower than its benefits. Individuals making this evaluation will naturally pursue their own objectives and not those of the state.

If the costs of access are such—considering the onerosity, delays, and other difficulties involved in formality—that they either become unaffordable for people with fewer resources or exceed the benefits of legal access, people will decide to remain in informality. Likewise, if the costs of permanence exceed the benefits of formality, people decide to opt out of the circuit despite having joined it: that is, they decide to go back to informality.

This explains why there are two specific types of informal workers: those who never joined the circuit because they could not afford the costs of access, and those who, having entered, leave it because of the high costs of permanence.

On the other hand, it must not be disregarded that informality has its own costs, in many cases especially high or dangerous, given the significant negative externalities affecting such activities as street trading or popular transportation. These costs of informality—the cost of lack of legal protection, the cost of being unable to apply to the courts, the cost of not having access to credit, the cost of lack of insurance, the cost of invasion, the cost of grafting and bribery, the cost of the definition of property rights, the cost of insecurity in contracts, etc.—are precisely those which argue the need to face the problem of informality as the principal one which the country is currently undergoing.

There is no doubt that modifying the institutional system will improve the effectiveness of the economy to the extent that it reduces its costs. Modification has become indispensable, given the high level of social pressure and frustration that these circumstances cause.

Some alternatives

Frequently, the problem raised by all these circumstances is summed up in the following dilemma: should informal workers be formalized, or should the formal workers become informal?

The dilemma is spurious: it is not convenient to have economic activities going on that do not meet the legal requirements at all, given the considerable costs and incitement to violence that this condition represents. Clearly, whatever is done on behalf of informal workers should benefit formally established activities. Establishing regimes of exception for the exclusive benefit of informal workers would have consequences as harmful to the country's economic organization as reviving the eradication of idolatries.

One alternative that suggests itself is to reduce the costs of access. Since illegality is generally the consequence of difficulties to cope with legal access to the market, it would appear mandatory to lower such access costs. To that effect, a deregulation program would be set up to remove all the hindrances that limit or prevent access to economic activities.

Obviously, deregulation would favour not only new businesses but also existing ones, since it guarantees fast movement of production factors and, as a result, the adequate appropriation of resources according to market incentives. At the same time, an attempt at effective debureaucratization would simplify the process of administration.

Secondly, lowering the costs of permanence would bring the expenses to levels at which they will not be stimulated to return to informality. Two specific measures are called for here.

The first ought to be an administrative simplification process directed, not at the formalities required to enter the market, but at all the others which businesses must satisfy in the course of their normal lives. It has been estimated that such formalities currently require an average of forty hours per work week from the managers of formally established companies. The second measure should be a thorough, simple and stable tax reform to cut rates to levels where the cost of paying the tax is lower than its benefit.

Similarly, an effective process of decentralization could be attempted: this should not be understood in a merely administrative sense but as a real distribution of power towards the provinces so that they can compete with each other as producers of legislation, coupled with the privatization of certain public functions to transfer responsibilities from governments to individuals.

The foregoing suggestions are quite general, but they may open the way for much more concrete proposals stemming from a recognition that the profusion of regulations may have contradictory effects if the poor are discriminated against and formal requirements are excessively expensive.

A package of reforms of this type would produce two types of economic effects. First, eliminating the limitations on informal growth and investment would raise informal productivity considerably—bearing in mind that it is currently equivalent to only one third of formal productivity. In the second place, eliminating superfluous rules and regulations would reduce the costs of formal workers and allow for the productive use of resources that are currently used up in unproductive expenses required to conform with the state. Both measures would finally lead to the growth of the GNP.

Although the real consequences are hard to gauge, an institutional reform eliminating the differential between the two levels of productivity would raise the GNP by up to 54 percent. Even if the differential could not be reduced by more than one half, the GNP would grow by 27 percent. If elimination took ten years, the annual growth rate of the GNP as a result of this single proposal would be 4.4 percent; if it were reduced by only one half in ten years, growth would amount to 2.4 percent. In either case it would certainly exceed the 1.8 percent per annum registered in the period 1973-1983.

It is therefore perfectly possible to use the so called "informality problem" to increase the collective wealth of our country: adequate institutional reform would enable every Peruvian to seek his own benefit and as a result serve and benefit the rest. It is a matter of thorough reform of the institutional framework that makes it more profitable to operate legally and thus stimulates the efficient appropriation of resources without which economic growth is impossible and social progress a farce.

A market cannot operate at its full capacity unless it has a "meta-market" that reduces its costs, internalizes externalities, stabilizes contractual relations, and guarantees property rights. Thus, the problem is being misconstrued when we refer to the growing importance of informality and the possibilities of its integration. Economically speaking, informality is not separate from formality. There is no such thing as the informal sector, autonomous and autarkic. Both formality and informality represent legal conditions of economic activities, not separate activities. In fact, the problem should be viewed from a different standpoint. It is the law that should be integrated; in other words, law must be adjusted to reality.

Law, democracy, and mercantilism

It is clear from the above that our institutional system is inefficient. It restricts legal access to and permanence within the formal economy. Further, its inadequacy imposes a series of expensive charges on informal activity. Through excess or insufficiency, it restricts the development of individual lives, discriminates against the less favoured—by definition, those who cannot afford the costs the law demands for its protection—and it divides markets and limits the movement of production factors. In sum, it gradually forms a legal order which, rather than consisting in general rules, tends to resemble a group of contracts between the state and small interest groups which regulate the different aspects of reality, doing absolutely without the participation of the other members of society.

We are convinced that a legal system like this is no accident in our country: it is bound up with the way the law is produced and, in the end, the nature of our political regimes. In effect, our lawmakers are adhering to a tradition of using the law as an instrument for the redistribution of wealth instead of its creation. The law is conceived as a mechanism that facilitates the distribution of a fixed "stock" of wealth among the various interest groups that demand it.

With legislation being produced in this manner, it goes unnoticed that beyond its immediate redistributive impact, every law affects the functioning of the economic system in its entirety. In fact, it enables our countries to organize themselves to compete, not in the economic marketplace, but in the political one, because Latin Americans know very well that they can obtain much more through a comfortable arrangement with government than through their own labours.

In the long run, all this affects both our means and objectives. In our countries, the laws discriminate against those who do not have either the organization or the resources required to participate in the process. Our countries compete for the benefit and privilege of the state rather than the benefit and privilege of the consumer. In our countries, the law does not limit power: it reflects power.

This is dramatically expressed in the legislative process. Nominally, our countries have a division and balance of powers in the best Western constitutionalist tradition. However, this is not true. In the case of Peru, for instance, the main producer of legislation is not the Congress but the Executive Power: in the last 40 years, an average 98.68 percent of the regulations produced annually came from the president and his ministers, not from the congressmen.

Certainly, in Latin America and Peru we all criticize our parliaments as inefficient, unreliable, and slow. But the executive lawmaking process lacks transparency and the public participation that parliaments are supposed to stand for. Regulations are "cooked up" in the consulting offices of the ministries or the Government Palace and are surreptitiously approved, making it impossible for anybody to oppose them until they are published, already mandatory, in the relevant official newspaper—if they are published at all.

Actually, it is quite usual in our countries for the drafts of decrees and resolutions to be written in the offices of the lawyers who represent interest groups and sent to the government with a calling card. If we coolly examine the historical process, we can see that legislative production by the Executive Power is constant between democratic governments and military dictatorships. In other words, our civilian presidents are as arbitrary as military dictators.

All the evidence tends to belie the democratic pretensions of our societies. Our institutional structures are such that the best we can expect is the right to vote for a president every certain number of years, but not the right to participate in the decisions made by the president or in his administration: we issue a blank cheque to the elected president to administer the country as he wishes.

The only way our institutional structures allow us to participate in decision making is by becoming involved in the political competition held by our interest groups for the redistributive power of the state. This leaves us with the option of trading reciprocal favours with powerful politicians, offering political support and votes in the nominal democracies or the capacity to call for assemblies and legitimacy in the exercise of power in our dictatorships. In any case, it becomes a matter of negotiating for legal regulations which, through different channels, will benefit the powerful by creating income in their favour. An insider licence to enter a market, a tariff raised, the technical modification of a tax calculation...

Looking at it in perspective, however, this way of governing and lawmaking is neither casual nor unique in history. In fact, it was typical of the Western world at least until the Industrial Revolution and the subsequent affirmation of market economy regimes. It is the system which economic historians call "mercantilism."

Now mercantilism has been defined in many ways. Usually, it is associated with more or less strict control of foreign trade. Nevertheless, consensus exists in economic history that it is much more than that.

UNESCO's *Dictionary of Social Sciences* defines it as the belief that the economic well being of a nation can be guaranteed only by a nationalist government. Other analysts prefer, however, to conceive it as the distribution of monopolistic privileges by the machinery of the state. In such a system, economic competition is transformed into a competition for privileges or revenues to be obtained from the state without the necessary presence of a productive counterpart. This competition for privileges limits access to the economy, segments markets, restricts the movement of production factors, and in general raises the cost of compliance with the law, which mainly affects people with the least resources.

The company as privilege, the law as discrimination, and property as restriction—all are typical of the mercantilism of France under the ancien regime, England under Cromwell, Russia under the Romanovs, and even Spain when ruled by Franco, as well as Latin America.

It is for this reason that Marxist Leninists erroneously believe that we are living in a society that dances to an imperialism which is the highest phase of capitalism. Latin American social democrats are also wrong in their belief, since the time of Haya de la Torre, that on our continent imperialism is not the last but the first phase of capitalism. The fact is that the first phase of capitalism we are living in is a mercantilism to which the informal entrepreneurs of Latin America are peacefully yet steadily offering resistance.

These millions of small entrepreneurs who have recovered the right to do business; these inhabitants of the emerging small towns, the poorest sections, the shantytowns of our cities who have recovered the right to private property; these vendors who invade the streets everywhere to illegally exercise the right to free commerce; these drivers who provide service without being under and protected by the law—all of these people represent a vigorous market economy that is moving right ahead. Informality is nothing less than an industrial revolution occurring in Latin America a hundred years after the European version.

Descriptions of Mexico City, Lima, or Bogota significantly resemble Charles Dickens's descriptions of London. Crowding, human migration, business activity are everywhere, but also the ignoble interventionist state trying to redeem the whole world when all it really does is negotiate the country's "stock" of prosperity in exchange for political profits, and the frivolity of a decaying bourgeoisie unable to realize that each poor individual facing it represents a private entrepreneur.

Of course, each historical experience is different. Mercantilism fell more violently in France than in England; it wore a corporative face for forty years in Franco's Spain; its sway was resolved by the installation of an even worse dictatorship in eastern Europe. There is no reason why we should follow any of these roads, but we cannot ignore the fact that in our countries the state already lacks legitimacy. Legitimacy now dwells in the street: in each poor dwelling where private property is rescued; in each street vendor's stand where free commerce is recovered; in each private enterprise where liberty is maintained.

And it will be only in the modification of our institutions, with the return of sovereignty to the people and the effective democratization of our societies, that the Latin American state will recover its legitimacy. In this process, the definitive fall of mercantilism and the triumph of our industrial revolution will afford all Latin Americans a chance to enjoy the benefits of liberty.

Learning from the Informal Sector

Ignacio Irarrazaval

Our subject here is the main lessons to be learned from the operation of the informal sector in Chile. Most of what follows is based on two empirical studies: the La Granja study of a low-income municipality of Santiago, directed by the author, which weighs the costs and benefits of becoming formal, and the MIDEPLAN study based on a sample survey of 415 microenterprises in the same Chilean city, which examines their operations and levels of regulation obedience.

We begin with a brief discussion of the term "informality" as it pertains to the Latin American setting before proceeding to survey some current estimates of the size of the informal economy in Chile. The final section presents the most important issues and lessons that can be derived from the local operation of the informal sector in Chile. What are the costs and benefits of informality? What has been done to tackle the problem of informality?

Approaches to the informal sector

The concept of informal sector is elusive: the literature offers a variety of interpretations. Since our main purpose here is to identify practical lessons to be learned from the informal sector, we will concentrate on two main approaches.

The International Labour Organization (ILO) approach views the informal sector as a result of the restructuring of labour and production worldwide. In the Latin American context, these processes occur in a situation of labour surplus. Competitive pressure from the labour force reduces wages and creates subsistence activities that are not linked with the dynamic sectors of the economy (Tokman, 1990). The informal sector supplies low-income markets that are incapable of accessing capital, training, and technology. In other words, the informal sector can be defined as the range of economic activities existing outside government regulation.

The ILO approach usually quantifies the informal sector in relation to various groups in the labour force. Traditionally, it views as informal all workers who are self-employed (excluding professionals and technicians), unpaid family workers, and workers in enterprises with fewer than five employees.[1]

Our second theory, the neoliberal or De Soto approach, is based on the observation that informal activities in developing countries are a by-product of inadequate legislation and excessive bureaucracy. Illegality and informality arise from difficulties with obedience to regulations and the costs they impose, rather than from any need to reduce production costs or increase production flexibility. According to De Soto (1987), government regulations are a barrier to the development of informal activities, and his well-known example of a potential street vendor having to secure more than 80 signatures or appeals speaks eloquently to this. Access to the more dynamic markets can be gained only through the legal and institutional machine.

The neoliberal approach sees informality, not in individuals, but in activities, which become illegal as a result of excessive government regulation. From this standpoint, informality and illegality are similar concepts. There are three main areas of illegality:

---

1   In some studies, a distinction is made between small enterprises (five employees) in services and trade and small enterprises producing goods. The former cases are considered informal only when the workers have no contract: in the latter, contracts are irrelevant.

- taxing illegality, reflecting the extent that a business is not a registered tax unit and/or is not paying taxes—it is possible here to further differentiate between central and local taxing illegality;
- environmental and physical illegality, reflecting non-compliance with health and environmental regulations, particularly important for food establishments, and non-compliance with an urban master plan in an establishment's physical features and layout; and
- labour illegality reflecting the absence, not only of contracts, but also of social security and health insurance for workers.[2]

Size and features of the informal sector

No studies exist of Chilean informality at the national level: most have concentrated on Santiago, the capital city of 4.2 million people. The available studies do not use the same definitions and data sources, making it difficult to form time series. In practical, methodological terms, this means that our general picture of informality has to rely on a variety of information sources and is constrained in some areas.

Before describing the Chilean case itself, however, we will need a broader understanding of the informal context in Latin America generally. This will also help to situate the Chilean sector in its regional setting.

Table 1 summarizes the findings of recent informality case studies in Latin America. The approach taken here adheres closely to De Soto's evaluation of the barriers to formality. The main variables assessed are time dedicated to administrative procedures and the financial costs involved. When looking at costs, we have to differentiate between cases in which the law requires alterations in the infrastructure for producing the goods and cases in which such requirements are minimal or nonexistent. Examples of this are regulations requiring special ventilation in

---

2   In the Chilean case, social security and health insurance are mandatory payments regardless of a firm's size. Both payments are financed by the employee and withheld directly from the employer's payroll.

kitchens or bathrooms exclusively for employees in industries employing more than three or four people.

How long does it take to formalize an economic activity? Measured in days of work dedicated to administrative procedures, this varies significantly among the countries reviewed. Bolivia, Brazil, Chile, and Uruguay impose relatively shorter periods for access to legality that range from a fortnight to three months. A different situation can be found in countries like Ecuador, Guatemala, Mexico, and Venezuela,

Table1: The Accessing Cost of Legalizing Informal Production

			Financial Costs			
			No Improvements		Alterations Required	
Country	Economic Sector	Time (days work)	Amount $	% Annual profits	Amount $	% Annual profits
Bolivia	Commerce	15 - 30	14	2.8		
	Industry	15 - 30	13	0.25-1.6		
	Services	15 - 30	26	0.25-1.6		
Brazil	Commerce	31 - 60	44	3.5-7.5		
	Industry	44	84	17.7		
	Services	31	99	-		
Chile	Commerce	12	110	-	5,308	128.3
	Industry	65	222	2.8-5.4	11,135	147.8
Ecuador	Commerce	60 - 75	32	15.5	70	33.8
	Industry	180 - 240	239	23.4	70	6.8
Guatemala	Commerce	179	216	4.2		
	Industry	525	894	8.6		
Mexico	Commerce	83 - 240	210-368	-		
	Industry	83 - 240	210-368	-		
	Services	83 - 240	210-368	-		
Uruguay	Industry	75 - 90	337	159.5	613	290.5
	Services	75 - 90	405	6.1-13	613-675	19.7-10.2
Venezuela	Commerce	170 - 310		5.1		21.5
	Industry	170 - 310		23.5		181.5
Source: PREALC, 1990.						

where access to legality can take from three to ten months. De Soto (1986) has estimated that it could take as long as 289 days to legalize a clothing industry in Lima. Thus, we can include Peru in the latter, slower group.

Regarding the financial costs of accessing legality, we again find important variations in actual amounts spent and their relation to profits. The previous country groupings hold here. In the first group of countries, Chile among them, the financial costs of access to legality are relatively low relative to annual profits. In the second group, average financial costs are twice as large. However, when the law requires alterations, accessing costs become increasingly high and in most cases prohibitive, since they can absorb more than the annual profits of the business. It is important to note that Chile places a high financial price on legality.

To summarize, we may conclude that Chile presents relatively low accessing costs for legality relative to other Latin American countries. However, this situation can be reversed if alterations costs are considered. As a result of this, many Chilean businesses fall into a "gray area" in which they have taken the initial steps towards legalization but have not incurred the additional and high costs of completing the process. In most cases, an entrepreneur's decision not to proceed will be related, not only to financial costs per se, but also to individual assessments and estimates of the areas in which the business can be more easily fined.

Informality in Chile

In analyzing the patterns in Chile over the last few years, we have used the ILO approach for measuring informal employment (see Figure 1). The figure highlights three main points:

- the Chilean informal sector measured by the ILO approach is about one third of total employment (32.5 percent in 1992);
- informal participation in total employment was very stable around the early 1990s and appears to be a structural constant in the Chilean economy.
- there seems to be no relationship between a country's informal sector and level of economic activity:[3] a decrease in

---

3   It is even possible to think of a positive relationship between GDP/PC and informality.

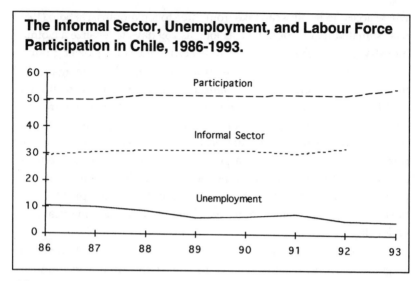

The Informal Sector, Unemployment, and Labour Force Participation in Chile, 1986-1993.

Figure 1

unemployment is not echoed by a decrease in the informal sector. As Leiva (1992) has pointed out, the urban informal sector is not necessarily a "refuge" for people becoming unemployed.

La Granja study

The Municipality of La Granja is one of the poorest in Santiago. Forty percent of its households are below the official poverty line. Per-capita municipal revenue is only half of the average for Greater Santiago. In 1991, La Granja had an estimated population of 151,681.

Our study was possible by an agreement between the municipality and the University of Chile's economics department.[4] The La Granja municipal tax inspectors first put together a list of the addresses of all businesses located within the municipal boundaries. This information

---

4   The bulk of the information in this study can be found in the B.Sc. Economics thesis of Ms. Aura Escudero, directed by the author (Faculty of Economics, University of Chile, 1991).

was then cross-tabulated with municipal data on industrial and commercial licensing fees and Internal Service Tax (IST) data on businesses that had initiated commercial operation (corporate and value-added tax). This simple cross-tabulation was possible because our three information sources recorded the owners' national identity numbers. Despite the obvious beneficial relationships that can be built up between the IST and the municipal finance department for collection purposes, this information is never shared due to special regulations. The La Granja case is in this sense a pilot study.

One important caveat is that our information relied on the "visual knowledge" of local tax inspectors and thus excludes a number of economic activities that have no "facades" or addresses, namely the small street vendors. This means that a significant proportion of small business was not considered in the study.

Our information enabled us to define three categories of formality in La Granja:

- *formal*, referring to businesses paying municipal and IST taxes;
- *informal to municipality*, referring to businesses paying only IST taxes; and
- *informal*, referring to businesses paying no taxes.

Table 2 presents the results of our cadastral survey of businesses in La Granja. It can be seen that of 1,635 businesses surveyed, almost 30 percent were totally informal and a further 12 percent were informal as classified by the municipality. This means that 42 percent of all known economic activities in this municipality were informal.

As noted in Table 2, by far the most common economic activity in this municipality was retail trade, followed by wood industries (furniture and carpentry), repair services, and services in general. Levels of informality varied among economic activities. Wood industries presented the highest level of informality, a situation stemming from zoning requirements in the urban master plan. In most cases, carpenters located their industries in the backyards of their residences, bypassing a residential land use requirement. The same situation also applied to repair services. In the cases of retail trade and other services, the most important constraint to formality related to environmental and health regulations (e.g., requiring a refrigerator for food). It is interesting to note that our "other services" included educational services. According

Table 2: Municipality of La Granja Type of Formality by Economic Activity (%)

Economic Activity	Formal	Informal Municip.	Total Informality	Total	Total (No.)	%
Agriculture	50.0	0.0	50.0	100.0	2	0.1
Mining	100.0	0.0	0.0	100.0	3	0.2
Food Processing	73.8	11.9	14.3	100.0	42	2.6
Clothing, Textile, Leather	39.1	13.0	47.8	100.0	23	1.4
Wood Industries	20.2	27.2	52.6	100.0	114	7.0
Chemical & other industries	51.0	17.7	31.3	100.0	96	5.9
Construction	0.0	100.0	0.0	100.0	1	0.1
Wholsale commerce	89.3	0.0	10.7	100.0	28	1.7
Retail commerce	66.0	8.5	25.4	100.0	1010	61.8
Restaurant-hotels	95.7	4.3	0.0	100.0	23	1.4
Repair services	29.6	28.0	42.6	100.0	125	7.6
Other services	50.0	9.2	40.8	100.0	120	7.3
Transport & storage	38.5	19.2	42.3	100.0	26	1.6
Electricity, gas & other	59.1	4.5	36.4	100.0	22	1.3
TOTAL	58.1	12.0	29.9	100.0	1635	100.0

Source: Own estimates from Cadastre municipality of La Granja.

to our information, La Granja had 13 informal schools. Although mostly small nursery schools, they did pose a question about the relevance of the regulatory requirements in this case.

The second part of the La Granja study was devoted to the costs and benefits of becoming formal. For this purpose, we conducted in-depth interviews with 10 businesses, questioning them about their perceptions of these costs and benefits. The project was evaluated over a period of 11 years, and we differentiated between accessing costs (period 0) and operating costs (periods 1 to 11).[5]

A summary of costs and benefits can be found in Table 3. On the benefits side, we worked with four main fields. Penalty savings reflected

---

5 The 11-year assessment of the formality project reflects previous studies showing that the expected lifespan of informal urban businesses is that period. See Corvalan (1983).

Table 3: Costs and Benefits of Formalization

ITEM	No. of Days	Costs/Benefits $
Accessing costs		
Municipal licence:		
Zoning	3	
Health report (*includes sewerage and water maps*)	45	50
Municipal certification	15	8
Infrastructure:		
Bringing workplace up to code	30 - 90	274 - 1373
		332 - 1431
Operating costs		
Rent		137 - 20
Income tax		0 - 68
Taxes and fees		
Municipal licence		38.5
Waste collection		17.3
Various fees		23.1
		284 - 367
Benefits		
Penalty savings		0 - 494
VAT absorption		0 - 791
Access to credit/loans		?
Access to markets (publicity)		?
		0 - 1285

the avoidance of fines for not complying with tax regulations. VAT absorption was the facility available to formal businesses of deducting VAT from the purchase of inputs for production and using this as a credit for the VAT to be paid on the sales of production. Informal businesses do not have this VAT facility, resulting in higher prices for inputs and thus higher final prices and probably less demand for production. The other two benefits were access to credit and access to markets. Some businesses perceived these as benefits, but it was impossible to estimate them monetarily.

Table 4: Municipality of La Granja Internal Rate of Return: Project "Becoming Formal"		
	Assets	**IRR**
Furniture 1	1,647	Negative
Furniture 2	1,098	12
Furniture 3	878	3
Furniture 4	4,117	12
Garment shop 1	2,196	100
Garment shop 2	2,059	30
Butcher shop	2,745	Negaive
Shoes	823	Negative
Handicraft shop	494	62
Food stand	274	Negative
Note: IRR estimated over a period of 11 years.		

Table 4 summarizes the results of the cost-benefit analysis of the "becoming formal" project. It is important to remember that this exercise considered costs and benefits as the businesses perceived them. This marked a departure from other cost-benefit estimates of informality. In our case, most owners repeatedly expressed no fears about municipal or IST penalties: we found only one tax penalty and shop closure experience.

As can be seen, there is no clear relationship between the assets of a business and the profitability of the project. The study required an IRR of at least 18 percent to consider a project viable, as this is the estimated inflation level for the period studied.

The MIDEPLAN study

The MIDEPLAN study was a semiprobabilistic sample survey of 415 microenterprises in Greater Santiago conducted by DESUC—the Institute of Sociology, Catholic University of Chile—at the request of MIDE-PLAN, the Ministry of Planning. An important feature of this study is that it considered businesses with no external identification, finding them by interviewing all the households in a randomly chosen block about the presence of businesses in their area.

In terms of the socioeconomic features of the microentrepeneurs, DESUC found the gender distribution of businesses strongly related to traditional occupations. Males tended to dominate wood and repair microenterprises, while women led in clothing and food microenterprises. At the same time, the study found no significative differences between the entrepreneurs' educational levels, even when controlling by area of economic activity and size of the business. Microentrepreneurs are not necessarily poor—only 28 percent of them reported incomes below the poverty line[6]—but higher concentrations of poverty were found in clothing and textile and food businesses, which exceeded the national average. An initial explanation for the subjects' relative prosperity is that a large proportion of microentrepeneurs, 43 percent, were former employees—an indication that these businesses tend to be created with an accumulation of previous experience. Again, this is less clear in the areas of clothing and food, which are basically subsistence or complementary activities.

Formality levels for Greater Santiago, reckoned with the ILO ap-

Table 5: Microenterprise Labor Formality

	Clothing & Textile	Equipment Repair	Furniture & Wood Products	Food	Total
With contract	42	67	74	91	68
Salary greater 1 MW	84	99	94	93	92
Soc. sec. payments	55	69	76	79	70
Source: DESUC (1993).					

proach, can be seen in Table 5. More than two thirds of the microenterprise employees had contracts and social security payments.

Table 6 shows formality levels by economic sector according to the De Soto approach. It can be seen that 40 percent of the microenterprises interviewed were in total informality, with an additional 12 percent in

---

6   The national estimate of population below the poverty line is 33 percent.

Table 6: Informality By Economic Sector and Tax Compliance

	Clothing & Textile	Equipment Repair	Furniture & Wood Products	Food	Total
VAT & municipal license	32	83	49	25	47
Only VAT	1	5	9	13	7
Only municipal license	8	3	7	3	5
No VAT or License	59	9	35	59	40
Total	100	200	100	100	100
Source: DESUC (1993)					

Table 7: Formality According to Age, Assets and Monthly Sales ($)

	Formal	Informal	Total
Age of Business			
1-2 years	54	46	100
3-5 years	50	50	100
6 years and more	66	34	100
Assets			
28-250	22	78	100
251-2470	56	44	100
2471 and more	94	6	100
Monthly Sales			
40-205	29	71	100
206-770	54	46	100
771 and more	93	7	100
Source: DESCU (1993)			

partial informality. It should be noted that clothing and textiles and food presented higher levels of informality.

The final table of this section shows the features of informal and formal businesses according to their ages, assets, and monthly sales. In contrast to the La Granja study, the MIDEPLAN study found initial evidence of a direct relationship between microenterprises' assets and sales and their levels of formality. In both variables, businesses in the higher brackets presented higher levels of formality. However, the table does not show a significant relationship by age: formality levels observed in the older group of businesses (55 percent of the sample) are not significantly higher than in the younger businesses.

Lessons from the informal sector

One of our intended contributions here is to relate perceptions of problems rather than their official definitions, thus providing a fresh view of traditional issues in the informal sector. Our brief review of the features of Chile's informal sector leaves us with seven major lessons from its experience.

The informal sector is relatively stable

Contrary to the conventional wisdom, the informal sector has maintained its share of total employment. At the same time, the MIDEPLAN study showed that more than 50 percent of the microenterprises included in the Greater Santiago sample had been operating for more than six years. Since the informal sector is apparently "here to stay," we can plan ahead with real incentives to help them become formal. A possible result of this suggestion might be an increase in the collection of municipal fees and the economic activities in which they are involved.

Accessing costs: bringing the workplace up to code

Accessing costs in terms of municipal licences or IST are not perceived as significantly discouraging formalization. The prohibitive costs are the ones involved in bringing the workplace up to code. This especially affects people working in the food and the furniture and wood sectors. Prohibitively priced though they may be, however, some of these requirements are unavoidable for safe working conditions or quality of production.

However, there is ample room to revise these regulations to consider the size of the economic unit. Regulations must be adjusted to reflect the scale of the hazard or problem that might be created. Is it possible to decentralize some standards? Can a bicycle workshop be treated the same as a car garage?

Operating costs might even create additional expenses

In general terms, the operating costs of being formal are not perceived as high, though an exception to this is added rent for a workplace. However, due to their severe lack of information, knowledge, and practice, most businesses had to ask for guidance in filling out tax returns and tax forms. In the MIDEPLAN study, of the few individuals paying income tax, over 90 percent hired an accountant to fill out the forms.

Municipal fees not perceived as benefits

An interesting example of popular knowledge arose in discussions about the importance of paying some municipal fees. People showed a clear perception of the concept of public goods and the impossibility of the municipal government excluding them. In only one case was an individual able to identify waste collection as a benefit to his business.

Benefits of becoming formal are not always perceived as such

In connection with penalty savings, we found only one case in La Granja of a business actually being fined by a tax inspector, closing the business for three days. The municipality has no enforcement policy and few tax inspectors, who concern themselves with the more profitable businesses, i.e. big industries. In addition, business permits form a small proportion of overall municipal receipts. Most municipal expenses are financed from central government transfers. The real incentives are to obtain those grants instead of disturbing local taxpayers (Irarrazaval and Scarpaci, 1994).

VAT absorption is also a theoretical benefit, but only one business was able to appreciate this as a potential gain. Most purchases are made in the informal market, so there is not much to absorb.

Intangibles remain intangible

Nearly three quarters of the microenterprises in the MIDEPLAN study had never applied for a loan. The most important perceived constraint is lack of collateral rather than lack of formality. Additionally, more than a third of respondents mentioned having fears of indebtedness. In fact, NGOs working with microenterprises have been awarding credit regardless of formality. However, the credit problem places a severe constraint on the growth of the sector.

According to the same study, more than 70 percent of sales were made in the place of production, with an additional 20 percent made at the client's address. These facts challenge the need for publicity. As is well known, most informal businesses are geared to local niche markets and show a poor integration with the modern sector of the economy. Even when this occurs, publicity is not needed because the whole business has been created as a result of a relationship with the purchaser.

Latin American solution: provisional licences

One interesting alternative for coping with informality would be provisional licensing. The strategy would allow tax inspectors to issue provisional municipal licences to most businesses except ones that presented clear dangers, for example in some areas of food processing and in cases of severe violations of zoning ordinances.

In this way, businesses could gain some of the benefits of being formal. When the firm became consolidated, the inspector could start to press for compliance with the rest of the requirements.

References

Ahumata, G. (1992), "Encuesta nacional de empleo y tamano de establecimiento," in *Revista Estadistica y Economia*, no. 5, INE Santiago.

De Soto, H., et al. (1987), *El otro sendero: La revolucion informal*: Buenos Aires, Editorial Oveja Negra.

DESUC-MIDEPLAN (1993), *Microempresas e informalidad*: Santiago, MIDEPLAN.

Irarrazaval, I. and J. Scarpaci (1994), "Decentralizing a centralized state: Local government finance in Chile within the Latin American context," in *Public Budgeting and Finance*.

Leiva, X. (1992), "El sector informal en Chile: analisis de sus componentes y mediciones posibles," in *Revista Estadistica y Economia*, no. 5, INE Santiago.

PREALC (1990), *Mas alla de la regulacion: el sector informal en America Latina*: Santiago, PREALC.

Tokman, V. (1990), "Sector informal en America Latina: De subterraneo a legal," in PREALC (1990).

The Russian Underground Economy in Transition

Michael Alexeev[1]

Introduction

Even prior to the introduction of market-oriented reforms in the late 1980s, a great deal of genuine market-economic activities used to take place in the Soviet Union. While some of these markets were legal, examples being the so-called kolkhoz markets for agricultural products, many were technically outside the law. Law enforcement, however, was generally lax and the risks of small-scale operation in many of these markets were negligible. For example, despite their commonplace occurrence, crimes of "speculation"[2] accounted for fewer than 2 percent of

---

1   The writer is grateful to Jim Leitzel and Vladimir Treml for their valuable comments and discussion. All remaining errors and omissions are entirely the author's responsibility.

2   Speculation was defined essentially as resale of goods at a profit.

all reported crimes in the 1980s.[3] According to Kozlov (1990), the Soviet researchers believed that only 1 percent of all crimes of speculation was reported to authorities, and even this estimate appears to be on the high side.

The Soviet underground economy was not, of course, limited to the resale of goods purchased or stolen from official vendors. Illegal economic activities permeated the entire Soviet system. In fact, the official system probably could not have survived for as long as it did without help from the underground economy. Besides greasing the wheels of the official economy and correcting its mistakes, the Soviet underground economy was also responsible for significant amounts of waste and distortion. As the official economy stagnated and the illegal sector grew rapidly during the 1970s and '80s, both the productive potential of the underground economy and its negative impact on the rest of the economy were becoming more and more apparent.

The market-oriented reforms that began, albeit haltingly, in the late 1980s and turned radical in 1992 were intended in part to bring these illegal economic activities above ground. Instead, however, the reforms further accelerated the growth of underground activities even though the main causes of this growth had changed from price controls to excessive regulation and high tax rates. In today's Russia, the underground economy continues to exert both positive and negative influences on the rest of the economy. It does appear, though, that in the current environment the negative effects of the illegal sector may have begun to overshadow its benefits.

The next section outlines the size and growth pattern of the underground economy in the USSR prior to market-oriented reforms and analyzes its impact on the traditional Soviet economy. After this, a brief description of the major developments concerning the Russian underground economy in the late 1980s and early 1990s is followed by a look at the role of illegal economic activities in the current environment and their implications for the future of reforms.

---

3   *Rossiiskaia* (1993), pp. 135-136.

The underground economy in the traditional Soviet system

The underground economy was always an important part of the Soviet system. According to Shmelev and Popov (1989), even during the height of the war, when private trade was prohibited and could be punished by summary execution without trial, black marketeers provided as much bread for Russian cities as state procurement did. Black markets continued to function in the postwar Stalinist period as well. They began to grow with particular rapidity in the mid-1960s, and by the mid-1970s the underground economy had permeated all areas of Soviet economic life.[4]

Comprehensive price controls accompanied by chronic shortages and the interdiction of most private economic activities were the main reasons for the growth of the Soviet black markets. Other incentives for turning to black markets included high taxation and excessive regulation of allowed private economic activities, the existence of a large amount of impersonal state property kept under inadequate custody, and the need of poorly paid individuals to supplement their incomes.

One of the commonest types of illegal activity in the USSR was theft of socialist property—i.e., property of governments, collective farms, "social organizations" such as trade unions, and so forth. This type of theft used to be taken for granted by the public and did not arouse serious social censure. Even the late Soviet President Brezhnev was quoted as saying to his aides: "You don't know life. No one lives on wages alone. I remember in my youth we earned money by unloading railroad freight cars. So, what did we do? For every three crates or bags unloaded we'd take one for ourselves. That's how everybody in the country lives."[5]

---

4   These illegal economic activities, as well as the so-called "second" economy in the USSR, have been extensively studied by Western economists since the pioneering works of Grossman (1977, 1979). By Grossman's definition, the Soviet "second" economy included all economic activities which were either performed directly for private gain, or illegal, or both. The illegal economy thus formed a major part of the second economy.

5   Burlatskii (1988), p. 14, quoted in Treml (1990).

A variant on the theft of socialist property was stealing time off work. Apparently this too was a Soviet commonplace. As a reflection of the importance of theft in the Soviet economy, wages in various occupations seemed to be vary inversely as opportunities to steal from the workplace. Treml (1990) has estimated Soviet workplace theft of materials at approximately 63.7 billion rubles in 1975 and 70.4 billion rubles in 1980, or between 3 and 5 percent of the Soviet Gross Social Product—defined as the value of output of all material goods, intermediate and final, valued at current buying prices.

Perhaps just as common was the phenomenon of "speculation," the technically illegal resale of goods for personal gain. Despite its illegality, speculation was practised virtually in the open. Large markets reminiscent of American flea markets existed in most large Soviet cities. Officially, their function was to allow individuals to sell unwanted goods, but in reality they became major outlets for selling stolen property and products from the underground economy as well as the resale of goods purchased at low state-controlled prices.

Significant amounts of production by individual artisans as well as entire underground factories also took place in the black economy. Workers often produced goods on their own account on company time, using equipment in their state-owned enterprises. There were armies of "moonlighters" repairing dwellings and appliances for private customers. Moonshine production was extremely popular in the countryside.

Such widespread illegality in what used to be called a police state could not have happened without rampant corruption in Soviet officialdom, including the police. The extensive existing literature on the "speculation" phenomenon makes it pointless to spend time here.[6] A quote from Grossman (1977, pp. 32-33) presents a good general picture:

> At the very least one can deduce that the purchase and sale of [official] positions for large sums of money signifies the profound institutionalization in the Soviet Union of a whole structure of bribery and graft, from the bottom to the top of the pyramid of power; that considerable stability of the structure of power is expected by all concerned; and that very probably

---

6   The standard references on Soviet corruption include Simis (1977-78, 1982) and Vaksberg (1992).

there is a close organic connection between political-administrative authority, on the one hand, and a highly developed world of illegal economic activity, on the other. In sum, the concept of *kleptocracy*, developed by sociologists with reference to corrupt regimes and bureaucracies in underdeveloped countries, does not seem inapplicable to at least certain portions and regional segments of the Soviet party-government hierarchy.

For obvious reasons, it is difficult to estimate the actual size of the Soviet illegal economy. According to figures based on a Berkeley-Duke survey of emigrants from the USSR, about one third of the urban population's income was derived from the second economy,[7] which employed 10 to 12 percent of the labour force.[8] Presumably, the bulk of this income was illegal. Soviet researchers themselves have offered various estimates of illegal turnover that range from 70 to 90 billion rubles to as high as 300 to 350 billion rubles in the late 1980s.[9]

The actual dynamics of the underground economy are even harder to discern. Koriagina (1988) estimated that the second economy had grown approximately fourfold between the late 1960s and the mid-1980s. The Treml-Alexeev research (1993) based on official retail trade and income data strongly suggests that the second economy was growing rapidly between 1965 and 1985, but no specific growth estimates could be provided.

We may argue over precise estimates of the size and growth of the Soviet illegal economy, but the fact remains that by the mid-1980s it was

---

7   Grossman (1987). The estimates refer to the late 1970s. The Berkeley-Duke survey covered 1,061 households from urban areas of the USSR in a sample that contained various biases such as self-selection of the émigrés and nationality—most of the respondents were either Jewish or Armenian. These biases, however, did not appear to be large enough to invalidate the reported estimates, which are, incidentally, quite conservative.

8   Treml (1992).

9   The first estimate is by Koriagina (1988). The second number, which approximated the offical retail trade turnover figures for the entire USSR, is from *Argumenty i fakty*, no. 37, 1989, p. 5. The aggregate official personal income in 1988-1989 was roughly 522 billion rubles. Rutgaizer (1992) provides a survey of Soviet research on the second economy.

clearly having a major impact on overall economic performance. To a considerable extent, illegal economic transactions obviated rationing in consumer markets. For example, Alexeev (1988) has demonstrated that despite the fact that state-owned housing had been one of the most strictly rationed consumer goods and seemingly simple to control, its allocation depended mostly on consumer ability to pay rather than the official non-price rationing criteria. Usually, this redistribution of consumer goods via black markets must have enhanced people's lives: after all, by its very nature it consisted in voluntary exchanges among individuals. Nonetheless, difficulties with disseminating information and enforcing long-term contracts make the underground economy a less than ideal distribution system. Also, in an otherwise highly distorted economy, the introduction of additional markets would not always result in more well-being. For instance, the possibility of the resale of officially purchased goods on the black market can easily lead to longer than necessary queues in the first economy when such resale is effectively prohibited.[10]

Besides redistributing goods in consumer markets, the illegal economy was involved in the reallocation of inputs and outputs in production.[11] Semi-legal or illegal trades among socialist enterprises often helped these enterprises to fulfil the plan by correcting initial input misallocations. At the same time, the possibility of diverting inputs and outputs to the black market must have lowered the official performance of at least some enterprises. More importantly, even if the black markets facilitated plan fulfilment, that does not imply that they were good for the economy. From the Soviet consumer's viewpoint, some state targets should probably never have been met.

In addition, the illegal economy was partly responsible for weakening and even destroying the feedback from the economy to planners. When a planner misallocated inputs but informal trades among state enterprises corrected this misallocation, the planner had no reason to change future input allocations. In effect, the planners were directing

---

10 See Stahl and Alexeev (1985) for a rather general model of this phenomenon, and Gang and Tower (1988) for a simple example.

11 For a description of the illegal economy in socialist industry, see Grossman (1982).

the Soviet economy with a highly distorted map of the economic situation.[12]

The underground economy also played a significant role in altering income distribution in Soviet society. As has already been mentioned, illegal opportunities tended to be inversely correlated with depressed official wages. This does not imply that illegal incomes reduced inequalities, however. Large and highly variable illegal incomes could increase inequality no matter how they related to official incomes. Based on the data from the Berkeley-Duke survey already cited, Alexeev and Gaddy (1993) have calculated that the inclusion of illegal income accentuated income inequality in Soviet regions with highly developed underground economies.

In addition to affecting resource allocation in the economy, the underground economy was responsible for shaping the Russians' image of free markets and providing training grounds for Russian entrepreneurs. In fact one survey found that Muscovites seemed to understand and appreciate the workings of free markets just as well as residents of New York did.[13] This awareness must have helped create a consensus for market reforms and promote their progress. However, underground markets do not adequately reflect the power of legal free markets reinforced by such modern market institutions as banks and stock exchanges. Perhaps for this reason, markets in Russia often have a bazaar-like image rather than the look of sophisticated mechanisms that can coordinate the smooth operation of a large modern economy.

Finally, we should mention what Cowell (1993) calls "a kind of demoralization crisis" that could be caused by a large underground economy. Illegal economic activities undermine a population's trust in the fairness of an entire system, whether socialist or capitalist. The perception of injustice in an economic system is detrimental to well-being in and of itself, even if this is difficult to fit into the more conventional framework of cost-benefit analysis.

---

12 Treml and Alexeev (1993) provide a more detailed discussion of the illegal economy's impact on Soviet economic performance.

13 Shiller et al. (1991).

Perestroika, market reforms, and the Russian underground economy

By the mid-1980s the Soviet leadership began to understand the significance of the underground economy. Even so, however, the leaders displayed a highly ambivalent attitude towards the informal sector during perestroika. On the one hand, realizing its potential for improving Soviet economic performance, the authorities wanted to bring many private economic activities above ground. On the other hand, they feared losing the remnants of their grip on the economy.

This ambivalence resulted in a slow, sometimes contradictory slackening of regulations against private enterprise. Thus, the November 1986 *Law on Individual Labour Activity* that widened the scope of legal private enterprise in the USSR was preceded by a campaign against "non-labour income" in May of that year. The legislation itself provided but slight relief from anti-private enterprise regulations: it continued to prohibit many private economic activities, gave regional legislatures broad powers to expand the list of prohibited activities, and required every individual who wanted to engage in individual labour activities to obtain a licence from local government.

Throughout the Gorbachev period, the Russian authorities continued to view genuinely private enterprise with deep mistrust. Instead, they lent their support to family-based and cooperative economic forms. Family-based contractual arrangements in agriculture and family contracts for running small state-owned service outlets were strongly encouraged by the authorities in 1987 and 1988. A more radical 1988 *Law on Cooperatives* opened the way for individuals into many areas of the economy that used to be, legally at least, the exclusive domain of the state.[14] Even this law, however, did not go nearly far enough to bring genuine legal markets into the economy.

The newly permissible cooperative activities were subject to various restrictions. According to the law, cooperatives had limited access to inputs and were forbidden to engage in some important economic activities. The state also retained the right to exercise significant control

---

14   "Zakon Soiuza Sovetskikh Sotsialisticheskikh Respublik o kooperatsii v SSSR," in *Ekonomicheskaia gazeta*, no. 24, June 1988.

over the prices charged by producer cooperatives. Local authorities were allowed to place further restrictions on the activities of cooperatives in their jurisdictions. All these constraints handicapped cooperatives in their ability to compete among each other and with state-owned enterprises. Particularly harmful to the goals of reformers were legislative reversals, as, for example, a December 1988 resolution by the Soviet Council of Ministers prohibiting cooperatives from engaging in a number of activities, including medical services, that had been permitted by the original cooperatives legislation. Changes in taxation were especially frequent.[15]

Yet even these half-hearted liberalizing measures were greeted by rapid developments in legitimate non-state enterprises.[16] This growth, however, did not take place at the expense of the "shadow" economy, to use the Soviet term. In fact, the partial legitimization of various private and crypto-private economic activities actually seemed to spur underground development. According to one Soviet researcher, legalization of about 800 million rubles' worth of the shadow economy in 1988 was accompanied by an increase of 1,400 million rubles' worth of various illegal activities.[17]

What led to such an outcome? As already mentioned, some actions of the Gorbachev government contradicted the general direction of reform. For example, the anti-alcohol campaign launched in May 1985 drove alcohol prices sharply upwards and restricted the production of alcoholic beverages by the state. Naturally, the result was an explosion of bootlegging and home brewing. Illegal alcohol sales reportedly increased 42 percent in the first 10 months of 1986. Some Soviet specialists maintained that the reductions in the state-controlled output of alco-

---

15 For a detailed discussion of the cooperatives during perestroika, see Jones and Moskoff (1991) and Murphy (1993).

16 By 1991, the number of cooperatives in the USSR reached 255,000. They employed almost 6.5 million people producing goods and services worth about 42 billion rubles.

17 This estimate by T. Koriagina was quoted in Grossman (1990).

holic beverages were fully offset by increased production of moonshine.[18]

Ironically, even the more radical measures proved to be counterproductive in their effects on the underground economy. In fact, it was the 1988 *Law on Cooperatives* which, with the 1987 *Law on State Enterprise*, probably bore the principal responsibility for the growth of illegal economic activities in the period 1988-1991. Prior to the *Law on State Enterprise*, Soviet state-owned firms conducted most of their financial transactions by adjusting their account balances in Gosbank, the state bank. The payment of wages was the only significant transaction conducted in cash. While state-owned enterprises operated under the so-called soft budget constraint for non-cash transactions, the central planners took special care in controlling enterprises' wage funds and cash budgets.[19] Separating the cash and non-cash money flows in the economy allowed the central planners to alleviate inflationary pressures in consumer markets.

The 1987 law afforded a large degree of autonomy to state-owned enterprises. In particular, it gave them greater independence in allocating their financial resources without imposing serious responsibility for failure. The *Law on Cooperatives* permitted and even pushed cooperatives and state-owned enterprises into close business relationships and associations. At the same time, state-owned enterprises were allowed to convert their Gosbank balances into cash for transactions with cooperatives. This essentially cracked the "wall" between the two types of money flows.

However, the conversion of non-cash balances into cash heightened inflationary pressures in the economy. What is more, given an environment of continuing price controls in the state sector, this strengthened incentives to engage in black market activities and divert outputs and non-cash balances from state-owned enterprises into cooperatives and private businesses. In other words, the conversion of non-cash into cash

---

18   See Treml (1987) and references therein.

19   The term "soft budget constraint" coined by J. Kornai essentially means that enterprises expected to be virtually automatically bailed out by the state if they ran out of money in the non-cash account.

was a self-promoting phenomenon that stimulated the growth of the underground economy. In addition, since the diversion of resources from the state sector was usually accomplished by means of at least questionable legality, this diversion itself contributed to the growing share of illegal economic activities.

In general, while the restrictions on private and cooperative businesses might have been imposed to combat the diversion of state sector resources, these restrictions only exacerbated disequilibria in the economy: helping to reduce competition and generate excessive profits, they promoted corruption and the growth of the underground. Corruption was further spurred by the fact that Soviet bureaucrats at all levels were in danger of losing many of their traditional privileges through either marketization or popular discontent. This gave them strong incentives to monetize their remaining perks and quickly convert the remaining rents associated with their positions into privately owned assets. Bribe taking, illegitimate privatization of state-owned assets, sweetheart deals between state-owned enterprises and cooperatives set up by local bureaucrats—these were the commonest examples of abuse of official power. Corruption was further facilitated by the dependence of private and cooperative enterprises on the benevolence of local authorities, a situation that often ruled out completely legal for-profit operations. At the same time, the state blessing for private and cooperative enterprise, at least in principle, provided an ideal front for expanding the scale and scope of illegal economic activities. For example, the creation of commercial banks presented opportunities for bank fraud that had been virtually nonexistent.

Another important obstacle to the legalization of the underground economy was the black marketeers' mistrust of the Soviet government's commitment to market-oriented reforms. In the absence of proven commitment, private entrepreneurs were afraid to reveal themselves and the extent of their operations. Such fears were supported by significant reversals in the progress of reforms and the persistence of many old anti-entrepreneurial statutes on the books.[20]

---

20 Thus, the blanket prohibition of "speculation" was not repealed until January 1992. Litwack (1991) and Boettke (1993) discuss the importance of credible commitment by the government for the success of reforms.

The underground economy in reforming Russia

The eventual acceptance in principle of the market economy came with the breakup of the USSR in late 1991. Following 1992 reforms, the Russian economy has no longer been centrally planned in the traditional sense.[21] However highly regulated contemporary Russian markets may be, a large portion of the Russian economy is supposed to be open to market forces. Nonetheless, a large and perhaps growing share of the economy continues to operate underground.

The flourishing illegal economy in today's Russia owes its existence to essentially the same factors as in the traditional Soviet economy, even though the relative importance of these factors has changed dramatically. Tax evasion appears to have become the main reason for operating businesses underground, while price controls, regulations, and the remaining prohibitions on private economic activity have become somewhat less significant.

To the extent that the Russian economy suffers from excessive regulation, the role of black markets in contemporary Russia resembles their role in the traditional Soviet economy. On the one hand, black markets help entrepreneurs to get around onerous regulations and thus enhance overall economic performance.[22] On the other hand, underground enterprises have problems with disseminating and acquiring information and with contract enforcement.

In some important respects, however, the role and impact of the underground economy in reforming Russia differ significantly from those in its Soviet counterpart. First, reforms brought an unusually high degree of uncertainty into the Russian economy about property rights and the future of the entire system. The admittedly inefficient and restrictive traditional Soviet system had been in many ways rather

---

21   One might argue that the Soviet economy was not really a planned economy even prior to reform (see, for example, Zaleski, 1980, and Roberts, 1990). Whether we call it central planning or not, commands from the centre used to play a significant role in the functioning of the Soviet economy.

22   In the words of Cowell (1993), "a world of perfect enforcement could be an intolerable place."

predictable. The elite could count on keeping their privileges through to old age, while ordinary consumers expected prices to stay low and shortages to persist. The system was relatively stable: even the underground economy enjoyed a large measure of stability that allowed black marketeers to plan for the future and put a premium on their reputations.

The volatility and turmoil brought about by radical reforms reduced the value of following the rules, thereby promoting the growth of the underground. However, uncertainty about the future undermines incentives for black marketeers to develop and maintain reputations for the high quality of their services. The generally high level of volatility in the economy not only facilitates illegal economic activities, but also shortens the time horizon for agents operating underground, making them likelier to cheat.

Secondly, growth in the underground economy reduces the tax base, promoting inflation and forcing the government to increase the tax burden on legitimate enterprises. Rising tax rates push even more businesses underground, which leads to still higher tax rates, and so on. Reduced tax revenues lead the government to print money and thus impose an inflation tax on citizens. Inflation in turn creates greater uncertainty with all its negative implications.

Thirdly, the underground economy attracts and promotes organized crime.[23] Organized crime or mafias could play a positive role in the economy—for example, by helping to enforce contracts and maintain order in the underground economy or any other circumstances where legal enforcement is not forthcoming.[24] Mafias, however, may impose serious costs on the economy as well. To begin with, some entrepreneurs may not want to deal with the mafia on moral grounds, or just as a matter of taste. If the only way to run a successful business is to pay protection money to organized crime, these entrepreneurs would not even bother to start up.

---

23 According to a recent Russian government report, 70 to 80 percent of private enterprises in major cities were paying protection money to organized crime. *New York Times*, January 30, 1994, p. 1.

24 For an insightful discussion of the economics of organized crime, see Schelling (1984), pp. 158-178 and 179-194.

Another problem with organized crime's involvement in the economy is its tendency to favour monopoly. Organized crime is interested in maximizing rents, and rents are maximized if the firm has a monopoly. For example, having one restaurant in a district may bring in significant income. If competition is allowed to work, some of this income would be siphoned off by other restaurants. Organized crime could use force to prevent other restaurants from opening.[25]

In addition, a large monopoly establishment may be easier than several small firms for organized crime to monitor. A similar argument was commonly used to explain the Soviet planners' preference for building large enterprises which often enjoyed a monopoly position in their segment of the industry. The monopoly advantage is somewhat offset, though, by the fact that competition helps organized crime to monitor enterprises it controls by providing a standard of comparison.[26] Finally, a monopolist might be less likely to complain to the authorities if organized crime shielded him from competition and left him at least a share of monopoly rents.

Organized crime is not new to Russia, of course. In many ways, the traditional Soviet "nomenclature" resembled an organized crime group, particularly with respect to illegal economic activities that took place in the USSR. The nomenclature used to hold a virtual monopoly on rent extraction from both the legal and illegal sectors of the Soviet economy. Underground entrepreneurs usually had to pay off government officials and law enforcement officers in order to stay in business. In this sense, the current situation is distinguished by a higher degree of competition among criminal groups and greater "disorganization" of the rent-extraction mechanism.[27]

---

25 This argument works if the mafia itself is running the restaurant. If, however, a criminal group controls the district and can collect fees from establishments located in it, the group may be able to raise higher revenues by allowing competition.

26 In more technical terms, competition eliminates the common uncertainty facing the firms' management, leaving only firm-specific uncertainty to influence its performance (see Holmstrom, 1982). Lower uncertainty leaves less room for the management of the firm to hide its true productive potential from the shareholders—or from the mafia, for that matter.

Despite the changing nature of the Russian underground economy, we could argue that the current situation is an improvement over the past in that a regulated market economy would perform better with the underground economy, all things being equal, than the traditional Soviet system would with the underground economy. While illegal economic activities exert essentially the same ambiguous influences on the rest of the economy, the more market-oriented nature of the official economy should hold an advantage over central planning.[28] On balance, however, the net impact of the black markets has probably changed from efficiency-enhancing to detrimental. Presumably, even the over-regulated market economy would perform better if it was largely legal than if much of it remained underground.

What are the implications of the existence of the large Russian underground economy in terms of evaluating the progress of market reforms and the likelihood of their success? The difficulties involved in quantifying illegal economic activities and incorporating them into the system of national accounts will distort our perceptions of both the pre-reform and the current situations. If the Russian underground has been growing rapidly over the last several years, this would mean that the official data on economic growth are understating the performance of the Russian economy.

Now such bias is particularly dangerous in the present volatile political situation. Any perception of the economic failure of reforms can easily become self-fulfilling by, among other things, weakening the monetary system, further increasing uncertainty, and driving even more entrepreneurs underground. The perceived link between reforms and economic crime provokes calls for limiting the freedom to engage in

---

27   The relatively disorganized nature of the current organized crime groups is evident from government data indicating that less than 1 percent of an estimated 4,000 "organized criminal groups" in Russia consisted of more than 10 individuals. More than half had only 2 or 3 members. *Statistika sotsial'nykh anomalii*, p. 19.

28   I do not want to take this argument too far. For example, the Soviet state might have been much more efficient at extracting rents from the underground economy while the contemporary mafia may do it in a wasteful manner.

private economic activities and other restrictions on individual rights. If the reforms become too closely identified with the illegal economy, the fight against crime may lead to serious reversals of reform progress.[29]

The underground economy modifies the effects of reform measures directed at the official economy. For example, an increase in tax rates may generate greater revenues for government if black markets are underdeveloped. They may, however, reduce revenues sharply if the underground economy presents a viable alternative for the entrepreneur.[30] For their policies to achieve the desired effects, Russian reformers must always try to take into account the existence of the large illegal sector in their country. Indeed, it might be precisely the recognition of the limits of their power in the face of the underground economy that is preventing the Russian government from imposing even more regulations and higher taxes on the Russian economy.

Reformers should also realize that the problems posed by the large and growing underground economy cannot be solved by tighter regulations and tax increases. On the contrary, the reduction of tax rates and the removal of most constraints on legal private activities is the route that can bring much of the illegal economy above ground and improve the performance of Russian markets. Since organized crime thrives on illegal economic activities, this would also reduce the role and power of the Russian mafias. The solution to the problem of economic illegality in Russia lies in the continuing advance of free market reforms.

---

29 A more detailed discussion of the relationship between economic crime and reforms can be found in Alexeev et al. (1994).

30 The recent rollback of cigarette taxes in Canada provides a vivid example of government recognizing the economic power of the underground.

References

Alexeev, M., "Market vs. Rationing: The Case of Soviet Housing," in *Review of Economics and Statistics,* vol. lxx, no. 3, pp. 414-420 (August 1988).

────── and C. Gaddy, "Income Distribution in the USSR in the 1980s," in *Review of Income and Wealth,* vol. 39, no. 1, pp. 23-36 (March 1993).

──────C. Gaddy, and J. Leitzel, "Economic Crime and Russian Reform," is forthcoming in the *Journal of Theoretical and Institutional Economics,* mimeo, Department of Economics, Indiana University, Bloomington, 1994.

Boettke, P. J., *Why Perestroika Failed: The Politics and Economics of Socialist Transformation*: New York, Routledge, 1993.

Burlatskii, F., "Brezhnev i krushenie ottepeli," in *Literaturnaia gazeta,* September 18, 1988, pp. 13-14.

Cowell, F., "What's Wrong with Going Underground?" in *International Economic Insights*, vol. iv, no. 6, pp.18-20 (November/December 1993).

Grossman, G., "Sub-Rosa Privatization and Marketization in the USSR," *Berkeley-Duke Occasional Papers on the Second Economy in the USSR,* no. 17, 1989.

────── "Roots of Gorbachev's Problems: Private Income and Outlay in the Late 1970s," Joint Economic Committee, US Congress, *Gorbachev's Economic Plans,* vol. 1, Washington, DC, 1987, pp. 213-229.

────── "The 'Shadow Economy' in the Socialist Sector of the USSR," in *The CMEA Five-Year Plans (1981-1985) in New Perspective*: NATO Colloquium, Brussels, 1982, pp. 99-115.

────── "Notes on the Illegal Private Economy and Corruption," in Joint Economic Committee, US Congress, *Soviet Economy in a Time of Change,* Washington, DC, 1979, pp. 834-855.

────── "The Second Economy in the USSR," in *Problems of Communism,* vol. 26, no. 5, pp. 25-40 (September/October 1977).

Gang, I. and E. Tower, "The Stahl-Alexeev Paradox: A Note," in *Journal of Economic Theory*, vol. 44, pp. 189-191 (1988).

Holmstrom, B., "Moral Hazard in Teams," in *Bell Journal of Economics,* vol. 13, no. 2, pp. 324-340 (Autumn 1982).

Jones, A. and W. Moskoff, *Ko-ops: the Rebirth of Entrepreneurship in the Soviet Union*: Bloomington, Indiana University Press, 1991.

Koriagina, T., *Voprosy ekonomiki*, no. 3, pp.110-119 (1990).

Kozlov, Iu., "Tenevaia ekonomika i prestupnost'," in *Voprosy ekonomiki*, no. 3, pp. 120-127 (1990).

Litwack, J., "Discretionary Behavior and Soviet Economic Reform," in *Soviet Studies*, vol. 43, no. 2, pp. 255-279 (1991).

Murphy, M., "Competition Under the Laws Governing Soviet Producer Cooperatives During Perestroika," in P. Patterson, ed., *Capitalist Goals Socialist Past: The Rise of the Private Sector in Command Economies*: Westview Press, 1993.

Roberts, P.C., *Alienation and the Soviet Economy*: New York, Holmes and Meier, 1990.

Rossiiskaia Federatsiia v tsifrakh v 1992 godu: Moscow, Goskomstat Rossii, 1993.

Rutgaizer, V., "The Shadow Economy in the USSR: Part 1. A Survey of Soviet Research; Part 2. Sizing up the Shadow Economy: Review and Analysis of Soviet Estimates," *Berkeley-Duke Occasional Papers on the Second Economy in the USSR*, no. 34, February 1992.

Schelling, T., *Choice and Consequence*: Cambridge, Harvard University Press, 1984.

Shiller, R., M. Boyko, and V. Korobov, "Popular Attitudes toward Free Markets: The Soviet Union and the United States Compared," in *American Economic Review*, vol. 81, pp. 385-400 (1991).

Simis, K., *USSR: The Corrupt Society*: New York, Simon and Schuster, 1982.

———— "The Machinery of Corruption in the Soviet Union," in *Survey*, vol. 23, 4(105), pp. 35-55 (Autumn 1977-1978).

Smelev, N., and V. Popov, *Na perelome: ekonomicheskaia perestroika v SSSR*: Moscow, Novosti, 1989.

Stahl, D., and M. Alexeev, "The Influence of Black Markets in a Queue-Rationed Centrally Planned Economy," in *Journal of Economic Theory*, vol. 35, no. 2, pp. 234-250 (1985).

Statistika sotsial'nykh anomalii: Moscow, Goskomstat RSFSR, 1991.

Treml, V., "Gorbachev's Anti-Drinking Campaign: A 'Noble Experiment' or a Costly Exercise in Futility?" in Joint Economic Committee, US Congress, *Gorbachev's Economic Plans*, vol. 2, Washington, DC, pp. 297-311.

—— "A Study of Labor Inputs into the Second Economy of the USSR," *Berkeley-Duke Occasional Papers on the Second Economy in the USSR*, no. 33, January 1992.

—— "A Study of Employee Theft of Materials from Places of Employment," *Berkeley-Duke Occasional Papers on the Second Economy in the USSR*, no. 20, June 1990.

—— and M. Alexeev, "The Second Economy and the Destabilizing Effect of its Growth on the State Economy in the Soviet Union: 1965-1989," *Berkeley-Duke Occasional Papers on the Second Economy in the USSR*, no. 36, December 1993.

Vaksberg, A., *The Soviet Mafia*: New York, St. Martin's Press, 1992.

Zaleski, E., *Stalinist Planning for Economic Growth, 1933-1952*: Chapel Hill, University of North Carolina Press, 1980.

Reform and China's Underground Economy

Yue-Chim Richard Wong

Progress of economic reform

Between 1978 and 1993, China's economy was incrementally liberalized and saw extraordinarily rapid output growth as real GNP expanded at an average annual rate of 9.5 percent.[1] The reforms started in agriculture with the replacement of the communes by a system of household farming on land leased from the state. Between 1979 and 1983, with over three quarters of the population still in agriculture, farm output surged by 8 to 10 percent a year.[2]

The dismantling of the commune system was not a matter of conscious policy or design. It was a process that started when local leaders

---

1   All figures quoted in this paper are derived from various issues of the *China Statistical Yearbook*.

2   See Johnson, D.G. (1990), *The People's Republic of China: 1978-1990*; San Francisco, ICS Press.

in Sichuan province decided to experiment with the household responsibility system in the absence of official sanction from the central authorities. When this experiment turned out to be a great economic success, it was rapidly emulated throughout the country. Within a year, the commune system had collapsed and agriculture became semi-privatized. The reforms were accorded ex-post legitimacy by the central authorities.

By 1984, the engine of rapid economic growth had shifted to rural light industry, which began to absorb much of the labour force released by productivity gains in agriculture. Small-scale private traders flourished alongside numerous new manufacturing enterprises that were mostly owned by local governments—townships and villages. These businesses, which became the backbone of the new market-driven non-state sector, operated outside the system of official price, output, and financial controls that still governed state-owned production. Non-state sector industrial output soared from 26.65 percent of total output in 1983 to 51.91 percent in 1992.

The central government has provided little support to the non-state sector. In particular, the state banking system has been highly reluctant to extend credit facilities. Total state bank loans to the non-state sector as a proportion of total outstanding state bank loans remained at around 12 to 14 percent from 1983 to 1992. Most growth in non-state enterprises had been self-financed during this period.

Foreign trade has been gradually liberalized through the establishment of special economic zones somewhat outside the control of the traditional state trading monopolies. The first and most important zones were in the Pearl River Delta area and connected with the Hong Kong trade.[3] They became more numerous and broader in the scope of their activities. In time, an export (and import) boom became China's new engine of economic growth. Exports as a share of GNP rose from 5.31 percent in 1979 to 18.76 percent in 1993. Bit by bit, the distinction between the special economic zones and the rest of the economy became blurred. A wide range of state-owned enterprises, township and village enterprises, and private businesses gained more or less equal access to foreign trade through the swap centres where they could buy and sell

---

3   See Sung, Y.W., P.W. Liu, Y.C.R. Wong, and P.K. Lau (1995), *The Fifth Dragon: Emergence of the Pearl River Delta*: Addison Wesley.

foreign exchange to finance transactions not included in the state plan. Until a unified foreign exchange market was set up in April 1993, the volume of foreign exchange transactions in the swap centres was reported to be almost 80 percent of total transactions in China. The official exchange rate depreciated significantly from RMB 2.5 yuan to US$1 in 1979 to RMB 8.7 yuan to US$1 in 1993. The depreciation reflected a gradual move towards market levels from an initial position of overvaluation. The process of foreign trade and foreign exchange liberalization was again incremental, responding to enterprises' most urgent needs as they arose.

Incrementalism and the underground economy

China's economic reforms were intended to promote economic growth and revitalize economic performance. The Chinese leadership recognized that their political legitimacy depended on delivering a better standard of living, though internal disagreements over the ultimate goals of economic reform and strategies to achieve those goals continue to rage. Not until 1993 did the creation of a socialist market economy formally become an official objective—and even then the socialist rider was retained, apparently because of the now chronic lack of consensus on goals and strategies.

The Chinese economy was running on a dual track where the traditional system co-existed with the new. Debates on price reforms, foreign exchange reforms, enterprise reforms, and the piecemeal nature of all reforms reflected ongoing conflicts within the leadership. Meanwhile, China's market expanded by diverting resources away from the state sector, growing out of the state plan. The economic reforms did not strip away the rents captured by major interest groups: they merely altered the way in which those rents could be secured. This evolutionary approach explains why reform has been incremental in China, starting with the easy and gradually progressing to the more difficult. Again, this was not a conscious gradualist strategy as is sometimes argued. A more appropriate way of characterizing the process of economic reform in China might be to call it a sequence of breaches in the traditional system at the points of least political resistance.

The massive shift of resources from the state to the non-state sector in agriculture and industry and the growing importance of foreign trade have combined to create a vibrant economy with more or less rational prices that are beginning to reflect economic scarcity. When the reform process began, almost all prices were controlled: today, less than 5 percent of prices are still controlled.

These impressive achievements notwithstanding, China remains a semi-reformed economy in which state-owned enterprises continue to produce almost half of industrial output. These state companies have become a major fiscal burden: one third of them are suffering losses that have to be covered by the state, while another third are being carried by state banks through low-interest loans. Reforming the state sector is the most difficult problem China has to solve before its economy can become truly efficient. There is a growing recognition in China of the need for fundamental change in the system.

Local governments have clearly been the most innovative force, experimenting with new reform measures and policy initiatives. Perhaps the farther from the political centre, the weaker the political resistance to reform. Successful local initiatives have subsequently been anointed by the central government, thus gaining political legitimacy and an enhanced possibility of surviving changes in local leadership.

The policy environment in China during the reform period was a peculiar one. The central bureaucracy, often identified with the interests of the state sector, was naturally hesitant to push ahead at speed. Local governments, generally identified with the interests of the non-state sector, were far more enthusiastic because they had incentives. Senior leaders at the political centre would forge alliances—sometimes with the central bureaucracy, sometimes with local leaders. This reform process resulted in great regional variations that were reinforced by the creation of the special economic zones.

The underground dimension

Defining the scope of the underground or informal economy in China is a daunting task. The Chinese system of law is in a permanent state of flux because of ongoing reforms. New legislation and regulations are constantly being drafted, and institutions are being created to implement and enforce these new laws and regulations. Since power has been devolved from the centre, local enterprises and authorities are often engaged in practices that have not been approved by the central authorities. Had they asked for permission ahead of time, it might not have been granted or been mired in lengthy delays. In consequence, there is an unavoidable element of ambiguity surrounding the legal status of all new local reforms. Indeed, local officials often try to enhance the legitimacy of their initiatives by lobbying senior leaders for support.

Regional and local variations imply that reform measures considered acceptable and legitimate in one area may not be acceptable in others. Provincial and local authorities have frequently approved or condoned practices that contravene policy regulations stipulated and even legislated by the central government. The best example here is the circulation of large amounts of Hong Kong currency in Guangdong province with almost no restriction, though this is in direct violation of central government regulations.

According to Feige's taxonomy (1990), China's underground economy has the features of being illegal, unreported, unrecorded, and informal.[4] Some activities are illegal: the growth of crime in many areas, including organized crime, is evident in most cities. Some activities are unreported, violating fiscal statutes: tax evasion is pervasive as a consequence of the introduction of the fiscal contract responsibility system whereby the central government engages in annual bargaining exercises to determine the level of taxes local governments and selected state-owned enterprises should pay. As to records, the distortions in China's economy and its evolving accounting system make it hard to measure the scale of economic activity: even estimates of the size of its GNP have a margin of error that is as large as 500 to 600 percent, depending on whether we use the conventional exchange rate conversion factor or the purchasing power parity measurements.[5] But the most significant underground economic activity is in the informal Chinese economy, where individuals and enterprises engage in widespread violation of legal and

---

4   Feige, E.L. (1990), "Defining and Estimating Underground and Informal Economies:The New Institutional Economics Approach," in *World Development*, vol. 18, no. 7 (July).

5   See "Chinese Puzzles," in the *Economist*, May 15, 1993, p. 79.

administrative rules. As in most developing countries, full compliance with these rules would make economic activity impossible.[6]

China today is a transitional economy in which private property rights are poorly defined and enforced. Regulations are pervasive but enforcement is not always effective. The coexistence of the state and non-state sectors in such conditions creates enormous opportunities for rent seeking and corruption. These activities take many forms, but a typical characteristic is the diversion of resources from the state sector, with its low private and social rates of return, to the non-state sector with relatively high rates of return. Liberalization has allowed bureaucrats and managers more freedom to capture profits that should accrue to the state and divert the resources of state-owned enterprises and banks into non-state businesses that they themselves control or own. Some of these businesses may even be incorporated overseas. For the economy as a whole, diverting resources from the state sector is economically efficient to the extent that it results in a higher social rate of return: in China, this is still largely true, so that we do not see perverse consequences in the economy.

Underground labour

Before the reforms, China had a rigid system of controlling population movements tied to a system of rationing essential consumer goods. This system has collapsed, and the country now has a growing floating population of individuals and households estimated at over 80 million living in major growth cities without residency rights.[7] These people are urban squatters in search of jobs. They have no access to social welfare, housing, or education without residency rights, but they are tolerated by local governments because economic growth has created tight labour markets in many coastal cities.

---

6   This problem is highlighted in De Soto, H. (1990), *The Other Path*: New York, Harper & Row.

7   Figure cited by Xuejin Zuo, "Socioeconomic Impacts of Floating Population in China: An Assessment and Policy Issues," Research Proposal, Shanghai Academy of Social Sciences, 1994.

Meanwhile, workers in state-owned enterprises who have attractive housing and welfare benefits but poor salaries are taking second jobs with non-state enterprises while holding on to their state-provided benefits. The magnitude of these labour markets is unknown but probably quite sizeable and will continue to grow over time.

Underground foreign trade and investment

Despite trade liberalization, China's tariff and non-tariff barriers remain quite high, a situation that has given rise to a huge smuggling problem. Statistics are difficult to obtain, but Hong Kong's proximity to China makes it a major conduit. It is reported that about 10 percent of all luxury cars in Hong Kong are being stolen and smuggled into China. According to an industry source, the amount of cigarettes smuggled into China is twice the amount officially imported. On the basis of Hong Kong import and consumption figures, it has been estimated that half the television sets imported into Hong Kong are subsequently smuggled into China. Smuggling between Hong Kong and China became so serious that the Hong Kong government was compelled to license high-powered speed boats in a bid to stem the flow of smuggled goods.

Taiwan fishermen routinely conduct barter trade with Chinese fishermen on the open seas. In a bid to regulate such trade activities, the authorities in Fujian province legalized them as "minor trade" in 1985 and stipulated that they take place in designated coastal mainland ports managed by customs officers. From Taiwan's point of view this is still smuggling, however, since the Taiwan authorities technically ban direct trade with China. In the elaborate trading system involving Taiwan, Hong Kong, and China created by this policy, indirect Taiwan trade through Hong Kong to China amounted to US $6.3 billion in 1992.

Actually, Taiwan does conduct three different forms of direct trade with China: transhipment, transit shipment or cargo-in-transit, and illegal direct shipment.[8] These three modes accounted for trade worth US $4.7 billion in 1992. In principle, Taiwan businesses cannot openly

---

8   See Y.W. Sung (1994), "The Economics of the Illegal Trade between Taiwan and Mainland China": Department of Economics, Chinese University of Hong Kong.

export to the mainland by transhipping via Hong Kong: transhipment usually involves a through bill of lading and would therefore constitute direct trade. Taiwan customs do, however, allow exporters to leave their final destination open and specify Hong Kong as the port of discharge whence the goods are to be shipped elsewhere. On arrival in Hong Kong, shipping companies can specify a mainland port as the final destination: the Hong Kong government usually allows such cases to pass as transhipment and exempts the goods from import and export tax. Such cases are known as "switch bill" shipments because another bill of lading, consigning the goods from Hong Kong to a mainland port, replaces the original bill consigning the goods from Taiwan to Hong Kong.

Transit shipment or cargo-in-transit involves those cases where ships carrying goods from Taiwan to China make stopovers in Hong Kong. Taiwan exporters claim that their goods are destined for Hong Kong when they leave Taiwan. On arrival in Hong Kong, the shipping company claims that the goods are destined for the mainland. The Hong Kong government treats these goods as cargo-in-transit.

Chinese reexports to Taiwan via Hong Kong amounted to US $1.1 billion and direct exports to Taiwan, US $1.2 billion in 1992. Chinese exports much less than it imports from Taiwan. Total trade between Hong Kong and China was worth about US $9.6 billion in 1993. This trade has served as a major conduit for capital flight from China through transfer pricing. Profits that accrue to Chinese entities are deposited in Hong Kong companies controlled by Chinese officials and entrepreneurs. Since these companies are incorporated in Hong Kong, they are treated as foreign by China though in reality they represent Chinese and not foreign capital. The Chinese call them the "false foreign devils."

When these companies invest in China, they enjoy the preferential tax benefits accorded to foreign investors. The tax rate on profits for foreign and joint venture companies is 15 percent when it can run as high as 50 percent for domestic companies. This simple mechanism provides a way of diverting Chinese government funds into foreign private funds controlled by Chinese officials and entrepreneurs. The percentage of foreign investment in China that is really domestic investment is unknown.

It is estimated that at least 15 percent of the currency issue in Hong Kong, US $1.5 billion, circulates within China where it can be deposited in Chinese banks as foreign currency. Since Chinese banks are not allowed to make foreign currency loans, these deposits are recycled into Hong Kong. It is reported that Chinese enterprises making deposits in China have indirect Hong Kong loan facilities that facilitate their financial transactions in Hong Kong and elsewhere.

Many state-owned enterprises in China are trying to raise funds by selling shares. If they are authorized to place those shares with foreign investors, they become foreign joint venture companies and can enjoy preferential tax treatment. These state companies thus have a huge incentive to sell their shares and assets at discounted values and obtain these tax advantages. Bribes can sweeten the pie, and a further twist may emerge if the foreign investor is in fact a "false foreign devil."

Financial reforms, underground loans, and macroeconomic instability

Prior to the economic reforms, banks were virtually the sole financial institutions in the Chinese economy. They were responsible for meeting planned objectives and in essence passively allocated credit in accordance with the economic plan, relying on the government to cover any loan losses. The People's Bank of China was charged with mobilizing resources from sectors that ran surpluses, mainly households, and passing them on for central allocation to industry and agriculture. China's banking system was basically a counting house: it had little to say about selecting firms to finance, assessing their creditworthiness, or monitoring them, and loan collection was of little concern since losses were routinely covered by the state. Under such a system, non-banking financial services would have been of little use.

In 1984, China started to reform its monobank system. The People's Bank, transformed into a central bank, handed over its day-to-day deposit and loan business to four specialized banks: the Agricultural Bank, the Industrial and Commercial Bank, the Bank of China, and the Construction Bank. Though there was change in the structure of the banking system, however, the process of credit creation remained unaltered. Bank loans were still regulated by a rigid system of quotas set by the central authorities to meet planning requirements. Interest rates on deposits and loans were also set uniformly. To attract deposits, the People's Bank would set interest rates at levels above the rate of inflation, but loan rates were often set very low to make the balance sheets of loss-making state-owned enterprises appear solvent.

As economic decision-making power was devolved to provinces and enterprises, the centre began to lose effective political control over the expansion of credit. Local authorities would pressure branch banks to make loans for local investment projects. When the centre did call for speeded-up economic reforms, the pressure from enterprise managers and local authorities on banks to expand credit increased. Banks would exhaust their lending quotas by mid-year, and the central government would be forced to seek monetary accommodation to meet its fiscal obligations.

A more significant change occurred in 1986 with the legalization of the interbank lending market. The market was originally developed for short-term lending among state banks to solve their liquidity problems, so that banks serving fast-growing regions and sectors with high loan demand could borrow from other banks with unused lending capacity. The imbalance between loans and deposits was a consequence of maintaining a system of rigid bank credit quotas as the economy became more and more liberalized. China's interbank lending market was intended as a mechanism for limited short-term financial flows across regions and sectors outside the plan, and it grew rapidly over time. By 1992 interbank lending had increased to 300 billion yuan, almost one seventh of the total volume of outstanding state bank loans. In 1993, interbank loans became an important cause of the overheating of the Chinese economy as banks sought to circumvent credit quotas by operating in the interbank lending market.

The overheating of the Chinese economy in 1993 can be traced to the enhanced pace of economic reform, which gathered momentum after Deng Xiaoping's trip to southern China in early 1992. In that year, real GDP rose by 12.8 percent, industrial output by 21.7 percent, fixed-asset investment by 37.6 percent, the general retail price index by 5.4 percent, and the cost of living index in 35 major cities rose by 10.9 percent. In the first six months of 1993, real GDP rose by 13.9 percent, industrial output by 25.1 percent, fixed-asset investment by 61.0 percent, the general retail price index by 10.8 percent, and the cost of living index in 35 major cities rose by 17.4 percent; all rates have been annually adjusted. It is worth noting that fixed-asset investment by state-owned enterprises rose by only 33 percent in 1992 but shot up to 70.7 percent in the first six months of 1993. This surge in fixed-asset investment, especially in state-owned enterprises, was the prime cause of 1993's overheated economy. It was reported in June 1993 that unauthorized interbank lending had risen to 200 billion yuan. State banking funds were being diverted through the interbank market into investment projects or speculation in the emerging securities and properties market. In some instances, even influential state-owned enterprises were able to gain direct access to the interbank lending market. The property development involvements of numerous banks and state-owned enterprises channelled much-needed resources from key infrastructure projects into speculative pursuits, spinning off heady opportunities for corruption.

Many problems can be identified. At the most superficial level, we can blame the diversion of bank funds on the poor state of banking regulation and supervision. Yet a more serious indictment of the inadequacies of China's monetary and banking system lies in the fact that banks suffer from undue political influence by powerful groups that impinge on credit allocation and decisions concerning monetary control. The lack of central bank independence, the arbitrariness of the credit allocation process, and the conflicting pressures arising from government support for state-owned enterprises and the market demands of the non-state sector are key policy matters that have yet to be addressed.

In the mid-1980s, the financial sector began to develop rapidly with a more diversified structure and a broader menu of financial instruments. Some state-owned commercial and development banks were established, first in the special economic zones and later throughout the country. Rural and urban credit cooperatives became more aggressive in loaning to the non-state sector. Numerous non-banking financial institutions were created: trust and investment companies, insurance companies, finance companies, financial leasing companies, and securities companies. These non-banking financial institutions were mainly subsidiaries of state-owned banks, state-owned enterprises, and central and provincial government offices.

Since these institutions operated outside the state plan, they had little incentive to lend to or invest in loss-making state-owned enterprises. Loans to the non-state sector as a percentage of total outstanding bank loans grew rapidly. Loans by rural credit cooperatives as a percentage of total bank loans rose from 2.33 percent in 1979 to 11.35 percent in 1992: the corresponding figures for urban credit cooperatives were 0.25 percent in 1986 and 1.75 percent in 1991. Loans by non-banking financial institutions rose even more rapidly, from 2.87 percent in 1986 to 6.71 percent in 1991.

These non-banking institutions undoubtedly played an important role in channelling resources to the more efficient non-state sector and contributed to the rapid growth of the more productive sectors of society. The state banking system's near-monopolistic control over loans was weakened, but this compounded the problem of macroeconomic control. In theory, these non-banking financial institutions are not part of the banking system and thus do not issue credit that constitutes money in the usual sense. Given the rudimentary regulatory framework in China, however, the real situation can be very different. It is clear that these institutions have access to the interbank lending market and have diverted these loans into investment projects and other speculative projects.

Corruption

Corruption has emerged as a pervasive feature of the Chinese economy. The recent reforms have created a dual-track system of state and non-state sectors. Economic liberalization has shifted decision making from the central bureaucrats to managers, entrepreneurs, and local bureaucrats. One consequence of this change is to make corruption easier: it has become difficult to monitor the behaviour of so many agents.

Corruption has improved incentives for bureaucrats and managers to enhance their enterprises' profitability and performance, especially in the non-state sector. Corruption has also improved the overall allocation of resources in the economy by diverting resources from the low-yield state sector to the high-yield non-state sector. As resources flow into the production of commodities with a higher social rate of return, the economy grows faster.

Given that most state-owned enterprises are losing money and have to be financed by state banks, growing corruption in the financial sector further complicates the problem with controlling macroeconomic stability. This threatens the momentum for reform. Pervasive corruption is socially disruptive and breeds discontent. As law enforcement agencies themselves turn corrupt, it becomes increasingly difficult to maintain law and order in society. With corruption institutionalized, it may be very difficult to maintain open and competitive markets.

Prospects for economic reform

From 1978 to 1993, China's central government revenue as a proportion of GNP fell from 35 to 15 percent. The fiscal deficit as a percentage of GNP was relatively small, and did not exceed 4 percent. However, the ambiguous financial position of the country's loss-making state-owned enterprises makes it hard for us to calculate the true fiscal deficit. Since policy loans represent forced lending to state-owned enterprises, often at very low interest rates, they should be included as part of China's fiscal deficit. The consolidated fiscal deficit that includes these loans is much larger, and in all likelihood exceeded 10 percent of GNP in 1993. Fiscal deterioration in China is a growing problem.

More than a decade of economic reform has failed to improve the productivity and profitability of state-owned enterprises, many of which continue to rely on the state to cover their losses. Increasing open and hidden fiscal deficits have been financed largely by loans from the state banking system. Macroeconomic instability has become increasingly difficult to handle and has from time to time resulted in open inflation and exchange rate crises that had to be managed with Draconian measures to cool off the economy.

Macroeconomic instability in China is a structural problem directly resulting from failure to reform the state sector. The transition to a market economy is still incomplete, and inflation and exchange rate crises are complicating the reform process by making it politically necessary to reintroduce price and exchange controls in the absence of any effective mechanism and the political will to curb credit expansion. Loss-making state-owned enterprises are the source of China's macroeconomic instability and put further economic reforms at risk.

The solution is not conceptually difficult. Unless the Chinese government is prepared to move quickly and boldly to prepare for the open privatization and restructuring of its state-owned enterprises, economic stagnation in the state sector cannot be averted. Interim measures to create a social security net for discharged workers are obviously needed to avoid widespread social discontent. Resources spent on services to displaced workers will be socially less costly than trying to prop up these unprofitable enterprises. An opportunity must be created for rationalizing the banking and financial system so that the problem of macroeconomic instability can be resolved. This in turn will make scarce financial capital available to the vibrant non-state sector instead of being wasted on the inefficient state sector. China's spectacular success of recent years would then become sustainable.

The current situation in China is best summarized with some recent figures for industrial output in the period January-April 1994.[9]

	Total RMB (billions)	Change (%) over same 1993 period
Total industrial output, of which:	1224	18.35
State enterprises	579	4.72
Collective enterprises	457	31.58
Other enterprises	188	39.65

In this period, state enterprises produced 47.5 percent of total industrial output, but their year-on-year growth rate was a mere 4.72 percent. The non-state sector comprising the collective and private, joint venture, and foreign-owned enterprises grew at a year-on-year rate of between 30 and 40 percent. The non-state sector is forging ahead with the state sector lagging behind.

Will the state sector quietly wither away? This is most unlikely. First, we have to recognize that the state sector includes many heavy and infrastructure industries that are state monopolies. Now the state sector

---

9   *China Economic News*, vol. 15, no. 20, May 30, 1994.

can be bled to death by simply diverting resources away into the non-state sector, but the same industries cannot be recreated in the non-state sector without a shift in policy. Privatizing major state enterprises and opening them up to competition has to be an explicit policy, not an implicit one. Financial arrangements affecting major investments cannot be successfully concluded without a more clear delineation of property rights. Privatization through the back door simply cannot work.

Secondly, if widespread social and economic disruption and macroeconomic instability are to be avoided, China needs a feasible strategic plan for reform that includes the establishment of social security nets for displaced workers in order to move the economy successfully towards the goal of creating a market system. Muddling through as in the past is really not an adequate policy response. The state has to embrace the private enterprise system and the market economy with no "ifs" or "buts." For all this to take place, political reforms are almost inevitable.

Section 4:
Some Policy Implications
and Insights

Policy Implications of Tax Evasion and the Underground Economy

Jonathan R. Kesselman

Introduction

There is little agreement about the size of the underground economy (UGE) relative to the total economy. No matter how small or how large the UGE might actually be, it has important implications for public policy.[1] These relate to matters of economic efficiency and distributional equity as well as the design, operation, and enforcement of the tax system. Even if the UGE were less than 5 percent of GDP, it could still be vital if its efficiency or distributional effects were significantly ad-

---

1   This paper concentrates on the public-finance and particularly the taxation implications of tax evasion and the UGE. For earlier analyses of UGE implications for macroeconomic phenomena, including cyclical fluctuations, price stability, economic growth, labour productivity, economic development, and monetary policy, see contributions in Gaertner and Wenig (1985) and Feige (1989).

verse. Conversely, a UGE as large as 15 or 20 percent of GDP could be of minimal concern if its efficiency and distributional effects were small or viewed as favourable.

The efficiency and distributional impacts of these overlapping but not congruent fields of tax evasion and UGE activity are of obvious interest in themselves. Yet we also need to consider the tax revenues lost to non-compliance and their economic repercussions. The lost revenues may be recouped through higher taxes on compliant taxpayers, or they may result in lower levels of public spending for various purposes. Each of these compensating policy reactions exerts its own efficiency and distributional impacts.

Since there is so much controversy about the scale of the UGE and tax evasion, we might expect knowledge about their efficiency and distributional effects to be hopeless at a quantitative level. However, economic theory and analysis can be helpful in identifying what features of UGE and evasion activities should be observed to cast light on these policy-relevant issues. We also need guidance about the kinds of evasion, the sectors of the economy, and the types of participants that should be of particular concern for policy purposes. Insights of these kinds should be instructive in guiding society's mobilization of resources to combat evasion and in designing effective strategies for countering these practices.

Such analyses must give due recognition to both the resource costs and the resource savings of alternative approaches to handling the UGE and evasion. Two major types of policy responses may be considered: 1) "ex post" policies related to information reporting, detection methods, and enforcement measures, based on a given mix, structure, and rate of tax; and 2) "ex ante" policies incorporated in the design of the tax system itself with its associated administrative structures and procedures.

In this paper, we draw on insights from an active and growing economic literature on tax evasion and the UGE. We address the policy-relevant issues described above in a relatively non-technical fashion. To provide a more precise context for these phenomena, a distinction will be drawn between UGE activity, which involves tax evasion, and pure tax evasion. We will then offer a discussion of the relationship of the

UGE and benefit fraud—the counterpart to tax evasion in the transfer system.

Following a review of some basic insights from the economic analysis of tax evasion and the UGE, we will examine the markets and mechanisms by which the efficiency and distributional effects of these activities operate. Finally, we attempt to extract some key implications of the analysis for the two major public policy aspects: enforcement (the ex post aspect) and tax and transfer design (the ex ante aspect).

UGE versus PTE

When attempting to assess the efficiency and distributional effects of tax evasion, it is useful to distinguish two forms. The first is tax evasion associated with activity in the UGE, which involves the productive supply of goods or services. This entails the use of labour, managerial, or entrepreneurial services, along with the requisite tangible capital, to operate a productive activity. The second is tax evasion not associated with participation in the UGE or the supply of labour or similar services. Such pure tax evasion (PTE) usually involves financial manipulation, the non-disclosure of capital or financial incomes, the overstatement of tax deductions, or misstatements of individual circumstances.

We will now briefly consider these types of tax evasion in greater detail, since each form has different potential effects on economic efficiency. The avoidance of taxes through such legal means as tax shelters and tax incentive provisions does not constitute evasion and therefore lies beyond our present scope.[2] Our treatment of the UGE does include the production of legal as well as illegal goods and services. The tax evasion associated with legal activities in the UGE is itself illegal, of course, and may be liable to criminal penalties.[3] Legal activities in the

---

2   See, for example, Slemrod (1994). The author of the present paper is undertaking an analysis of tax avoidance behaviour using general equilibrium techniques described later.

3   A telling commentary on this point was expressed by the chairman of a Vancouver brokerage house, Peter Brown, when a client of the firm was found to have evaded taxes: "There was no money laundering here. I associate money laundering with criminal activity. Lots of people cheat on their taxes." *Globe and Mail*, July 29, 1994, p. B1.

UGE include a wide range of goods and services that are also produced in the legitimate or "above-ground" economy. Common examples are home repair and renovation, food and entertainment, auto repair, gardening, babysitting, and the like.

The illegal portion of the UGE includes such "productive" activities as distributing illicit drugs, smuggling and trading in contraband goods, prostitution, and unauthorized gambling. These items constitute goods and services that are transacted between willing buyers and sellers, even though they are illegal per se. By contrast, purely "appropriative" activities are illegal but are excluded from our notion of UGE activity because they do not add to society's total level of consumer satisfaction. Examples here include extortion, blackmail, and many forms of theft such as robbery, shoplifting, embezzlement, fraud, and forgery. Participants in the illegal UGE evade taxes mainly to conceal their illegal activities; conversely, those who participate in the legal UGE are motivated largely or primarily by the evasion of taxes or benefit fraud.

Pure tax evasion involves non-reporting, understatement, or misreporting of taxable income, profits, or sales, but unlike UGE activity, PTE involves no labour input or no change of mode of business operation relative to the legitimate economy. Some PTE activity is related to extreme financial manipulation that goes beyond the bounds of legal tax avoidance. Other PTE occurs in conventional, legitimate businesses that underreport their receipts or overstate their expenses. Still other PTE stems from misreporting such events as intrafamilial transfers for tax purposes or misrepresenting the type, source, or timing of receipts. Although PTE does not directly affect the allocation of labour or capital resources or the methods of business operation, our later analysis will indicate how it can nevertheless affect the overall allocation and distribution of economic resources.

The distinction between UGE and PTE activities is not always clear-cut. For example, an established jeweller who understates receipts from cash sales but does not significantly alter his mode of business operation to conceal such sales is closer to PTE than the UGE. An individual who repeatedly buys, renovates, and resells homes while claiming the capital gains exemption on principal residences in Canada is probably closer to the UGE than PTE.

Benefit fraud and the UGE

For several reasons, we might expect the size of the UGE to be conditioned by benefit fraud as much as by tax evasion. Public transfer programs—including cash transfers, tax-linked benefits, and in-kind benefits—have grown substantially over the past thirty years. Most transfer benefits are conditional on reported incomes using implicit marginal tax rates (MTRs). When the MTRs of several programs are added together, the total rate can exceed that of the highest rate of personal income tax.

In Canada, the principal transfer programs include provincial welfare, unemployment insurance, and subsidies for child care, housing, and health care benefits. It is not unusual for the total MTR to approach or exceed 100 percent, providing a strong incentive for benefit fraud by working in the UGE.[4] Benefit fraud has been further fuelled by such phenomena as rising numbers of unmarried couples and other unconventional families and the secular growth of welfare dependency. Higher rates of family fragmentation and child support obligations have driven others, particularly non-custodial fathers, into the UGE.

Echoing the distinction between the UGE and PTE for tax evasion, benefit fraud can involve either participation in the underground economy or simple non-reporting of income from the "above-ground" economy. However, since most candidates for public transfers have little capital other than consumer durables and possibly home equity, their income will be overwhelmingly derived from labour earnings. The visibility of most work in the above-ground economy will tend to drive such persons into the UGE if they hope to conceal their earnings from the transfer authorities. Something analogous to PTE can arise in benefit fraud when a beneficiary conceals assets that would be counted against benefits or fails to report capital or investment income. Such "pure benefit fraud" can also arise in cases where two-parent households

---

4   Some observers have applied the term "benefit fraud" solely to multiple welfare claims and similar manoeuvres, arguing that concealment of earnings from the welfare authorities is understandable and non-culpable in view of the low level of benefits and the high penalty on earnings. This view mirrors one cited in the last note that tax evasion is commonplace and not really a criminal activity.

present themselves as single-parent families to conceal one partner's earnings. In such cases, the second parent can work in the above-ground economy with less risk that visible earnings will be traced back to the partner who is claiming the transfers.

Economic framework

An economic framework for explaining tax evasion and UGE participation will be based on rational decisions by individuals. These decisions are affected by preferences—including attitudes towards risk, honesty, and alternative occupations—as well as policy, market, and institutional factors. The simplest form of behaviour to model is PTE, which involves no substantive productive activity or occupational choice. Pure tax evasion hinges on a calculated weighing of gains from the concealment of a taxable receipt, sale, or purchase against perceived risks and penalties if detected.

Attitudes towards risk play a pivotal role in the extent to which various individuals will evade taxes. Persons who are risk-neutral will evade to the point where the taxes saved equal the potential penalties; risk-averse persons will evade to a lesser extent. Views about public morality, influenced by perceptions of the value of public services and the fairness of the tax system, may also condition PTE. It is commonly thought that higher tax rates will augment PTE and the associated revenue losses, and yet economic theory finds that this outcome depends on attitudes towards risk. Under certain conditions—"diminishing absolute risk aversion"—higher tax rates will actually decrease PTE.

UGE activity is more complex to explain than PTE since it involves decisions about occupations (often self-employment) and markets with both producers and consumers. To conceal tax evasion, UGE participants also have to conceal the activity that generates their income. This attempted secrecy affects the scale of underground businesses, their modes of operation, and their production technologies, with key implications for economic efficiency that will be discussed below.

In addition to the risk of being apprehended for tax evasion, self-employed UGE participants further bear the risks of being in business. Since the range of industries and occupations that lend themselves to small-scale covert operation is limited, personal tastes and skills in those lines of work will affect decisions about entering the UGE. The goods and services produced in the UGE must be sold, and the tastes of consumers for them as against the output of the legitimate economy will affect relative pricing and the distribution of UGE gains.

The size of the UGE is conditioned by the balance of the benefits versus the costs of moving into that sector. The benefits of working in the UGE include taxes evaded; the costs of working there include lower gross earnings, the expenses of concealment, and potential tax penalties. The need to conceal activities and occupations in the UGE will also mean psychic strain for many individuals. In equilibrium, UGE participants will tend to be, relative to their counterparts above ground, less averse to risk, less honest, more efficient at concealment, and/or more productive in those occupations or industries that are most amenable to tax evasion. Many who are compliant in equilibrium would actually be evaders were it not for the presence of others who are more predisposed to or efficient at evading. A populous UGE drives marginal returns down to the point where it is not attractive for others to enter. The marginal entrant gains little or nothing from participating in the UGE.

In the context of UGE as against PTE activity, it looks more likely that higher tax rates will raise levels of non-compliance. Tax increases will affect decision-making under risk, and the outcome again hinges on the precise characteristics of individual attitudes to risk. In the UGE, however, tax increases also raise the relative profitability of working covertly rather than in the tax-compliant sector—a situation that will attract more people to move productive activities underground. A new equilibrium will be established when the relative prices of UGE output have fallen to the point where no additional individuals find it advantageous to go underground. Note that this process of adjustment reduces the returns to all previous participants in the UGE as well, so that their incremental savings from evading at a higher rate of tax are offset by lower gross returns from their production.

Efficiency effects

PTE and UGE activities both distort the allocation of economic resources and may thereby reduce economic efficiency. That is, they may produce a lower level of material well-being than would prevail in their absence. However, it is also possible for such activities to enhance economic efficiency, particularly in cases where taxation or regulatory systems are highly coercive or confiscatory. For example, if taxes are imposed on incomes at very high rates, even short of 100 percent, the adverse effects on incentives to produce may be so severe that tax evasion yields higher-valued economic activity than tax-compliant activity would.

Whether the effects on economic efficiency are mainly negative or positive will hinge on the institutional, tax, and regulatory environment of a particular economy. In a rigid, centrally planned economy, we might expect PTE and the UGE to enhance overall economic well-being. At the other end of the spectrum, in a low-tax, relatively unregulated economy, non-compliance is likely to erode economic well-being. In advanced economies with substantial tax and regulatory burdens, the net efficiency impact of non-compliance has not been clearly determined.

Since PTE does not in the first instance involve substantive economic activity, its effects on efficiency are more roundabout than those of evasion within the UGE. If PTE is randomly distributed across the industries and sectors of an economy, it is unlikely to affect resource allocation other than through the need to recoup revenues lost through higher tax rates. Conversely, if PTE is concentrated in particular industries or sectors it will raise net returns from activity in those sectors, and this will in turn tend to expand those sectors and their products as against the efficient pattern arising with uniform compliance. This efficiency cost may be partially offset by the fact that evasion raises net returns on savings and investments, thereby mitigating tax distortions in those activities.

Evasion involving the UGE also involves inefficiencies from channelling excessive resources into the sectors or industries most amenable to evasion. The UGE further entails economic inefficiencies that arise directly from the altered production and sales methods businesses have to use for covert activities. Typical UGE operating styles will include smaller-scale production, fewer workers, less specialization of functions, less subcontracting, fewer tools and equipment, and more time wasted between jobs. For example, an off-the-books plumber will spend more time travelling between jobs than a legitimate plumbing firm with radio-dispatched trucks that can schedule its crews to adjacent jobs. Additionally, UGE operators will have to use less efficient means of advertising and incur more costs of concealment, such as changing phone numbers and addresses more frequently to reduce the risk of apprehension.

More than workers in the legitimate economy, UGE participants may also have their consumption and investment choices biased. They may be inclined to consume a high proportion of their current incomes rather than accumulate savings or large consumer durables that would be visible to the taxman. The composition of their savings and investments will be biased towards underground or offshore activities so as to prevent detection of the original cheating. UGE participants will also invest less in the human capital associated with their underground activity if they perceive greater risk to their business lifespans due to apprehension for taxation, regulatory, or licensing offences. Economic rents garnered by UGE participants may be dissipated through bribes to officials, especially in developing economies. To the extent that this practice diverts officials from their primary duties, it decreases the efficiency of the public sector.

Goods and services produced in the UGE carry less in the way of guarantees and general consumer protection than their legitimate-sector counterparts. With informed consumers, this factor is presumably reflected in lower prices. The UGE offers opportunities to individuals who might not be able to enter conventional production because of licensing or union barriers. If the conventional markets have monopolistic or non-competitive elements, the presence of the UGE may provide effective competition. Such competitive pressure can actually make the above-ground suppliers more efficient.

Of course, many regulations have to do with safety, health, and environmental standards which may be shortchanged by UGE producers. One might argue that consumers of UGE products are willing to accept lower standards for a lower price. Even if they are fully aware of this, however, there may be external effects on other people who are compromised by UGE activity. For example, a home built below the established standard may be a fire risk for the next-door neighbours, or substandard plumbing will be hidden in walls so that subsequent purchasers are unable to gauge its quality.

Even if the positive and negative efficiency effects of PTE or UGE activity offset each other, there would still be an impact on economic efficiency through the public finances. Public revenues lost because of these activities would have to be either recouped through higher taxes in the compliant economy or reflected in lower levels of public spending. Raising rates will simply exacerbate tax distortions of economic decisions in a variety of areas. In other words, the marginal cost of raising public funds is increased over what it would be without tax evasion.

If, on the other hand, revenues lost through non-compliance are reflected in reduced public spending, this would ordinarily be construed as an inefficiency.[5] This view assumes that the outcome of the political and bureaucratic process is to supply the optimal amount of public goods and services relative to the public's preferences and willingness to pay taxes. Yet for those who believe that governments tend, Leviathan-like, to oversupply public goods and services, reduced public spending resulting from PTE and the UGE might be regarded as enhancing efficiency.

Distributional effects[6]

A common assumption of lay observers is that tax evaders and UGE participants pocket all of their ill-gotten gains. Our review of the economic framework and efficiency effects has showed however that these gains may be dissipated in a variety of ways and that the beneficiaries may include other individuals in the affected markets. In particular, consumers of goods and services that are augmented through PTE and UGE activity stand to gain.

As in our previous analysis, it will be useful here to look at the movement of distributional effects separately for PTE and the UGE. One might expect PTE to be more concentrated at upper income levels, since it typically involves capital rather than labour. However, individuals of modest means can also underreport their receipts from interest, dividends, or rents. Conversely, given the markets and occupations in-

---

5   The higher cost of raising public funds due to non-compliance should itself induce an efficient public sector to choose a lower level of public spending. Fewer prospective public projects will survive a cost-benefit test when revenues are more costly to raise.

6   Any policy assessment of the distributional effects of tax evasion must contain ethical judgments about the relative weights to be assigned to gains enjoyed by compliant and non-compliant individuals.

volved, UGE activity might be expected to occur more frequently at lower to middle income levels. Of course, exceptions will arise with high returns to some participants in the criminal sector of the UGE.

The distributional effects of PTE hinge on its dispersion or concentration across the economy. When it is so dispersed as to be almost random across sectors, PTE perpetrators enjoy most if not all of the benefits. No market reaction arises to offset their gains, and the losers are either compliant taxpayers who have to make up the lost revenues or else people who suffer from curtailed public spending. At the other extreme, with PTE highly concentrated in a few sectors, the cost of capital will be depressed in those sectors and the expansion of goods and services produced in them will benefit consumers. Hence, the net gains to PTE practitioners will be less than their apparent savings from evasion, because they will accept lower gross rates of return in order to invest in sectors or industries that are conducive to evasion. This case is similar to the outcome of legal tax avoidance, where tax shelters for particular sectors depress their gross rates of return to the point where marginal investors gain nothing from the preferential tax provisions. With PTE, some of the gains will be dissipated in costs of concealment; in tax avoidance, the gains are partially spent on professional tax advisors.

The UGE has two distributional aspects that interest us here. The first is the distribution of gains between UGE participants and persons in the legitimate sector. This is the issue of UGE producers versus consumers of UGE goods and services, whether or not these buyers work in the UGE or the legitimate sector. If underground output is perfectly substitutable for the counterpart goods and services of the legitimate economy, it will sell at the same price and consumers will not benefit. But if the UGE output is so large as to lower the prices of those goods and services on the legitimate market, consumers can benefit even with homogeneous products. If the UGE output is imperfectly substitutable for consumers, it will command a lower price and consumers will benefit thereby. One would expect typical UGE output to be imperfectly substitutable, if not because of differences in quality or other characteristics, then at least because of the lack of warranties or legal recourse for consumers.

The second distributional aspect of interest is how gains are spread across UGE participants. Here, we apply the concept of "evasion costs" for individuals—costs like risk aversion, the psychic stress of evading or working in the UGE, concealment, and lower productivity. The critical point for distributional effects in the UGE is the degree to which evasion costs vary across individuals. If everyone—at least, everyone in the UGE in equilibrium—bears the same evasion costs, then everyone will benefit to the same degree. Yet in equilibrium, the marginal UGE entrant will derive no benefit from the UGE; fully homogeneous evasion costs mean that no underground workers are better off than they would be working legitimately. However, in the much more realistic case of heterogeneous evasion costs, the people with the lowest evasion costs gain the most from UGE work, with successively smaller gains for those with higher evasion costs.

Any policy assessment of the UGE must be concerned with the characteristics of UGE participants with low evasion costs. Some elements of evasion costs—particularly concealment and productivity losses in the UGE—might be lowest for groups such as youth, recent immigrants, and persons with anonymity in communities set apart by ethnicity or language. Many of these individuals are disadvantaged when it comes to finding work in the legitimate sector or in markets with unions or other entry restrictions. Hence, policies that would effectively address tax evasion in the UGE could have a disproportionate effect on disadvantaged individuals. Still, some industries are so dominated by UGE activity that forcing workers out of the underground would increase opportunities for many of the same individuals in the legitimate sector of the same industries.

The other distributional effects of PTE and UGE activity arise from the government response to lost tax revenues. As already mentioned, a government can respond by raising tax rates or trimming public spending; an increase in the public deficit can be regarded as an increase in future tax rates. We cannot form general conclusions about likely responses or their distributional effects without reference to the type of party in power or fiscal structure. In governments pressing against the political limits of the tax burden and seeking ways to curtail spending and control deficits, the likely response to revenue losses from evasion will probably be more spending curtailment. Similarly, effective policies to reduce evasion would probably reduce constraints on spending sooner than tax rates on compliant taxpayers. To the extent that public spending programs are typically tilted in favour of lower and middle income households, revenue losses from evasion are more than likely regressive in their ultimate effects.

Implications for enforcement policy

Policies to enforce the provisions of the tax system against PTE and UGE activities face a diverse matrix of factors. These include individual and social psychology, strategic behaviour by evaders, political pressures on public policy, and ethical issues concerning the appropriate balance between law enforcement and personal freedom. Efficiency and distributional outcomes have to be considered when defining an optimal enforcement policy. The economic and psychic costs of enforcement must be weighed against the benefits, and each needs to be evaluated at the margin to determine policy. The marginal benefits of increased enforcement should also include the deterrent effect on other evaders as well as the incremental revenues collected from the ones who are apprehended. The emphasis to be placed on the well-being of tax evaders is equally relevant to the distributional assessment of enforcement policy. At one extreme, evaders would be totally ignored in computing social welfare, while a more individualistic approach would encompass their well-being.

We will first examine the factors affecting enforcement policy for pure tax evasion, many of which will also apply to policy for the UGE. The penalty rate and the probability of detection both raise the anticipated costs of evasion, and an optimal policy will choose an appropriate combination of the two elements.[7] Raising penalties is costless for society, whereas enhancing detection efforts entails expensive audit resources. It might therefore appear desirable to raise penalty rates sky high while reducing resources spent on audits. One observer has called this a policy of "hang tax evaders with detection probability zero."[8]

---

7   Penalties can be lump-sum fines but are more commonly expressed as fines related to amounts of tax evaded.

8   Benjamini and Maital (1985, p. 254) attribute this statement to Serge-Christophe Kolm.

This extreme strategy is limited by several considerations. The acceptable penalties for evasion may be constrained by penalties applied to other criminal offences of comparable severity. Unduly severe penalties are also ruled out by the possibility of, for example, the government or an offender being mistaken as to when an act of evasion took place. The complexity of tax laws increases the likelihood of "honest mistakes" through poor advice, misinformation, or misjudgment. The possibility of erroneous conviction for tax evasion will make Draconian penalties unacceptable.

So how stringent should a detection program be? One measure of stringency is the *expected* penalty for the act of evasion—the punishment multiplied by the probability of detection. Even if audits or other means of detection were costless, an optimal enforcement policy would stop short of attempting to eliminate evasion altogether. Policy actions to decrease evasions may, beyond some point, reduce the level of society's well-being, because they reduce the utility of risk-averse evaders. In the optimum there should be positive marginal tax revenues from raising either the penalty rate or detection probability. Only if the welfare of evaders does not count should enforcement be pursued so as to generate the maximum total revenues. Considering the resource cost of tax enforcement will also reduce the optimal stringency.

The economic hypothesis of PTE decisions by risk-neutral individuals suggests that much tougher penalties may be needed to deter evasion than are currently in force. For an act of evasion that saves one dollar of tax, a risk-averse person will choose to evade so long as:

$$1 - P > P F,$$

where P is the probability of apprehension and F is the fine per dollar of tax evaded. In other words, deterrence of evasion requires that fines be levied at a rate of

$$F > (1 - P) / P.$$

If the probability of detection is as high as 50 percent (P = 0.5), then fines of just over 100 percent (F = 1.00) will suffice. This is roughly in line with penalties for evasion in many countries. However, a more realistic appraisal of the chances of being caught for many kinds of evasion will suggest that penalties at the above rate are woefully inadequate. For example, if the perceived probability is just 5 percent, then the requisite fine should be over 1900 percent, or 19 times the amount evaded.[9]

Tax enforcement in the UGE involves the same factors as with PTE, but policy makers must also examine the effects on real resources absorbed in underground activity. The old saying that "an economy breathes through its tax loopholes" can be extended from tax avoidance to tax evasion. Excessively stringent enforcement can reduce productivity, output, and work incentives in the UGE and possibly in the economy as a whole. The effects on total economic performance are more likely to be adverse if cracking down on the UGE pushes labour into leisure time or tax-free household production activities rather than into the above-ground economy.

Another dimension of enforcement policy for the UGE has to do with detection methods. If the tax authorities investigate and apprehend only individuals who have filed tax returns or had taxes withheld on regular jobs, some of them will be induced to go completely underground. Such persons have been called "ghosts" since they have no official existence as far as the tax authorities are concerned. UGE participants will have a greater risk of being caught if they also report or engage in regular work. Tightening enforcement for these non-ghosts may propel enough of them into the ghostly state that total tax revenues actually decline. The obvious solution here is to organize an appropriate effort to seek out and apprehend the ghosts, possibly by following up on tips from the public and pursuing underground workers through their classified ads.

Other strategies for tax enforcement also follow from the economic framework reviewed earlier. Publicity campaigns based on evader convictions can raise the perceived probability of detection without increasing public spending for audits. Appeals to morality and public-spiritedness may also play a role, but are less likely to be effective with today's jaded taxpayers. There are high returns from improved knowledge about what signals to use for focussing tax investigation and audit resources. As indicated above, these signals should include elements that will

---

9   The formula also shows how an unconstrained, optimal strategy is to "hang tax evaders with detection probability zero": $P = 0$ implies an infinite value for F.

detect ghosts as well as individuals with reported earnings. Moreover, the strategic aspects of evader behaviour need to be better understood by the enforcement authorities. More creative penalty schemes could also play a role in deterring tax evasion. For example, someone with a recently detected offence could be subjected to detailed retrospective investigation for previous years; this would greatly increase the expected penalties for recurrent evasion.

Implications for tax and transfer policy

The existence of PTE, benefit fraud, and the UGE has significant implications for the design of tax and transfer policies. Most enforcement problems are primarily the result of inadequacies in the basic design of these policies. Compliance cannot be stronger than the policy design supports in terms of information reporting, source withholding, and related incentives for taxpayers and other parties. Of course, compliance should be just one major concern in the design of tax and transfer policies; it should not be allowed to dominate other key objectives such as efficiency and equity. Still, poor compliance itself poses inequities across taxpayers and raises the costs of operating the tax system.

Compliance will also be affected by broader issues of tax policy and public finance as well as specific tax structures and rates. For example, taxpayers will be better motivated to pay if they perceive that they are getting good value for their tax dollars in public goods and services and that the tax system is basically fair. Replacing general taxes with user charges—at least within the limited range where they can sensibly be applied—also reduces incentives for evasion since payments are attached to the receipt of particular goods or benefit entitlements.[10]

The design of a tax or transfer system contains several elements that have a particular bearing on compliance and enforcement. The first is the base of the tax in both the theoretical and implementation senses. Two taxes can have the same formal base and be equivalent in their

---

10 User fees are limited to those goods and services provided by governments that do not have any of the following characteristics: "pure public goods," "merit goods," or other social externalities, high costs for excluding non-payers, and distributional goals for their use or consumption.

economic content and predicted effects but still differ radically in their operational and compliance characteristics. For example, a flat-rate consumption tax can be implemented either as an indirect tax like a value-added tax or as a direct tax, like a personal income tax with a full deduction for net savings. The second element is the intended rate structure and degree of progressivity. The third comprises definitions of the taxable unit, whether it be the individual, family, or some other notion. The fourth includes the methods of tax collection, tax remittances, and source withholding or self-reporting with installment payments. These are essential aspects of tax design for compliance purposes, and they imply systems for information reporting and verification. Parallel issues arise in the design of transfer programs, such as defining the measure of need and verifying reported needs.

Information reporting and source withholding are particularly important for achieving high rates of tax compliance. The income types that are subject to withholding—wages and salaries—have higher rates of voluntary compliance than types subject only to reporting, such as interest and dividends. The lowest rates of voluntary compliance are found in income types that require neither withholding nor reporting by an agent independent of the taxpayer—rent receipts, capital gains, and self-employment income. Yet requirements to withhold and report must offer the parties genuine incentives. For example, most firms have a strong interest in withholding and reporting the correct amounts of personal tax from their employees since they can claim deductions for payrolls from their own taxable incomes. Most firms face comparable or higher rates of tax than their employees, so there are few incentives for collusion between employer and employee to underreport payroll .

The weak link for compliance with most taxes arises at the final stage—purchases by households and sales of goods and services directly to households. Company-to-company transactions usually have the built-in safeguard that they are tax-deductible by the purchasing firm, so that a revenue paper trail leads back to the vendor firm. This point has often been cited in support of the credit-invoice method of value-added taxation exemplified by the Canadian goods and services tax. Households, however, do not ordinarily need receipts for tax purposes. This is one reason, along with the small scale of production for many services purchased by households, for the high incidence of evasion related to the sale of services to households. An interesting exception is the requirement that Canadian households claiming the child care tax deduction must report the names, addresses, and social insurance numbers of persons paid for child-minding services.

It is useful to examine four issues of tax design to see how they are affected by the presence of PTE and the UGE. First, we consider optimal progressivity and levels for personal income tax. Choices here hinge on the value of public spending at the margin and the trade-off between efficiency costs and distributional effects of taxes. Since evasion itself reduces the distortions of high tax rates, its presence does not necessarily imply that a less progressive rate structure is desirable. The existence of the UGE also does not necessarily mean that marginal tax rates should be reduced—the reason here being that the UGE is distorted by penalties imposed on evaders, which can mean a less than optimal supply of labour and other resources for this sector. Hence, an increase in tax rates on the legitimate economy can in some circumstances improve efficiency by driving a more optimal level of resources to the UGE. While the presence of evasion can raise the levels and progressivity of tax rates, it unambiguously reduces the optimal total level of tax revenues for program spending.[11] This is because PTE and the UGE raise the marginal efficiency cost of taxes. Their presence also clearly reduces the total income and spending of a government that acts like a Leviathan.

A second issue involving tax design has to do with relief for individuals at lower income levels. The main methods in use are personal exemptions for an initial amount of income and taxing all incomes from the first dollar while providing an offset through either payments or refundable tax credits. The latter method allows the extension of source withholding to many additional types of income, including interest and dividends, thereby improving compliance rates. The personal exemption method makes it more difficult to withhold taxes at a uniform rate from such payments, since many persons with low and moderate incomes, including retirees, would have tax withheld on interest and dividend receipts and need refunds. The use of a flat rate of tax, at least over lower to middle income levels, further facilitates the use of with-

---

11 However, the optimal level of gross tax revenues including those needed to finance tax enforcement can be higher with tax non-compliance.

holding at source. A flatter rate schedule would support the extension of withholding to purchases from independent contractors; a penalty could then be applied to purchasers who failed to withhold. Australia has required homeowners buying home repairs or renovations over a threshold level to withhold and remit tax.

A third tax design issue is the appropriate revenue mix of direct and indirect taxes. It has commonly been asserted that the presence of evasion should prompt greater reliance on indirect taxes, particularly the value-added type. While direct personal taxes can be evaded in numerous ways, indirect taxes of both the retail and value-added types are also amenable to a variety of evasion manoeuvres. It is said that shifting the mix from direct to indirect taxes would allow taxes to be collected on the consumer spending of people who evade income tax. Yet the authorities find it as difficult to apply an indirect tax on UGE output as to collect direct tax on the earnings of UGE participants. This implies that the effects of such additional indirect taxes will be felt mostly or entirely by workers in the legitimate sector. The economy will reach a new equilibrium in which the competitive prices of goods and services from the legitimate sector fall relative to UGE prices. UGE workers would pay the indirect taxes on their purchases from the legitimate sector but be fully compensated by a fall in the prices of those items.

Empirical studies of the Canadian economy support the theoretical prediction that a shift in the mix from direct taxes toward greater use of indirect taxes will not improve tax compliance or reduce the size of the underground sector.[12] Changes in indirect taxes have been found to account for most growth of the UGE since 1964. Moreover, the change in form of the federal sales tax in 1991, from a single-stage tax on manufacturers to a multi-stage value-added tax, has been associated with a large increase in the UGE even without a shift in the direct-indirect tax mix. Estimates of the resultant impact on the Canadian UGE range form 1 percent to nearly 4 percent of GDP.

A fourth issue around tax design is the appropriate use of excise and property taxes. The presence of PTE and the UGE suggests that greater

---

12   The results cited here are based on Hill and Kabir (1996) and Spiro (1993, 1994).

reliance on particular forms of those taxes could improve overall compliance. By raising taxes on the purchase or use of items that are large, visible, and registered, governments can be relatively assured of collecting their money. The shift allows them to reduce rates on taxes that apply to other items such as earnings, which can more easily be concealed. In the optimum, this strategy should be pushed to the point where the social gains from improved tax compliance, measured in efficiency and distributional terms, are just offset by the marginal inefficiencies and distributional effects from the distorted consumption patterns of taxing a few selected commodities more heavily. Two natural targets for this kind of tax policy are automobiles and homes or real estate; both are highly visible, with ownership registered and valuations either already available or readily obtained.[13] The US pursued a tax strategy of this kind in 1991 by imposing excise taxes on purchases of higher-valued cars, boats, airplanes, jewellery, and furs.

Benefit fraud has major implications for the design of transfer policies. Here we will focus on fraud in the form of undeclared or underreported earnings. In contrast with tax policies, one can design transfer policies in a way that provides incentives for full reporting of earnings.

Traditional welfare programs provide net benefits that are negatively conditioned on reported earnings. For this reason, beneficiaries have a strong incentive to conceal or underreport earnings, a practice that is facilitated by working underground. For employable individuals, the transfer scheme can be structured as a wage rate subsidy with benefits that rise proportionately with hours worked but fall with hourly wage rates. An individual who has no earnings receives no benefits. It is far harder for the public authorities to detect unreported earnings than to verify the existence and level of reported earnings.

Another way of structuring transfer policies that discourage work in the UGE for the purpose of underreporting earnings is to attach a work requirement to the payment of benefits. This approach has a variety of forms that range from special public employment to community work. By taking up the beneficiary's regular working hours, such a

---

13   Also relevant to the formulation of this kind of policy is the correlation of consumption of these items with the incidence of evasion of other taxes.

policy sharply raises the cost of taking UGE employment. Of course, workfare or work-for-welfare policies can offer other benefits such as socially useful output, the maintenance of skills and work habits, skills training, and the dignity of beneficiaries. Careful design of the content and operation of the work program will be required to achieve all these goals and avoid stigmatizing recipients.

Conclusion

Pure tax evasion and the underground economy pose fundamental questions about the effects of taxation. Benefit fraud poses analogous questions about the transfer system. The importance of these phenomena for public policy cannot be judged by their scale alone; it stems from the magnitude and nature of their associated efficiency and distributional effects. Even a relatively small underground sector could generate serious inefficiencies and inequities. However, our analysis suggests that most of the benefits associated with the UGE are in fact more widely dispersed to consumers as well as underground producers.

With pure tax evasion, which is not highly concentrated in particular sectors of the economy, greater inequities may arise between compliant and non-compliant individuals. The efficiency costs of noncompliance include distortion of overall resource allocation, low productivity from petty producers trying to conceal their operations, public enforcement costs, and reduced public provision of otherwise desirable goods and services. Offset against these inefficiencies are the potential efficiency gains from economic activity in a sector free of tax distortions and the possible reduction of excessive activities by a Leviathan-like government.

PTE and the UGE also raise important questions about the design, operation, and enforcement of tax and transfer systems. Many policy decisions can be made at the enforcement stage in the form of increased audit or penalty rates and changes in reporting or withholding requirements. Yet our analysis stresses the importance of considering compliance factors at the initial design or major reform stages of tax and transfer policies. The feasibility and cost of source withholding depend very much on tax structure, and the basic design of a tax determines what kinds of information need to be reported to the authorities. Furthermore, it is vital to consider the incentives for third parties such as employers, payers, or purchasers to comply with withholding or reporting requirements.

No matter how many resources a society spends on enforcing tax and transfer provisions, it will ultimately be limited by the integrity of its policy design. And there are economic and social considerations that should restrain a society from devoting excessive resources to enforcement. These factors include the efficiency and distributional impacts of enforcement as well as concerns about individual privacy and Draconian justice.

References[14]

Alm, James, "The Welfare Cost of the Underground Economy," in *Economic Inquiry* 24 (April 1985), pp. 243-63.

Benjamini, Yael and Shlomo Maital, "Optimal Tax Evasion and Optimal Tax Evasion Policy: Behavioral Aspects," in Gaertner and Wenig (1985), pp. 245-64.

Besley, Timothy and Stephen Coate, "Workfare versus Welfare: Incentive Arguments for Work Requirements in Poverty-Alleviation Programs," in *American Economic Review* 82 (March 1992), pp. 249-61.

Clotfelter, Charles T., "Tax Evasion and Tax Rates," in *Review of Economics and Statistics* 65 (August 1983), pp. 363-73.

Cowell, Frank A., "Public Policy and Tax Evasion: Some Problems," in Gaertner and Wenig (1985), pp. 273-84.

―――, "Tax Evasion with Labour Income," in *Journal of Public Economics* 26 (February 1985), pp. 19-34.

―――, *Cheating the Government: The Economics of Evasion*: Cambridge, MIT Press, 1990.

Erard, Brian and Jonathan S. Feinstein, "Honesty and Evasion in the Tax Compliance Game," in *Rand Journal of Economics* 25 (Spring 1994), pp. 1-19.

Feige, Edgar L., ed., *The Underground Economies: Tax Evasion and Information Distortion: Cambridge, Cambridge University Press, 1989.*

――― and Robert T. McGee, "Sweden's Laffer Curve: Taxation and the Unobserved Economy," in *Scandinavian Journal of Economics* 85 (1983), pp. 499-519.

Feinstein, Jonathan, "An Econometric Analysis of Income Tax Evasion and Its Detection," in *Rand Journal of Economics* 22 (Spring 1991), pp. 14-35.

Fortin, Bernard and Nguyen M. Hung, "Poverty Trap and the Hidden Labor Market," in *Economics Letters* 25 (1987), pp. 183-89.

---

14 This bibliography provides key references for the economic literature on pure tax evasion but focusses on the smaller body of studies exploring the linkages between evasion and the underground economy.

—— and Guy Lacroix, "Labour Supply, Tax Evasion and the Marginal Cost of Public Funds: An Empirical Investigation," in *Journal of Public Economics* 55 (November 1994), pp. 407-31.

Frey, Bruno, "How Large (or Small) Should the Underground Economy Be?" in Feige (1989), pp. 111-26.

Gaertner, Wulf and Alois Wenig, eds, *The Economics of the Shadow Economy*: Berlin: Springer-Verlag, 1985.

Gordon, James P. F., "Evading Taxes by Selling for Cash," in *Oxford Economic Papers* 42 (January 1990), pp. 244-55.

Hansson, Ingemar, "Tax Evasion and Government Policy," in Gaertner and Wenig (1985), pp. 285-300.

Hill, Roderick, and Muhammed Kabir, "Tax Rates, the Tax Mis, and the Growth of the Underground economy in Canada: What Can We Infer?" in *Canadian Tax Journal* 44 (no. 6,1996), in press.

Jung, Young H., Arthur Snow, and Gregory A. Trandel, "Tax Evasion and the Size of the Underground Economy," in *Journal of Public Economics* 54 (July 1994), pp. 391-402.

Kaplow, Louis, "Optimal Taxation with Costly Enforcement and Evasion," in *Journal of Public Economics* 43 (November 1990), pp. 221-36.

Kesselman, Jonathan R., "Income Tax Evasion: An Intersectoral Analysis," in *Journal of Public Economics* 38 (March 1989), pp. 137-82.

—— , *Rate Structure and Personal Taxation: Flat Rate or Dual Rate?* Wellington, New Zealand, Victoria University Press for the Institute of Policy Studies, 1990.

—— , comment on "Taxation and the Service Sector" (by John Whalley), in Richard M. Bird and Jack M. Mintz, eds, *Taxation to 2000 and Beyond*: Toronto, Canadian Tax Foundation, 1992, pp. 286-94.

—— , "Evasion Effects of Changing the Tax Mix," in *Economic Record* 69 (June 1993), pp. 131-48.

—— , "Compliance, Enforcement, and Administrative Factors in Improving Tax Fairness," in Allan M. Maslove, ed., *Issues in the Taxation of Individuals*, a volume of research studies for the Ontario Fair Tax Commission: Toronto, University of Toronto Press, 1994, pp. 62-84.

Lemieux, Thomas, Bernard Fortin, and Pierre Fréchette, "The Effect of Taxes on Labor Supply in the Underground Economy," in *American Economic Review* 84 (March 1994), pp. 231-54.

Persson, Mats and Pehr Wissén, "Redistributional Aspects of Tax Evasion," in *Scandinavian Journal of Economics* 86 (1984), pp. 131-49.

Pyle, D.J., "The Economics of Taxpayer Compliance," in *Journal of Economic Surveys* 5 (no. 2, 1991), pp. 163-98.

Sandmo, Agnar, "Income Tax Evasion, Labour Supply, and the Equity-Efficiency Tradeoff," in *Journal of Public Economics* 16 (December 1981), pp. 265-88.

Schweitzer, Urs, "Welfare Analysis of Excise Tax Evasion," in *Journal of Institutional and Theoretical Economics* 140 (June 1984), pp. 247-58.

Slemrod, Joel, ed., *Why People Pay Taxes: Tax Compliance and Enforcement*: Ann Arbor, University of Michigan Press, 1992.

——"Fixing the Leak in Okun's Bucket: Optimal Tax Progressivity When Avoidance Can Be Controlled," in *Journal of Public Economics* 55 (September 1994), pp. 41-51.

Spiro, Peter S., "Evidence of a Post-GST Increase in the Underground Economy," in Canadian Tax Journal 41 (no. 2, 1993), pp. 247-58.

——"Estimating the Underground Economy: A Critical Evaluation of the Monetary Approach," in Canadian tax Journal 42 (o. 4, 1994), pp.1059-81

Usher, Dan, "Tax Evasion and the Marginal Cost of Public Funds," in *Economic Inquiry* 24 (October 1986), pp. 563-86.

Watson, Harry, "Tax Evasion and Labor Markets," in *Journal of Public Economics* 27 (July 1985), pp. 231-46.

Yaniv, Gideon, "Withholding and Non-withheld Tax Evasion," in *Journal of Public Economics* 35 (March 1988), pp. 183-204.

Benefit Principle and Taxation: Possible User Taxes and Fees in Canada

François Vaillancourt

Introduction

The purpose of this paper is to examine the possibility of increasing the role of user taxes and fees as revenue sources for governments in Canada. This is of interest in the context of an examination of the underground economy, since it is argued that the current tax mix contributes to the growth of that economy. We begin by reviewing the conceptual framework used for assessing revenue sources and then look at the revenues and expenditures of governments in Canada, ending with some ideas for a few possible user taxes.

Conceptual framework

Governments finance themselves in three major ways: seigniorage income, also referred to as the inflation tax; deficits, covered by domestic or foreign borrowing; and general revenues encompassing taxes, fees, returns on investment, and other sources of current income. With inflation running at under 2 percent, the first method is not significant in Canada at present. Deficits and general revenues are the two major sources of income.

Deficits emerged as an important source of financing in the 1970s with the oil shocks of 1973 and 1979 and came into full bloom in the '80s with the recession of 1981-1982. They now, depending on our exact definition of the public sector and the year considered, account for about 20 to 25 percent of government spending. The general revenue source is over 80 percent made up of taxes.

Taxation has been founded for generations on two major principles: ability to pay and benefits received. Early on, the main emphasis was put on benefits, with income sometimes called on as a measure of benefits, not of ability to pay. In the early part of this century, the generalization of the progressive income tax, justified in part by arguments that equal sacrifice required increasing proportions of income because of the decreasing marginal utility of income, was accompanied by a greater and indeed almost exclusive emphasis on ability to pay as a basis for taxation. An example of this is a recent Quebec government paper on taxes and expenditures where the benefit principle is not even mentioned in the list of tax principles.

From our perspective, the three interesting questions to be asked with respect to taxation are:

- What are user taxes/fees and when should they be used?
- How are they currently being used? and
- What can be done?

We address the first question below and the other two in our next two sections.

"What are user taxes/fees?" is more easily answered for fees than for taxes. User fees are payments for specific and clearly identified units of goods or services such as so many cubic metres of water delivered to a specific outlet, parking permits valid for given streets for limited time periods, fishing or hunting licences for particular seasons, and so on.

User taxes, on the other hand, are not conceptually well defined. They must be earmarked insofar as they are linked to a well-defined expenditure. However, not all earmarked taxes are user taxes, since by our definition user taxes are taxes paid directly by users of specific public programs, or on their behalf by others such as parents or employers, for access to the benefits—goods, services, transfers—provided by the programs.

User taxes can be solely entry-restrictive: they can also be benefit-defining. Entry-restrictive user taxes must be paid to gain access to benefits, but once payment has been made the value of benefits does not depend on the amount paid. With benefit-defining user taxes, the amount of benefits is tied in some way to the payment by rules about benefit duration and so on.

"When should taxes/fees be used?" is at least partly a normative question and thus difficult for economists to answer. Nonetheless, we can argue that:

- User fees/taxes are an appropriate way of charging for private goods and services provided by government when their provision cannot be privatized. Why? User fees/taxes act as pricing mechanisms and thus help to allocate resources optimally over various goods and services. This does not mean that publicly provided goods and services will not be produced at too high a cost: what is does mean is that the quantity produced may not be too great. Proper pricing would set the fees/taxes to cover the costs of producing these goods and services privately. Any excess cost, associated with the inefficiency subsidy arising from public production, should be raised from general revenues.
- User fees/taxes must take into account, not only the efficiency gains of using them rather than general revenue sources, but also their associated administrative and compliance costs. Thus, it may be appropriate to offer individuals and small businesses a bundle of services for a flat inclusive fee.
- User fees/taxes should not be used for redistributive purposes. Redistribution should be explicit: in some cases, it will result in individuals or families being fully compensated for user payments.

Revenues and expenditures of governments in Canada

Table 1 presents the most recent data on expenditures and revenues for all levels including local governments. The most important expenditures are social services (22 percent of all governments) followed by debt charges (20 percent), health (14 percent), and education (13 percent): these four spending areas account for about 70 percent of the total. The revenue field is dominated by personal income taxes (36 percent for all governments) followed by general sales taxes (13 percent) and health and social insurance levies.

Table 1: Government Own-Source Revenues and Expenditures Canada, 1993-1994 ($ millions)			
Revenues	**Federal**	**Provincial-Local**	**Total**
Income taxes	76,507	43,506	112,426
Personal	64,173	38,690	96,519
Corporate	11,000	4,816	14,635
On payments to nonresidents	1,334	—	1,272
Property and related taxes	—	31,877	31,877
Consumption taxes	29,731	28,151	58,019
General sales	19,000	19,643	37,949
Motive fuel	3,470	5,797	9,453
Alcoholic beverages and tobacco	3,090	2,418	5,818
Customs duties	3,390	—	3,652
Other	781	293	1,146
Health and social insurance levies	19,300	9,649	27,882
Petroleum and natural-gas taxes	—	—	—
Miscellaneous taxes	391	4,386	4,833
Natural-resource revenues	60	5,584	5,643
Privileges, licences, and permits	376	4,684	5,094
Sales of goods and services	3,766	11,903	15,091
Return on investments & otherrevenue (consolidated in 1993-1994)	6,005	19,179	26,067
Total consolidated own-source revenue	136,136	158,920	286,932

Table 1 (continued)

Expenditures	Federal	Provincial–Local	Total
General services	7,562	12,041	19,603
Protection of persons and property	15,822	11,106	26,248
Transportation and communications	3,789	12,703	16,317
Health	8,331	46,846	47,820
Social services	59,458	33,587	85,616
Education	4,914	42,685	44,420
Resource conservation and industrial development	6,683	8,986	14,573
Environment	751	7,315	8,049
Recreation and culture	1,347	6,000	7,328
Labour, enployment and immigration	2,689	851	3,487
Housing	2,135	1,776	3,910
Foreign affairs and international assistance	3,924	—	3,924
Regional planning and development	485	1,233	1,706
Research establishments	1,584	350	1,934
Debt charges	37,982	26,820	64,739
Transfers to own enterprises	11,460	—	—
Other	2,123	2,956	5,086
Total consolidated expenditures	171,039	215,254	354,761

Source: *Finances of the Nation 1995*, Toronto, Canadian Tax Foundation, Tables 17.1 and 17.3.

The information in the table does not enable us to comment on the relative importance of user fees/taxes. An interesting paper by Thirsk and Bird (1993) attempted to measure the importance of earmarked taxes in Canada, some of which are user fees, but they were unable to come up with a precise figure. They concluded that user fees were more important at the local level than at other levels of government. If we examine the four main areas of spending identified above, it can be seen that debt charges, health benefits and elementary and secondary education are financed from general revenues. User fees are often present in postsecondary education (the exception being the CEGEPs in Quebec) but they account for only a small part of total expenditures.

With respect to social services and user taxes, there is a link between payroll taxes and benefits received in terms of eligibility for worker's compensation benefits (WCB), unemployment insurance (UI) and Canada/Quebec Pension Plan (CPP/QPP) benefits. Employees of uninsured employers cannot receive WCB benefits and non-contributors cannot collect UI or CPP/QPP benefits. In these last two cases, individual benefits are weakly (UI) or strongly (CPP/QPP) linked to contributions. In 1994, about $40 billion in user taxes, representing about 15 percent of all government revenues, covered a part of social services expenditures in Canada—UI=$18 billion, CPP/QPP=$15 billion, and WCB=$7 billion.

Potential user fees/taxes for Canada

Before addressing the question of potential new fees and taxes for Canadian jurisdictions, we want to mention a few points to be kept in mind when introducing levies of this kind:

- Borrowing should be the method used when governments are buying multiyear capital assets. In a steady-state economy we could see total borrowing increase while per-capita debt remained the same as the population increased. Depending on technological change, real debt and assets could rise in the economy. Thus, introducing user fees/taxes does not imply a balanced budget.

- A checklist financing system would seem appropriate for advocacy programs and specific semi-public services. At income tax time, the government would attach to the tax return a list of programs to be publicly financed. The initial list would reflect the status quo, while subsequent lists would evolve in part according to funding received. Individuals would use this list to determine a level of support for each program. For example, the Consumer Association of Canada and the Canadian Broadcasting Corporation would receive financial support equal to the sum of all amounts contributed with a one-year lag.

- User fees should be introduced as widely as possible. For instance, all municipalities should be required to sell metered water and, when operating transit systems, levy charges to reflect distances travelled. Similarly, users of downtown access roads should be charged for downtown access permits or, ideally, by electronic monitoring of actual use.

Let us now turn to possible user funding in the fields of social services, debt charges, health, and education. In suggesting user taxes, we will assume that:

- Existing programs remain more or less unchanged, although user financing may reduce demand for some services.
- As the term "taxes" (rather than "fees") indicates, participation is compulsory. The freedom to choose not to be covered by public health insurance or pension plans does not exist. This is important, as we would otherwise move away from taxes to premiums and from a public monopoly to a private market.
- User taxes can pay the full costs of each plan examined. This might be achieved in part through a redistribution of income from the rich to the poor to cover the relevant user taxes.

Income security / social services

In general, we wish to distinguish between three types of transfers: those to unemployables, those to employables, and those to retirees (once employables).

The key point with unemployables will be to identify them as precisely as possible to avoid free rides by other groups. We would argue that individuals should be presumed employable and thus need to prove that some serious physical or psychological problems prevent them from working. The basic needs of unemployables should be met out of general revenues, not user taxes.

In the case of employables, premiums paid by workers should be used to fund an employment income insurance system that integrates the various existing schemes such as UI, WCB, and welfare for employables (Vaillancourt, 1994). Benefits would be set at a basic minimum with some topping off to reflect premiums accumulated in the fund. Unfunded benefits would then be recovered, possibly from future premiums. This would be a user tax with a strong link between payments and benefits.

In the case of retirement income, CPP/QPP should become fully funded from individual contributions at a given point in time for everyone then aged 45 or less. To begin with, people would receive statements of their accumulated and projected benefits: they would have the right to make extra contributions over the ensuing 25 years to make up for the shortfall in expected pensions resulting from this change in the rules.

Also from that changeover date, individuals aged 25 or less would be told that they no longer had access to OAS/GIS: they must contribute more to CPP/QPP. If people are free to contribute, then society must be willing to let them suffer, if not die, from lack of resources. To ease the transition, CPP/QPP funds should be invested to earn the market rate of return (Prince, 1993). Again we have a strong link between taxes paid and benefits received.

The use of individual premiums to finance both employment income insurance and retirement income would make it more advantageous to declare income for tax purposes and thus reduce the size of the unreported economy.

Debt charges

At first blush, it may seem strange to make a connection between debt charges and user fees/taxes. But in Canada, debt has been incurred to finance either infrastructures—and should therefore be paid by appropriate user fees and taxes—or current spending. If the latter was the case in the 1980s and through into the 1990s, and we would argue it was (Trahan, 1993), then it is incorrect to raise the taxes of the young or cut the services available to them in order to finance the spending of the old: the young could not vote on these borrowings.

In other words the older generation, having failed as trustees of the nation and misused their borrowing power, must pay an ex-post user tax. The following three possibilities are offered in increasing order of feasibility:

- sending each Canadian aged 35 or more a debt bill to be paid now or at the time of departure from Canada or death (applied against his/her estate). Life/departure insurance would have to be paid by anyone electing not to pay the bill on receipt;
- imposing an age-specific (say, 35 to 70) income surtax for a limited time period (10 to 20 years) to pay off this consumption-related borrowing.

- taxing pension fund earnings at a flat rate (say, 25 to 40 percent) on the grounds that people with access to pension funds are the better-off 35- to 60-year-olds. They will thus see their retirement savings and income reduced.

Age 35 was chosen as the minimum age to make those who voted repeatedly for free-spending governments in the 1980s and '90s pay up for the misuse of their borrowing power.

Health

In this area we need to distinguish the three classes of illnesses and injuries: genetic, natural, and self-inflicted.

- Genetic illnesses are passed on by parents. Some are detectable before conception, some early after conception so that abortion is possible, some are detectable right after birth, and some are detectable only when they materialize. Assuming that society does not wish to coerce women into having their foetuses tested, let alone having abortions, genetic illnesses should then be covered by per-capita health premiums.
- Natural illnesses are complaints such as colds, ear infections, and so on that occur in the natural course of our lives. Little if anything can be done to prevent them, although their severity may vary among individuals. Again, these conditions should be covered by per-capita health premiums.
- Self-inflicted illnesses or injuries should be covered by premiums set to reflect high-risk behaviour. For example, smokers and those who share living quarters with them would pay a Tobacco Consumption Health Premium (Vaillancourt, 1994a). The premium would be collected on the basis of an annual declaration: falsification would lead to ex-post collection of the real premium and, if this could not be paid, denial of services.

Education

Here we should distinguish between elementary/secondary schooling on the one hand and postsecondary education on the other. In the first case, we can argue that basic abilities are a public good, and while user fees should be levied to finance, say, one fourth to one third of the costs of that educational level, general revenues should also be tapped. In the second case, private returns from postsecondary schooling at the bachelor's and master's levels are such that full fees should be charged in combination with an income-contingent repayment scheme. When it comes to PhDs, an argument cay be made for R&D externalities to justify subsidies from general revenues for at least some fields of study.

Conclusion

We have argued here that it is possible to make greater use of user fees and user taxes to finance governments in Canada. This should somewhat slake the thirst for general tax revenues and income taxes in particular, opening the way for reduced tax rates that would diminish incentives for tax evasion and thus the size of the underground economy.

References

Prince, M. (1993), "Reforming the Public Pension System in Canada, Retrospect and Prospect," Centre for Public Sector Studies, University of Victoria.

Thirsk, W. and R. Bird (1993), "Earmarked Taxes in Ontario: Solution or Problem?" in A. Maslove, ed., *Taxing and Spending Issues of Process*: Toronto, University of Toronto Press,.

Trahan, F. (1993), "Réflexion sur le contrôle des dépenses et la comptabilité générationnelle," M.Sc. term paper.

Vaillancourt, F. (1994), "Income Distribution, Income Security and Fiscal Federalism in Canada," in *Future of Fiscal Federalism*, R. Banting, ed., Queen's University School of Policy Studies.

Vaillancourt, F. (1994a), "Cigarette: No thanks, I haven't paid my premium," Toronto *Globe and Mail*, February 17, 1994, p. A19.